Primitive and Universal Laws of the Formation and Development of Language. A Rational and Inductive System Founded on the Natural Basis of Onomatops

PRIMITIVE AND UNIVERSAL

LAWS

OF THE

FORMATION AND DEVELOPMENT

OF

LANGUAGE.

A RATIONAL AND INDUCTIVE SYSTEM FOUNDED ON THE
NATURAL BASIS

OF

ONOMATOPS.

BY

CALLISTUS AUGUSTUS COUNT DE GODDES-LIANCOURT

AND

FREDERIC PINCOTT.

Verba ex "onomatopoieiâ" oriuntur.
Naturâ revoluta, ad Naturam revertuntur.

LONDON:
WM. H. ALLEN & CO.,
13, WATERLOO PLACE, PALL MALL.

1874.

LONDON:

GILBERT AND RIVINGTON, 28, WHITEFRIARS STREET, AND
52, ST. JOHN'S SQUARE, CLERKENWELL, E.C.

TO

Dr. G. W. Leitner,

PRINCIPAL OF THE GOVERNMENT COLLEGE, LAHORE, REGISTRAR OF
THE PUNJAB UNIVERSITY COLLEGE, AND FOUNDER AND PRESIDENT OF
NUMEROUS LITERARY AND EDUCATIONAL INSTITUTIONS,

AS A TESTIMONY TO THE

AUTHOR, LINGUIST, REFORMER

AND

DISCOVERER OF LANGUAGES,

THIS WORK IS RESPECTFULLY INSCRIBED BY

THE AUTHORS.

CONTENTS.

INTRODUCTION.

WHILE in Rome—1840—occupied in establishing a "Humane Society" on the Flavum Tiberim, and lecturing on the art of bringing the asphyxied back to life, I[a] had the honour to breakfast with Cardinal Mezzofanti, and an old friend, Count Martorelli, minister of Hohenzollern. The reader will easily imagine that I did not lose the opportunity of conversing on idioms and symbols, &c., in company with such excellent scholars. His Eminence having made a characteristic mimical sign to his servant, I at once approached the subject. The quick perception of the Cardinal soon outran me, and he said, "Mimicry acts powerfully on man, and on the lower animals generally. They not only comprehend the expression of the acted thought, but they penetrate our modelling of the expression itself." I then rejoined as follows: "Does not your Eminence believe that Greek actors had really, at one time, conquered the art of mimicry, so as even to occasion hysterical fits in those assembled to witness their performances, and to induce the magistrates of the Republic to suppress pantomimes?" "I have no doubt that the history is true, and so is also the enactment of the magistrates of the Athenians."

[a] De G.-Liancourt.

B

"Then," I added, "mimicry, as a sub-faculty of our intelligence, seems to me one of the probable crude forms of language. Does not your Eminence think that monosyllables must be *onomatops*?" "Yes, I do; there is certainly a good deal in onomatops, and I will consider that interesting subject at the earliest opportunity." The Cardinal then, pointing to a chair where I was to sit, asked me what were the equivalents of *poêle* and *chaise* in Picard. Had I been foreign to Picardy[a] I should have wondered at this singular question; but we had before us an *omelette aux fines herbes*, and, though much puzzled, the link of the ideas passing in his Eminence's mind was soon discovered. "In Picard," I replied, "the vocables *poêle* and *chaise* are called *pa-ielle* and *ca-ielle*."[b] "Just what I wrote this morning!" exclaimed Mezzofanti; and a marked joy conveyed to me that the association of ideas was not to him a mystery.[c]

To speak of the birth-place of language is, seemingly, a mere assumption; but where the human genus was formed, or transformed, in times that baffle all calculation, there man began to exercise the won-

[a] Another Cardinal in London made a sharp remark about this celebrated Mezzofanti: "Perhaps his Eminence knew the fact by consulting a biography."

[b] *Pa-* found in *pa-bulum*; and *ka-* or *ca-* in καθέδρα; *-ielle* is the termination that marks the Picard patois.

[c] Finally, the Cardinal told me that he was just come from Bologna, where he had met several Cochin-Chinese princes, who afforded him a good opportunity for working at his Cochin-Chinese Dictionary. I have never once heard of this work since

derful faculty he possesses in common with other animals. But man, amongst all other creatures, is certainly the only one who had the astonishing power of enlarging the gift of nature to an unlimited extent, from, so to speak, the cry of pain to the melopoeia of joy. Furthermore, man only can symbolize in a thousand manners and ways, the whole creation of which he is *princeps.*[a]

The process of learning to speak is far from a rapid one. We have seen many ploughmen and woodmen who could never imagine what a musical note was; who had never reflected one single minute on the resources of language; and had never uttered more than 200 different words in their lives. We asked some of them what God was, Jesus, England, France, &c. Their answers were, "I can't say," "I don't know," "I have never seen them." This state has been most improperly called the state of blessed ignorance. In a part of the country about twenty miles from London, we have known men of forty, fifty, and sixty years old, looking stupid and unable to express a single idea. Speech—so near to the mind; the instrument for the expression of thought; the instrument so necessary for all the operations of man's intellect; the instrument which imparts to its possessor the power of thinking within himself and with his fellow-men; the greatest of intellectual feats—among these poor people

---

[a] Plato was the first who introduced the vocable ὀνομαωργον and ὀνοματοθετην.

is more than barbarous, or negative. By the side of such degraded beings let us place a Mithridates, who could speak twenty-two tongues; or a Themistocles, who learned how to speak Persian fluently in one year. The *memoriæ felicitas* of that illustrious warrior was so wonderful that he used to say jocularly, "I wish some one could teach me how to forget; because I recollect things I would have forgotten, and I cannot forget things which I would not recollect." These wonders of past ages have been surpassed by Mezzofanti, late Librarian of the Vatican. This astonishing man, the son of a carpenter, when on the very eve of engaging in the same business as his father, was rescued from manual toil by a monk, who had discovered a great power within him. The monk interested himself in the welfare of the little Mezzofanti, and sent him to school. At the age of twenty-two the student had acquired a knowledge of Latin, Greek, Hebrew, French, German, Spanish, Portuguese, Dutch, Swedish, English, and Russian. Ultimately he acquired about forty languages, and could have travelled round the world without an interpreter, for he could express himself even in African and American idioms. It must be confessed, however, that as soon as Mezzofanti was led into a conversation the subject of which was alien to polyglottism, the good man ceased to be a cardinal point in the horizon of science.

Our friend Elihu Burritt was a blacksmith's apprentice when he picked up some leaves of a foreign grammar, and became, so to speak, suddenly a professor of

Coptic, Phœnician, Persian, Syriac, French, English, German, and Italian, with a good range of other accessory knowledge.

Stanislas Julien was, another wonder. He was keeper of a little shop on the Place de l'Estrapade, close by the Panthéon at Paris. Once a snow-storm overtook Julien near the Collége de France, not far from the Estrapade, and he took shelter in the establishment. The storm increasing in intensity, Julien ventured to enter a room on a level with the ground floor, and finding a stove burning went forward to warm himself. Shortly after an old gentleman entered carrying several books under his arm; the books he quietly placed on a kind of pulpit, and joined Julien at the fire. In a few moments he said, "Well, sir, I thought I should have to lecture to the four walls, but I see with pleasure that to-day I have one pupil in attendance." "I beg your pardon, sir," replied Stanislas Julien, "but I am not a student. Surprised by this storm I ventured to take refuge here, and to warm myself in this deserted room." "Do not trouble yourself, young man, I am happy to receive you in this my lecture-room, and, should you like it, I shall be glad to teach you Chinese and to furnish you with the necessary books. I see you have a quick eye; you might make rapid progress: it will cost you nothing." Julien accepted the generous offer, became very proficient, and, when the excellent lecturer not long after died, Julien was elected professor, with a salary of £400 a year, and a yet more distinguished reputa-

tion. Stanislas Julien, who recounted the above circumstance to us himself, could speak Chinese to the
Chinese, a miracle that his venerable and learned
professor could never perform.

These very remarkable men, with the utterly ignorant and uncultivated labourer by their side and in
contradistinction to them, represent the whole range
of the power of our race. It is as wonderful to
observe Mezzofanti, Elihu Burritt, Stanislas Julien,
and others like them, plunging at once into the abyss
of language, as it is to witness the English labourer
living during three generations without being able to
acquire the elements of a single one.

The problem of the origin of speech is one of the
most interesting that can engage the human mind.
In it is involved the examination of that rudimental
germ or autelechy whence sprang all the lofty conceptions of Homer, the divine guide of the sublime
triad of tragic poets; of Plato and Aristotle, the fer-
vent and immortal worshippers of eternal beauty; of
Pindar, Virgil, Horace, Cicero, Archimedes and *tutti
quanti*, the founders of our present intellectual greatness—men who never caused a tear to be shed by their
myriads of admirers during thousands of years, except
those tears provoked by gratitude, love, and admiration.
By contemplating the heroes in all branches of art and
science, it is easy to see that all that man is and has
beyond his animal nature is the gift of language.
This it is which marks in an indelible way the line

of demarcation between man and beast—the rubicon which no other animal has ever crossed. Bereft of language, man would be still following his animal instincts, ignorant alike of past and future, incapable of progress, because incapable of communicating advancing thought. From considerations such as these the early Hindûs raised speech to the rank of deity, and prized the acquisition with feelings of reverential awe.

When the mind has been once awakened to the consciousness of the mysterious and potent agent now so obedient to its command, a feeling of surprise overtakes the thinker as he reflects on the little notice bestowed upon the subject, while so much time and pains are given to cognate branches of science. The intangibility of words no doubt accounts for much of this neglect; and the subtle nature of the bond linking sound and sense, eluding all but the closest scrutiny; so that it required the combined labours of a succession of such men as Leibnitz,[a] Horne Tooke,[b] Pritchard,[c] Schlegel,[d] Rask,[e] Grimm,[f] Adelung,[g] Bopp,[h] Burnouf,[i] Humboldt,[j] Bunsen,[k]

[a] Dissertation on the Origin of Nations. [b] Diversions of Purley. [c] Researches into the Physical History of Man.
[d] Essay on the Language and Philosophy of the Hindoos.
[e] Ursprung der Altnordischen oder Isländischen Sprache.
[f] Deutsche Grammatik. [g] Mithridates.
[h] Vergleichend Grammatik des Sanskrit, Zend, Griechischen, &c.—Glossarium Sanskritum.—Kritische Gram. des Sanskrit.
[i] Commentaire sur le Yaçna. [j] On the Kawi Language.
[k] Christianity and Mankind.—Egypt's Place in Universal History.

Max Müller,[a] Eichoff,[b] Pictet,[c] J. E. Renan,[d] L. Delâtre,[e] E. Duponceau,[f] P. Renouard,[g] N. F. Wiseman,[h] &c., &c., to demonstrate the great fact that speech is a homogeneous whole.

Setting aside ancient unreasoning assumptions, three hypotheses have been propounded to account for man's possession of language. The first of these is what Professor Max Müller aptly styles the Bow-wow Theory, according to which man, originally mute, hearing the sound of the lamb, the wolf, the wind, the thunder, &c., &c., sought to imitate them with his vocal organs.[i] The most able exponent of this theory was the late Baron Bunsen, who, in his great work on "Egypt's Place in Universal History," announces this as the final result of his studies. In despite, however, of so high an authority, this ingenious theory must fall to the ground, as it has never been explained, firstly, why man should have been the only mute animal; secondly, how it was that he possessed vocal organs for an indefinite period without the power to use them; and, thirdly, how any process of imitation

[a] The Science of Language.
[b] Parallèle des Langues de l'Inde et de l'Europe.
[c] Les Aryas Primitifs.   [d] Orig. des Lang. Sémitiques.
[e] Français et Sanscrit dans leurs rapports.
[f] Langues Indiennes et Chinoises.
[g] Science and Religion, 1856.
[h] On the Influence of Words, 1856.
[i] There is in French a sort of *grun*, or *grum, cru-cru*, very often resorted to. There is no articulation; the mouth is not open; but it means, *Look at this*, or *that*, or *I notice you*, &c. It would not be fair to call it language; it is simply an onomatop.

could have given to man the faculty of speech, without which his imitative instinct could never have come into play.

The second hypothesis has been called the Pooh-pooh Theory, because, according to it, articulate speech arose from the interjections of pain, joy, surprise, wonder, and admiration, which start out from the very nature of animated beings. Now there is a fatal objection to such a limited basis for language, viz. that existing words cannot be brought back to interjectional forms. We never speak of oh ! or ah ! but of pain, grief, vexation; we do not say ha ! ha ! but laugh, smile, pleasure, merriment. Horne Tooke justly observes, that "Language is built upon the downfall of interjections."

The third method of accounting for language is that of Professor Max Müller. In the opinion of this eminent scholar, man, by his very nature, and as one of his proper qualities, is possessed of a few hundred vocal sounds, each of which has an inherent sense, which man has no more the power of acquiring or of altering than he has the power of adding to his own stature, or of endowing himself with eye-sight, hearing, taste, feeling, or smell. With respect to this theory, it need only be remarked, that it leaves the question unanswered. It brings the inquirer up to the original bases, and teaches him to believe that all existing languages took their origin from a small number of cognate or possibly identical bases, and then the theory leaves him with the assurance that these bases are inexplicable.

But the explication of these bases is, unfortunately, the very problem a solution of which philosophy demands. To treat them as inexplicable is, in effect, to assert that, although the mental and moral faculties are reducible to system, and are acknowledged to have been developed by natural processes, yet that language, one of the agents by which these faculties operate, is beyond the ken of the human mind. There is, furthermore, this fatal objection to Professor Max Müller's very orthodox theory, the indisputable fact that people born deaf never speak, although the organs of speech may be quite unimpaired. Now if bases were man's *natural* inheritance, he would express his wants by their means without tuition, in the same way that he looks with his eyes, eats with his mouth, and reaches with his hands. One born deaf is, however, quite oblivious of the use of language, and resorts to gesture as the appropriate means of communicating with others. Neither does it dispose of this matter to say that the faculty is dormant from inability to appreciate uttered sound; because people afflicted in the way spoken of do make noises (pure onomatops) for the purpose of arresting attention, expressing anger, &c. The noises they utter, are, however, not Aryan bases with inherent sense, such as when uttered can be at once understood by other Aryans. We never hear anything like *vid*, or *paś*, or *kṛi*, or *dâ*, or any other base, issue from their lips. Yet this is what we should hear if bases were natural to man, even if we allow that all grammatical inflexion is matter of convention. On the contrary, the sounds these poor creatures utter are all of a purely animal character, a gurgling, snarling, shapeless kind, such as it is impossible to write, and painfully sad to hear. One such natural fact as this is more conclusive than many arguments, and it proves incontestibly that what we call *bases* are in reality as much acquired as are the methods of inflecting them, and that all that we can fairly consider to be the natural gift of man is the power of making noises with certain organs which we call vocal.

Furthermore, if bases were intuitive, all nations would speak one language; for each individual would be born with the common stock of words, and would at once apply them in their unalterable senses, in the same way that all races of mankind use their hands, feet, and eyes, in precisely identical manners. So, also, it would be right to argue that each nation would be able to speak the languages of every other nation without special tuition; for though certain clusters of individuals may have habituated themselves to the use of a limited number of the common natural stock of bases, yet they could not fail to understand perfectly any of the others that might be uttered by strangers to their society.

The real objection to the imitation and interjection theories lies against their too narrow foundations. Man is an imitative animal, it is true, but not purely imitative; he possesses also an impulse to spontaneity. This latter impulse is taken as the one basis of lan-

guage by the advocates of the Pooh-pooh theory.
Onomatopoieism is all imitation ; and Interjectionalism
is all exclamation ; neither of these theories, nor does
that of Professor Müller, take cognizance of the numerous sounds emissible by man that express, by neither
imitation nor interjection, the many and ever varying
animal sensations.

It has often been said that an infant expresses all
its wants by crying. This is true only of the first few
weeks of infancy, when all that the child is conscious
of is the desire for food, and the sensations of personal
pain. No sooner does the animal nature develop
sufficiently to let the little creature know of other
things and beings beyond itself, than the power of
expression at once enlarges, and every mother hears
and understands the many modulations of tone,—the
murmuring, cackling, hissing, puffing, and such-like
indescribable sounds by means of which the little
infant expresses its wants, its approbation, and its
disapproval. A more instructive lesson on the origin
of language can scarcely be imagined than that afforded
by the significant noises of a child of about a year old,
before it is capable of uttering a single articulate
word.[a] One half-hour's observation will astonish a

---

[a] Though well known, we must recall to memory the little history of Psammeticus. That prince, wishing to detect the origin of
language, and its comparative antiquity, confided two poor children
to the keeping of a herdsman. They were shut up in a small
house by themselves, and completely isolated, in order that they
should forget everything. At the end of the period of isolation the

discerning mind with the almost incredible volubility and expressive character of the natural onomatops which such a child will pour forth.[a] These utterances, alike in all times and in all places, form the natural and true basis of articulate speech. The germs of all past, present, and future generations are contained one in the other, as if packed up in a succession of boxes.[b] This was Cuvier's idea of the developments of form, and the same remark seems to apply to mental evolutions. Certain it is that the only sounds natural to man are those which each child utters in its first

herdsman reported that, when he visited the poor creatures they repeatedly said " Bécos! Bécos! " the Phrygian word for *bread* (Gr. βέκ).

[a] " Os tenerum pueri balbum que poëta figuras." "The poet fashions the tender and lisping accents of the boy." The Romans recognize the services of poetry. The ancient Greeks used, rightly, to make children at first learn by rote the moral sentences of the poets, so as to accustom their ears to sweetness and propriety, and to compel them to pronounce with exactness. Horace argues that poetry renders great service to ethics, enabling men to bear uncomplainingly the infirmities of old age and ill health, and teaching them admirably how to sustain poverty itself under the scorn and insult of contumelious opulence.

[b] Godfrey Wilhelm, Baron de Leibnitz, two centuries ago, propounded the theory of the cosmologic system of *monads* (μόνας), which was, and is, the most rational hypothesis, but also the most subtle, which was ever suggested, to explain the formation of the world. The difficulty of understanding the *schema,* or principle, essential to the existence of every *monad* or *unity-perfect,* has been much more against Leibnitz than against the truth of his cosmologic doctrine, the honour of the discovery of which was claimed by Newton.

efforts to convey its meaning; and these are always uttered for purely animal purposes.

That profound philosopher, the late Baron Bunsen, supplies the demonstration to this simple reasoning, in his work on Christianity and Mankind. He there says,[a] "In surveying all the languages of which we have records, we find the constant phenomenon, that the physical sense is the substratum of the metaphysical." And again, he states that the evidence of language points " to the fact that all intellectual, moral, and spiritual notions are found to be only the secondary signification of the respective words, their primary sense being physical, sensual."[b] The plainest proof that the abstract arose from the concrete.

This fact being established, our ground is circumscribed and cleared for the final investigation. All language is reducible to the concrete ὄνομα, otherwise called *roots* or *bases*, simple monosyllabic sounds. In the words of Professor Müller, "They are *phonetic types* produced by a power inherent in human nature,"[c] and articulate speech is fabricated from these stems by man, "guided only by innate laws, or by an instinctive impulse."[d] No one will contest this who has studied the efforts of a young infant to express

---

[a] Vol. iv. p. 133.

[b] "Nomina verbaque non positu fortuito sed quadam vi, et ratione naturæ facta esse."—A. Gellius, Noct. Attic. l. x. cap. iv. Naturalia magis quam arbitraria.

[c] Science of Language, Part I. p. 370.　　　　[d] Ibid. p. 296.

its meaning by *sound*. Indeed, this scholar admits the whole question for which we contend, and definitively confutes his own final speculations when he says, "In fact, interjections, together with gestures and movements of the muscles of the mouth and the eye, *would be quite sufficient for all purposes which language answers with the* MAJORITY *of mankind;*"[a] and again, "We cannot deny the possibility that *a* language might have been formed on the principle of imitation."[b] These admissions, coupled with the assertion that "nothing in nature exists by accident,"[c] beget surprise in the reader that so acute a reasoner as Professor Muller did not perceive the only rational conclusion deducible from them. Still more marvellous does this become when we find the same author relating the experience of Moffat, the African traveller,[d] who states that the inhabitants of isolated villages in the desert tracts of Africa are frequently compelled to travel to great distances from their homes; "on such occasions, fathers and mothers, and all who can bear a burden, often set out for weeks at a time, and leave their children to the care of two or three infirm old people. The infant progeny, some of whom are beginning to lisp, while others can just master a whole sentence, and those still further advanced, romping and playing together, the children of nature, through their live-long day, *become habituated to a*

---

[a] Science of Language, Part I. p. 353. [b] Ibid. p. 346.
[c] Ibid. p. 18. [d] Ibid. p. 53.

language of their own. The more voluble condescend
to the less precocious; and thus, from this infant
Babel, proceeds a dialect of a host of mongrel words
and phrases, joined together without rule, and, *in the
course of one generation the entire character of the
language is changed.*"

Such facts lay bare the whole process of, and the
reason for the existing diversity among tongues; for
the African villager of to-day is the reflex of what
civilized man was some 5000 years ago. The first
tendency of language was unquestionably to un-
bounded variety; and of this we have yet remaining
evidence in the superabundance of synonyms found
in ancient dialects. If we take so modern a form
of speech as the Sanskrit, we find that the more
primitive is the idea, the more words are there to
represent it. The proof of this axiom is found in
some statistics of the Sanskrit language published in
the "Notes and Queries," June 20, 1870. The writer
[F. P.] had arranged the Sanskrit bases under English
vocables as a kind of reversed dictionary, including
in the arrangement every fairly established radical in
the language. The conclusions are given in the following words:—

"There are between 1700 and 1800 *original* Sanskrit roots.
The exact number will be about 1780. These have been
registered under 645 English vocables; but as many of the
roots have been repeated under synonyms, and from difference
of conjugation, &c., it results that the arrangement includes
5658 apparent roots, giving an average of 3·2 meanings to
each radical. Now these 5658 apparent roots are most

unequally divided over their 645 English representatives. 180 words have only *one* root each; on the other hand, one word (*go*) has 439 roots to itself. There are five vocables with more than 100 roots each :—

(1) go	439
(2) injure	270
(3) sound	165
(4) shine	141
(5) speak	129
	1144

It will be seen that a large part of this total can be deducted from the 1780 *original* roots, as the ideas expressed differ too much to allow of much repetition. Thus we have the curious result that the major portion of the radicals express but five simple ideas. But deducting 1144 from the gross apparent number 5658, we have 4514 roots remaining. Selecting vocables which have between 50 and 100 radicals registered under them, we have—

(6) kill	75
(7) bind	54
(8) cut	56
(9) divide	50
(10) abuse	62
(11) throw	75
(12) tremble	57
(13) collect	61
(14) cover	56
(15) surround	61
	607

The primitive nature of these words will be noticed, and also that the two lists of only *fifteen* words comprise 1851 of the roots, or just one-third of the whole number.

There are *seventeen* words which have between 30 and 50

radicals registered under each, which I give in two divisions, as a new class of idea appears :—

Rougher Idea.

(16) break	. . . .	39
(17) burn	. . . .	31
(18) despise	. . . .	49
(19) join	. . . .	37
(20) firm (be)	. . . .	36
(21) give	. . . .	47
(22) take	. . . .	38
		—— 277

Gentler Idea.

(23) love	. . . .	32
(24) play	. . . .	36
(25) please	. . . .	31
(26) praise	. . . .	35
(27) worship	. . . .	31
(28) serve	. . . .	37
(29) desire	. . . .	41
(30) wish	. . . .	32
(31) increase	. . . .	40
(32) eat	. . . .	49
		—— 364
	Total . .	641

Descending lower, I find 39 vocables with between 20 and 30 radicals a-piece, comprising as a total 922 more of the gross number. It would make this communication too long to set these out at length ; but they contain the yet more developed ideas of 'adorn,' 'dwell,' 'flow,' 'know,' 'obtain,' 'preserve,' 'purify,' &c.

Beyond these there are 70 vocables with between 10 and 20 roots under each, which absorb 937 radicals among them, and introduce to us the yet more refined notions of 'colour,' 'cook,' 'finish,' 'fry,' 'learn,' 'prosper,' 'proud,' &c.

Now, collecting the foregoing totals, we have—

Vocables.				Roots.
Registering		No.		No.
100 +	. . . .	5	. . . . .	1144
50 to 100	. . . .	10	. . . . .	607
30 to 50	. . . .	17	. . . . .	641
20 to 30	. . . .	39	. . . . .	922
10 to 20	. . . .	70	. . . . .	937
Totals	. .	141		4251

Therefore, out of the whole number of words (645) under which the 5658 roots are registered, 141 words (or 21 per cent.) appropriate 4251 (or 75 per cent.), leaving only 1407 to be divided among the remaining 504 vocables, or an average of 2·79 roots a-piece. It is further seen that the simpler the idea, the larger is the number of roots found to express it; the whole illustrating in an unforeseen way the primitive character of the Sanskrit language.

The laws by which language has been developed from primitive articulations are few and simple; as, indeed, are all the operations of nature when we reach their real source.

Sir C. Lyell thus expresses himself on this question :—

It becomes a curious subject of inquiry, what are the laws which govern not only the invention, but also the selection of some of these words or idioms; giving them currency in preference to others ? Although when we observe the manner in which new words and phrases are thrown out, as if at random or in sport, while others get into vogue, we may think the process of change to be the result of mere chance,—there are nevertheless fixed laws in action, by which, in the general struggle for existence, some terms and dialects gain the victory over others.

c 2

Words change their forms by *Combination* and *Compression*, and their meanings by *Metaphoric usage.*

By *Combination* we mean the joining of two sounds, so as to produce a compound with a sense differing from that of either of the components taken separately, as, *up-rise, up-right.* By *Compression* we mean the blending of two or more sounds into one syllabic instant, which may or may not be accompanied with a change of sense; as, to *prise* (*i.e.* up-rise) a board. *Piplu* for *apiplu,* and *pidhána* for *apidhána,* are instances in Sanskrit. Under *Metaphor* we would include every change in the use of a vocable; for the assumption of a dynamic character by a static word, or its adverbial employment, are clearly metonymical processes. When we say, "*Hand* me a chair," the action requires the hand; but the employment of the word in this sense is as much metaphoric as it is when we speak of a *handy* tool.

The laws of the development of language are set forth in the following table :—

       1. Combination.
          a. Compounding.
          b. Reduplicating.
          c. Inflecting.
       2. Compression.
          a. Phonetic.
          b. Metastatic.
       3. Metaphor.

The process of *Combination* operates in several

ways. Sound is added to sound with a view to intensify the meaning. This process belongs to a very
early form of language, although it is a law of change
in full operation at the present day. As soon as
sounds were become consolidated into words,[a] they
could be added to each other for the purpose of more
precise definition; and a sound that successfully defined one thing would readily be applied to define
other things. Hence it results that these "definers"
would be among the first vocables to sink into mere
conventionalities; and this satisfactorily accounts for
the fact that what are termed "demonstrative bases"
(*i.e.* pronouns, &c.) are among the most petrified
fossils of language.

A further stage in the development of language
would be marked by the addition of word to word
with the object of qualifying or extending the meaning. These true compounds could be formed at a time
anterior to the separation of verbal, nominal, and demonstrative stems. Human speech must have passed
through such stages before it reached even the biliteral form of Arabic bases; because, as we think the
present inquiry will demonstrate that no more than one

---

[a] More will be said anon about the origin of words. It is, however, convenient to state here that so keen a thinker as A. W. von
Schlegel had no doubt on the subject. He says, "As regards inven-
tion, I find no difficulty in that either, since in order to comprehend
the absolute origin of language, we have no choice between having
recourse to a miracle, and conceding to mankind an instinctive
power of inventing language."—*Trans. Roy. Soc. Lit. U.K.* vol. ii.
p. 433.

letter can be safely allowed as the base of any word, it must follow that a base containing even two letters is the product of combination. The word "letter" here, and elsewhere in this book, means the uttered sound, and not the written character representing the sound.

Upon arriving at the stage just spoken of language became grammatical (see p. 29), that is, the knowledge of the origin of vocal symbols was entirely lost, and a conventional meaning existed for a number of sounds sufficient to express the simple wants of a primitive people. Fresh sounds doubtless would obtain currency, but from that time forward language would mainly develop by the *combination* of existing vocables, and by their application to new uses. It has been long ago known that the complex of modern speech arose from a very limited number of bases,— about two or three hundred stems proving a sufficient foundation on which to erect the Chinese and Semitic dictionaries respectively; and Professor Max Müller conjectures that some similar number will be found to be sufficient in the case of Aryan words. This conclusion has been arrived at by a comparison of words with actual bases; but, if we were to consider mere possibilities, then only eight or ten bases, by mutual combinations, would produce an infinitely greater number of words than is contained in the richest of languages. The actual number of words, then, in every language being much smaller than the possible combinations of the smallest number of bases ever likely to be seriously proposed for them, we have no difficulty in believing that when man's vocal utterances settled into conventionalities, the subsequent development could be effected by a mere word-building process. This view is further strengthened by considering the natural disinclination to indulge in useless toil. It is easier to combine two vocables together as attributive and nominal, than it is to cast about for a new and appropriate vocal symbol. A people possessing equivalents for *big* and *man* would be more disposed to place one before the other, than to invent the new term *giant*. So, doubtless, our remote ancestors, starting from the sound *i* = move, accompanied its pronunciation with a rattling of the tongue to indicate rapidity, and so produced the form *ṛi* = go quickly. It has been long ago remarked that the letter *r* gives a sense of rapidity to a vast number of Aryan words; and the quivering of the tongue upon the palate is certainly the simplest and most natural way of expressing rapidity by sound.* The word *ṛi*, then, would be an intensive, and, as familiarity breeds contempt, by usage it would gradually lose its intensive power, and at last be used as synonymous with *i*, 'go;' as we find, in Sanskrit, to have been actually the case. The sound *pă*, produced by a puff of breath

---

* Once, the great Talma, who was to the French stage what J. Kemble was to the English, said to one of us: "If you shut up your ears when we speak, keeping them open only to hear the buzz, you will remark that there is a continual vibratory sound through that *litera canina* (R), as Persius used to call it."

through the lips, would aptly convey an idea like *forth*,
forward, &c., and, as a matter of fact, the letters *p*, *v*,
f (which mutually interchange) enter into a large
number of words having such a meaning. Now, by
simply prefixing this sound *pă* to *ri* we orally describe
the idea *forward-go* or *move-on*. It seems certain
that such was the origin of the Sanskrit base *pri*, to
go forth, expand; and of the Sanskrit preposition *pra*,
the Greek πρὸ, the Latin *per*, the Teutonic *for*, *forth*,
fore, &c., &c.

These stages of formation had been traversed before
the records of language we possess came into being;
even the Egyptian inscriptions, the most solid bases
of antiquity, are written with words in the main of
settled formation, but which, as will be shown anon,
throw much light on the process just described.
Egyptian bases are biliteral in form, but so constantly
lose one of the letters in combining with each other,
that special inquiry may reduce them all to a few
uniliteral primitives. Here it will be sufficient to remark that the words of the Hieroglyphic language
were modified by many adjuncts or servile letters, the
origin and meaning of some of which have been traced.
The letters *d*, *r*, and *m*, are of this class. By their
insertion bases are modified materially in their meanings as well as forms. Thus, by way of example, *hān*,
to incline, becomes ᴅū*hān* and ʀo*hān*, 'to stand.' Of
these two serviles, the *r* is derived from an independent base aʀi or eʀ, 'to do;' and the *d* is from ᴅū, 'to
give,' a base found also in the word ᴅūt, 'the hand,' that

which gives; the *t* in this last word being also servile. The servile letter *m* is from ᴍū, ' to give,' and is similarly used. Thus the forms ᴍū*hān* and ʀo*hān* mean, literally, "to give an incline," and ᴅu*hān* is a true causal meaning "to make incline." Now when we find that it is possible to trace the servile letters of a language up to substantive vocables, we have actual demonstration of the reasoning before advanced.

Beside the addition of word to word so as to change the meaning, a love of Exaggeration is so natural to the human breast, that it will occasion no surprize to find its operation constituting a law in the building up of words. The meaning of a word can be exaggerated in two ways, (1) by the addition of other words which repeat the idea in another form, giving rise to such locutions as *hurly-burly*, *chitter-chatter*, and to such still more demonstrative words as the Hindî *tan-badan* = the body, in which both *tan* and *badan* have separately the sense of " body," and their combination only produces a bigger word. We say to children in France, " Allez faire *do-do* " (*dormire*, Latin).

This principle underlies the formation of the reduplicate preterite in Sanskrit and Greek, and such words as *did* (= do-do) in English. Nations with more primitive mental organism than our own avail themselves largely of this method of intensifying. Thus in India at the present day *achchhá achchhá* means "very good," *dúr dúr*, "very far," and so

on.* In the same way in ancient Sanskrit *gri*, to swallow,
was first fortified with a sibilant (by the same process
that converts *run* into *rush*), and assumed the form
gra-s; an asper still further intensified it, and it
became *ghas*. This last form when doubled, as in
the preterite, by common Indian euphonic laws, becomes *ja-ghas*, or, when rapidly pronounced, *jaksh*.
Hence this verb makes *jaghása*, "he swallowed," and
jakshuh, "they swallowed." The habit of exaggeration caused the idea of reduplication to be lost in the
case of this among other verbs. It became more common to say *eat-eat*, or *eat-up*, than to say *eat* only.
In consequence of this the form *jaksh* was ultimately
treated as a primitive word, and we find it separately
conjugated, as *jakshiti*, "he is eating," *jakshishyati*,
"he shall eat;" and in the preterite it is reduplicated
for the second time, and becomes *jajaksha*, "he did
eat."

This process of intensifying words, and when they
become familiar re-intensifying them—which we are
able to trace in the Sanskrit, because so many stages of
the literature of that language have been preserved,—
has been a powerful engine in the operation of those
changes which make the discovery of primitive bases
so difficult in our day. But through all its diversified
forms the onomatop is to be found, living on through

* The French, also, rarely content themselves with one *oui*, they
prefer a series, *oui, oui, oui;* and in this case, also, the sense of exaggeration is lost.

all changes like the vital principle animating the organic creature, and from the *grí* of the Rig-Veda to the modern English *gree-dy*, the sound *gă*, suggestive at once of the throat by which alone it can be produced, is for ever present to attest the impulse which first stamped this ὄνομα with sense.

The second method of exaggeration is easier, and no doubt more primitive, consisting of the simple expedient of repeating the word itself. As instances, we may cite the words GORGE, the throat, Fr. GORGE, It. GORGO, Germ. GURGEL; and to GUGGLE or GURGLE, Fr. GLOUGLOU, Swiss GUNGELN, Modern Greek ΚλουΚλου. Both these words are formed by a repetition of the base found in Sanskrit under the form *grí* or *gal*, to eat, the parent of *gala*, the throat, Lat. *gula*, Fr. *gueule*, and all the thousands of derivatives which arose in boundless profusion from this highly suggestive sound. So fully recognised is this method of repetition in Sanskrit that every base in the language admits of reduplication in a frequentative or intensive sense. The rule being general, it would be useless to cite special examples; and the words *gorge* and *gurgle* are mentioned merely to show that, like the *Bourgeois Gentilhomme*, we are continually performing a feat without knowing it.* Similarly, the Hindûs say *dug-*

---

* Numerous other such words readily suggest themselves, as the Greek γορ-γὸς, γαρ-γαρίζω, γαρ-γαρισμὸς, γαρ-γαρεὼν, γόρ-γυσμὸς, Γαρ-γαφία (a gurgling fountain in Bœotia); the Latin, *gur-ges*, *gur-gustium*, &c.; the French *gar-gote*, *gar-gotier*, *gar-gouille*, *gar-gousse*; the English *gar-gle*, &c.

dugáná, " to beat a drum," *khilkhiláná,* " to burst out laughing," *lakhlakháná,* " to gasp, pant," &c., &c.; and the Arabs say, *taftafat,* " weakness," *sinsin,* " thirst," *dardar,* " eating," &c. &c.

We will now, however, seek the assistance of those marvellous old hieroglyphs of Egypt, and trace this phenomenon to a conscious process. The well-known Egyptologist, M. G. Maspero, says,[a] "Repetition is the simplest manner of increasing the sense of a root; and, therefore, in Egyptian, as well as in most languages, radical repetition is sometimes intended to mark an increase of the action. Q⁰N, *to beat,* develops itself into Q⁰NQ⁰N, *to give somebody a sound thrashing.* But this is rarely the case: repetition ordinarily is a modification of the word without any modification of the idea. S⁰NS⁰N, *to breathe,* B⁰NB⁰N, *to spring,* have no more value than S⁰N, B⁰N: they are both of them mere variations of the words, corresponding to no particular shade of variety in the fundamental thought. The sole difference between them is that S⁰N is a monosyllable, while S⁰NS⁰N is a dissyllable." This is another way of stating, and of proving, our proposition that words are repeated so as to intensify their meaning, and that a certain amount of usage evaporates the exaggeration originally intended. The laws of Compression then operate, and pave the way for fresh inflation. The Egyptian words just cited may be compared with the following from Sanskrit:

---

[a] " The Academy," vol. iii. p. 377.

gam = go, *jangam* = go repeatedly; *pí* = drink, *pepí* * = drink excessively—and so on, every Sanskrit base being subject to a similar exaggeration.

A third method of combining word-sounds is that intended to express the relations which words bear to each other. This is the principle underlying all grammatical inflexion and syntactical arrangement, and is one of the most obscure processes in the science of language. Fortunately it is not necessary to enter into much detail, as the result of the study of comparative philology has produced a pretty [general impression among scholars, that unquestionably all grammatical formatives originated in independent vocables.

Prof. Max Müller is very clear on this point : "We know that grammatical terminations, as they are now called, were originally independent words, and had their own purpose and meaning." [b] Again: "We are accustomed to the idea of grammatical terminations modifying the meaning of words. *But words can be modified by words only ;* and though in the present state of our science it would be too much to say that all grammatical terminations have been traced back to original independent words, so many of them have, even in cases where only a single letter was left, that we may well lay it down as a rule that all formal elements of language were originally substantial." [c]

* *Pépie* has passed entirely into the French " avoir la pépie" = to feel the want of drinking.

[b] Science of Language, Part I. p. 202.   [c] Ibid., p. 215.

Such are the views of a scholar at the head of the
modern school of philology, so that as we also arrive at
the same opinion by independent processes, it must be
admitted that the theory has a claim to be received as
established fact.   Let us now quote M. Maspero on
the working of this law as illustrated in the development of the Egyptian language.   That learned scholar
thus writes :[a] " Egyptian roots are not, properly
speaking, nouns, adjectives, or verbs :[b] they express
the idea independent of grammatical category, and
may, according to their relative position, play the
same part that nouns, adjectives, and verbs, play in our
modern languages.   Thus √ÂA may signify *great*,
greatness, *to be great;* s°M, *to hear* (*to obey*),
obedience, *obedient*, and are therefore not definite
nouns, adjectives, or verbs, but only possibilities of
nouns, adjectives, or verbs.   Their grammatical category resides not in their material form, but in the
mind of him who speaks or hears.   Hence it comes
that the Egyptians possess nothing which we may
say corresponds exactly to our declinations or con-
jugations.   By dint of personal pronouns affixed as
signs of the subject to the roots of appellative value,

[a] " The Academy," vol. iii. p. 378. This excellent journal always
gives the last results of modern scholarship, and its articles are,
therefore, of even greater authority on the subjects treated than
are the works of the scholars who write them.

[b] The same is also true of Chinese and Sanskrit roots. As the
Egyptian language is Semitic, and the Chinese Turanian, we have
thus the oldest forms of each family of language agreeing in the
power to be ascribed to their primitive bases.

they contrived to build small phrases Mᵉʀ-ᴀ, Mᵉʀ-ᴋ, by which they devolved the possession of the idea expressed by the root upon one of the three persons, but without creating any definite grammatical category. Mᵉʀ-ᴀ, Mᵉʀ-ᴋ, signify, after a general fashion, *love-o'mine, love-o'thine;* but we were not right to interpret them, when taken isolatedly, by *I love, thou lovest,* more than by *my love, thy love:* it is only their position in a sentence which determines the special value we are obliged to give them for the nonce, and enables us to see whether they are to be rendered by one of our substantives or by one of our verbs. Mᵉʀ-ᴀ ᴀᴛᵉw-ᴀ is translated, 'I love my father;' and we say that Mᵉʀ-ᴀ is the first person of a verb, the regimen of which is ᴀᴛᵉw-ᴀ. But Mᵉʀ-ᴀ and ᴀᴛᵉw-ᴀ are two locutions constructed on exactly the same pattern, and which, when isolated, express the attribution to the first person of the general ideas *love, father;* being united in the same proposition, they become the two terms of an equation, Mᵉʀ-ᴀ $=$ ᴀᴛᵉw-ᴀ, *love-o'mine=father-o'mine,* where the relative position of the factors induces us to bestow upon Mᵉʀ-ᴀ the quality verb, *I love,* while in another equation, ᴍᴀ̄ᴀ̄ ɴᴜ̂ᴛᵉʀ Mᵉʀ-ᴀ, *God sees my love,* we would be obliged to give it the substantive value of *my love.* Mᵉʀ-ᴀ being alike a substantive or a verb, may, in its verbal impersonations, denote the past as well as the present, and the future as well as the past. The Egyptians contented themselves with indicating the fact of the action being done, and with naming the doing person; they left to the hearer's or reader's mind the care of ascertaining, according to the tenor of the phrase, the moment of duration in which the action is, has been, or will be present."

M. Maspero also describes a further development, by which the Egyptians gave a more definite character to their words. Four roots, *a*, *p*, *t*, *n*, when vocalized with the vowel *ú*, were used to give a verbal signification to bases, but when vocalized with the letter *ā* produced forms with a power similar to that of the definite article. These prefixes were used by no means indiscriminately, though we need not here be minute in our description of their grammatical functions. It is enough, by way of illustration, to say that TĀZ°D-A or TĀ-A Z°D represented "my word," while TÚZ°D-A or TÚ-A Z°D meant "I speak;" so also NĀAR-A = "my deeds," and ÚN AR-A = "I do." The personal pronoun A = "I, me, my," can, as we have just seen, change its place in Egyptian. It can, indeed, be used along with the auxiliary in three ways: by being added (1) to the auxiliary itself, AÚ-A M°R, *the being-of me love* = *I love*; (2) to the verb, AÚ M°R-A, *the being love-of-me* = *I love*; (3) both to the auxiliary and to the verb, AÚ-A M°R-A; *the being-of-me love-of-me* = *I love*.

We shall only touch upon one more point of Egyptian grammar, and that is the evolution of a participial form. The auxiliary ÚN, *to exist*, (curiously like the Sanskrit *an*, to breathe, the base of *an-imus*, &c.) was used, without the vocalizing helpmate *ú*, also to express existence. In this form it followed verbal stems and gave to them the sense of participles. Thus ûn-*n* AMEN meant " the being *which is* Ammon," or " Ammon's being; " and ûn-*n*-A = " the being *which is* me," or " my being." The use of the auxiliary expressed an insistence on the idea which enabled it to perform the office of a past tense. An idea of " possession " underlies all verbal inflection— "I walk " means that the walking is mine, " I shall eat " that the eating will be mine, and so on. In the same way an insistence on actual possession would fairly convey the idea of the past tense, that is, the possession which is possession. Therefore the form ûn-*n*-A meant not only *my being* but also *I was* (or " the being actually being mine "), in the same way M˙R-A, *loving of me*, or *I love*, becomes much stronger in the form M˙R-*n*-A, *the loving being (actually) mine*, or *I loved*. The future tense was formed in a similar rational manner, by the addition of the base R, *to do;* thus, Aû-A-R M˙R = *I am to do the loving*, or *I shall love*.

Theory is quite superfluous after such lucid facts. We need no longer speculate on the possible origin of grammatical formatives when the whole process is made manifest by the structure of the venerable language preserved on the monuments of Egypt.

It will, we think, be interesting to show that the very processes found in Egyptian, and which may have seemed somewhat mysterious to the reader, are to be seen in operation at the present day in Turanian languages. The construction of these languages allows their formations to be more easily separated and examined than is the case with the more highly organized Aryan forms of speech. Not to weary with details we will content ourselves with an instance from Turkish. This language possesses no verb equivalent to the English *to have*, to express which relationship the Turks employ an impersonal verb *var*=" existing," precisely as is the case in Egyptian. This base *var* is joined with the genitive and a form of the verb *dur-mak*="to stand, to be, to remain." Thus we get *binim-var-dar* "of me there is the being"=*I have ;* *binim-var-edi*, " of me there was the being"=*I had*, and so on, in striking analogy to the method of the hieroglyphs. This impersonal verb *var* is to be deduced from the regular infinitive *ol-mak*, ' to be,' by the common change of *l* into *r*, the proof of this alliance being found in the fact that, in the future and imperative, the regular verb is used: thus, *binim-ol-ur*, " of me it will be,"=*I shall have ; binim-ol-is-un*, " of me let it be."[a] The change of *ol* into *var* is not so great as at first sight may appear. Another verb from Turkish will show how the change came about,—the infinitive " to beat " though written *or-mak* is pronounced *vour-mak*. The fact, however, with which we are mainly concerned, and which is perfectly clear, is that the idea of possession is expressed in both Turkish and Egyptian by the insertion, as a verbal

---

[a] The verb *to have* or *hold* is almost peculiar to Europe. Indian languages supply its place in precisely the same way as the Turkish does.

inflexion, of a base of which the primary sense is "being." The French say phraseologically *C'est à moi* to convey the same idea.

The Chinese language is not chosen for illustration, because, as is well known, it contains nothing that at all approaches our ideas of an inflection. It is an interesting example of the theory of Survivals found in language, one perfect word being modified by the juxtaposition of another perfect word, just as we say was the case originally in all other languages.

In the preceding remarks we have confined ourselves to a few examples illustrating the formation of verbal inflexions, because they are among the most obscure of all the changes that words have undergone. The personal terminations in most languages can readily be referred to the personal pronouns. In Semitic grammars rules are actually given for the modification of personal pronouns so as to fit them to become the terminations of verbs. In Turanian languages, also, apocopated forms of these pronouns are regular verbal affixes; and in the Aryan languages the same thing can be recognized, though with greater difficulty. When we see how an idea of personality is imparted to Semitic and Turanian bases, there can be no longer a doubt that the termination ·*m*· for the first person of all Sanskrit tenses, and the tenses of so many other Aryan languages, is identical with the ·*m*· found in all those languages as the pronominal *me, my, mine,* Greek *è-μός,* Latin *meum,* Span. and Ital. *mi-o,* French *moi,* Persian *man,* Hindî *main,* Sanskrit *mám,* &c.

So again, the termination ·*t*· of the second person singular is the base upon which *thee*, *thou*, Latin *te*, French *te*, Persian *tú*, Hindî *tain*, Sanskrit *twam*, &c., have been erected. The personal terminations blend so completely with the stems in Aryan languages that it is impossible to separate them more distinctly than in the indefinite way above given. The dot before and after the *t* and *m* may be taken to stand for some unknown vocalizing element, which may have preceded or followed the consonant.

What we have just advanced about conjugation is equally applicable to declension; but on this point we will content ourselves with citing Professor M. Müller. He says, " Originally declension could not have been anything but the composition of a noun with some other word expressive of number and case."[a]

As it is not our object to trace grammatical forms to their origin, but only to adduce such facts as will support the general laws we enounce, the foregoing details are amply sufficient for the purpose. We hope our illustrations, and the authority of Professor Max Müller, will have satisfactorily proved the fact that the relations which words bear to each other are expressed by the addition of word to word, and are not the result of any mysterious or incomprehensible process.

The foregoing will be enough to show the existence of combining principles in the formation of language; and but few words are necessary to establish the com-

[a] Science of Language, Part I. p. 205.

pressibility of compounded sounds. This latter law of growth is, indeed, so patent that it has never, to the writers' knowledge, been doubted. It is, nevertheless, a process of much interest to the student of language, as it affords historical evidence of undoubted truth, whence certain laws of permutation may be deduced, by which hypothetical forms of words can be constructed carrying the inquirer back, logically and scientifically, to primitive onomatopic bases. Horne Tooke spoke of what is here called a law of compression as arising from a desire to abbreviate the labour of utterance; we shall, however, be able to show that it is not due solely to this cause. "There are not only signs of sounds," says Horne Tooke, "but signs of those signs one under the other in a continual progression."

It will, perhaps, be sufficient if we mark two fairly distinct laws of compression: 1. Phonetic corruption; 2. Metastasis.

Words are in a perpetually unstable condition from the operation of phonetic corruption. All the vast machinery of social intercourse, of schools, and of literature, is impotent to stop the powers of nature*; the Word passes on from mouth to mouth for ever subject to the varying aspects of the speakers' mental constitutions. The speakers are quite unconscious of the changes which they themselves are operating. They hear the word and think that they repeat it ac-

* Since this book has been in the press, Dr. Fitzedward Hall has illustrated this truth with remarkable clearness, in his work on "Modern English."

curately, but yet unconsciously modify it. In early times no effort was spent on exactitude, and no institutions preserved traditions of what once was ; accordingly words then changed more rapidly than is the case in these days. The long word *folium*, found in the Latin *trifolium*, dwindles down to *fl* in the French *trèfle;* the Sanskrit *madhya,* Latin *medium,* Greek μέσος, French *milieu,* English *middle,* sinks to *mi* in the French *à mi-corps,* half-length. We have elsewhere adduced reason for believing that the letter *f* in the word *lift* is all that remains of the words *above, over, up,* and that the word *lift* meant originally *lay-up,* the *p* undergoing a change similar to that which educes the French *cuivre* out of *copper.* It must not be supposed that we imagine for a moment that the French word *cuivre* arises from abortive attempts tó pronounce the English word *copper ;* on the contrary, it is our firm conviction that there is much less of this kind of derivation in the world than is generally supposed. It seems almost certain that no language whatever was ever derived from any other language by a relationship akin to that of mother and daughter. The spoken languages of to-day had their original at the parent fount of universal speech quite independent of classical mediation. The dialects of the dominant tribes in the peninsulas of Greece and Italy acquired a fictitious importance from the martial conquests of their speakers, and from the literature clothed in their dress; but it must not be forgotten that other ethnically cognate tribes inhabited both Greece and Italy along with those who finally gained the political superiority. These independent colonies never derived their languages from what we call Greek and Latin; although, after their absorption, their languages were necessarily modified by the genius of their masters. The different dialects of modern Italian and modern Greek carry the indelible marks of the independence of these primitive colonies, and are thus of equal value to the philologist with their more renowned rivals. If the dialects of Italian are not derived from Latin still less can the speech of the Goths, Vandals, Franks, Gauls, Lusitanians, &c., be derived from that language. The commonly prevalent teaching on this matter is, therefore, unsustainable.

As a remarkable instance of phonetic corruption let us take the English copula *and*. In German this word is written *und;* in Dutch the *d* is dropped and it becomes *en;* in Latin the *n* is lost, and it is pronounced *et;* in French, though still written *et,* it is sounded like *ay;* in Italian the last consonant is rejected, and it is written *e* while preserving the French sound; and, finally, in Spanish the sound is further modified to the vowel sound of *y*. Thus we see that the word *and* by phonetic corruption alone becomes *y*. But what is this word *and*? and whence does it derive its sense of copulation? To answer these questions we must trace it through its Indian forms. In Bengalî we find the same idea expressed by *o*, and in Hindî by *au* and *aur*. In these words no trace is found of the medial *n*, and the vowel has the *u* sound as in the German *und.* But the Hindî form *au* or *aur* also means "other," and through this sense points to its derivation from the old Sanskrit word *antara,* which means "different, separate." The word *aur* is a phonetic corruption of *antara,* just as the English *or* comes from *other.* Thus we see that the word *and* is an abbreviated form of the Sanskrit *antara,* Gothic *anthar,* Anglo-Saxon *oþer,* and that its original intention was to mark a difference between two objects. And it is really a sense of difference that we recognize in the word *and.* "This and that" means, etymologically, "this other that," *i.e.,* "this thing with that other thing." The word *other,* as will be perceived, preserves both the form and sense of the parent better than its rival *and.*

It is almost superfluous to prove that *or* and *other* were originally the same, still we may as well cite a case: thus, in Higden's Polichronicon we read, "for þis nyȝt I schal assaye wheþer I schal overcome oþer be overcome." We also read, "I douȝte wheþer I schulde be wroþe eþer no;" which shows that *either* is another form of the same word; as are also the compounds *whether* and *neither.*

Mr. Wedgwood with much ingenuity argues that *and* is a possible form of *even,* and was intended to place two objects on a level, and so mark their connectedness; but the foregoing and following remarks will, we think, show that such a view is untenable. The word *antara* is also found in Sanskrit deprived of its nasal, in the word *itara,* and this latter word has exactly the same meaning and use as the former. But *itara* reveals its origin, because in this shape we are able to resolve it into the two parts, *i* and *tara*, the first being the proximate definite explained at the end of the Præfamen, and the second being the Sanskrit noun expressing "passage, crossing," derived from a verbal base, *trí*, "to cross over." The same noun, *tara*, also forms the termination of the comparative degree of adjectives in Aryan languages ; as the Persian *bih-tar*, English *bet-ter*, Sanskrit *puṇya-tara*, English *pur-er ;* but it dwindles, by phonetic corruption, to the letter *r* only in such words as the Latin *melio-r*, and the English *mo-re*. As the sign of comparison it means " beyond," and this is also the sense which the same base, *trí*, bears in the Latin prefix *trans-*, and the French *très*. Hence we see that *i-tara* means " beyond this," a very rational expression for the ideas still conveyed by *other, and,* &c.

The primitive meaning of *trí* is, however, " cross over ;"—it is a compound formed of *·t·*, the remote definite="there "+*ri*="go," and is, therefore, equivalent to " go there," *i. e.*, "motion to that place." This analysis satisfactorily accounts for its use in another sense, as in the word *antar-ála*, Sanskrit ; *inter-vallum*, Latin ; *inter-val*, English, for where *this* crosses to *that* there must be *inter*-vening space. A similar line of reasoning shows the origin of such Sanskrit words as *anya*, other ; *antra*, intestine ; *antar*, within ; *anta*, the end ; *antima*, last, &c., &c. ; and the Latin *inter-us*, *inter-ior*, *alt-er*, *ulter-ior*, *ult-ra*, and the thousands of derivatives that will readily suggest themselves to the reader.

The changes of which we have been speaking are caused by the attrition of use, and arise, in some respects, from a disinclination to take more trouble than is necessary to make oneself understood. It is a law of abbreviation very manifestly marked in the language of the Egyptian Hieroglyphs. The Egyytians, it seems, had an affection for monosyllables, so that the process of intensifying by reduplication, though gratifying a natural love of exaggeration, was irksome in the utterance. "To overcome that difficulty,"—we again quote M. Maspero,—"the Egyptians had no resource left but to drop one of the three last radicals, the first being always respected. Thus, QᵉʙQᵉʙ becomes QᵉQʙ, by dropping the second radical; QᵉʙB and QBᵉʙ, by dropping the third; QᵉʙQ or QBᵉQ, by dropping the fourth; so that each biliteral monosyllable, being raised to the square, turns out to be the common stock for three triliteral monosyllables, all of them signifying the same thing."

Phonetic corruptions such as those above described have played an important part in the development of language. By their means, primitive bases, in originating derivatives, have lost their first form; the altered form, in possibly an altered sense, has given birth to new derivatives yet further departing from the parent type; and these last, becoming tertiary bases, have produced other derivatives, able in their turn to carry on the process of development in ever-widening circles.

One thing these changes impress upon our minds in an especial way, and that is the unwisdom of the clamour made by some philologist about the essential distinction between termination and base. It is abundantly evident that in no language have the ultimate bases been as yet discovered, and this fact has caused even the best scholars to draw an arbitrary line at a certain period in the development of language, and to assert that the bases then existing were part of man's nature, and among his ingenerate attributes. Such an idea is pure mythology. Our researches lead to the conviction that the primitive bases exist now only as single letters; whenever two letters, certainly whenever two consonants, are joined together, there we have the remains of two or more bases. The number of these bases must be very small,—they are all contained in the alphabet of the universe,—and will in each case be found to be the natural expression of a material fact, that is, a true onomatop.

The desire for abbreviating the labour of speaking would of itself suffice to make an originally homogeneous language break up into rapidly diverging sections. The impulses of man's nature being ever the same, we can readily understand that long before historic time began, the whole form of language had been repeatedly changed, broken down, and renewed, leaving behind no traces of its former states. But the same being operating with the same means, and propelled by the same desires, would, however, con-

tinually remodel the same natural forces to a like
result, and thus how repeatedly soever the elements
were combined and dissolved, they would be for ever
present, awaiting only the labour of the scientific
analyst to resolve the compounded mass, and to separate
it into primary atoms. Διπλοῦν ὁρῶσιν οἱ μαθόντες
γράμματα.

The complete fluidity of language was brought
to an end by civilization. The utterly savage state
would allow of any amount of diversity, so long as
the needs of the passing moment were subserved; but
the first approach to civilization implies community of
interest, with some amount of fixedness in occupation,
in abode, in ideas, and therefore fixedness in vocal
symbols.

Metastasis is another form of phonetic corruption.
By this process the letters composing a word are
not rubbed off or blended into new sounds; they
remain in the word, and are changed only in position.
After metastasis has taken place, however, a word is
still liable to ordinary phonetic corruption, so that
in the course of time its identity is completely de-
stroyed. This law of change is the most obstructive
to the student of language; for as long as the letters
remain in their natural order they can be tracked
through an indefinitely long series of permutations,
but if any part of the series is traversed by metastasis,
the clue to the labyrinth is gone, and is only recovered
by a lucky hazard. Instances of genuine metastasis

are happily somewhat rare, but are sufficiently numerous to prove their undoubted existence. Such are
the following:—

Lat. sᴘᴇcto becoming in Gr. σΚέΠ-τομαι.
Eng. ᴘoт ,, ,, Germ. тoᴘƒ.
Eng. ʙᴜтt ,, ,, Eng. тᴜʙ.
Eng. ʙᴜтt* ,, ,, Lat. тᴜʙᴜs, тᴜʙa.
Eng. ʙᴇʟly ,, ,, Germ. ʟᴇiʙ.
Lat. ꜰoʟium ,, ,, Eng. ʟᴇaꜰ.

A milder form of metastasis is frequently present,
giving rise to duplicate forms in the same language,
such as *blabber* developed from *babbler*, *board* from
broad, *bird* from the older *bridde*, and *bocla* from
bloca the Provençal for a knob. In Sanskrit words
ending in *ṛi* regularly change that termination to *ir*
in the past participle; thus *kṛi*, to scatter, becomes
kirṇa; *gṛi*, to eat, becomes *gírṇa*, and so on.

These metastases arise in some part from carelessness,
and in some part from physical peculiarities. We have
known boys continually to say "regually" for "regularly," and be apparently quite unconscious of the
difference. We have here nothing to do with the
cause, we only chronicle the fact; and the single
example of *spec-* becoming σκέπ- is sufficient to prove it.

Words change their meanings as well as their shapes,
and a change in meaning frequently occasions some

---

* These words, *pot*, *butt*, proceed from the base *pá* or *pí*, 'to
suck,' as is shown by their Hindi forms *pípá*, a barrel or butt, and
pípí, a tube or pipe. This is seen clearly in the expression "a
pipe of wine."

changes in form which in the original sense could never have taken place. The science of language concerns itself as much with the meanings of sounds as with the sounds themselves, hence it follows that what operates such changes of a meaning is a law in the development of language. We think that all such changes of meaning arise from *Metaphor*, that disposition which man invariably manifests to describe that for which vocables are wanting by such words as he has at command,—speaking of the analogic unknown in the likeness of the known.

Dr. Daniel Wilson, in his work on Præ-Historic Man, brings before our minds a remarkable historical instance of the development of language by the application of existing vocables to new objects. "In the slow migration of the human family," he says, "from the great central hives, language imperceptibly adapted itself to the novel requirements of man. But, with the discovery of America, a new era began in the history of migration. In its novel scenes language was at fault. It seemed as if language had its work to do anew, as when first framed amid the life of Eden. The same has been the experience of every new band of invading colonists on its first arrival in the new world. That its English settlers, after occupying the continent for three centuries, instead of inventing root-words wherewith to designate plants and animals, as new to them as the nameless living creatures were to Adam in Paradise, apply in an irregular and unscientific manner the names of British and European flora and fauna. Thus the name of the English *partridge* is applied to one American tetranoid (*Tetras umbrel-lus*); the *pheasant* to another (*Tetra cupido*); and that of the familiar British warbler, the *robin*, to the *Turdus migratorius*, a totally different American *thrush*." So also E. A. Eyre, says, "When an Australian sees an object unknown to him, he does not invent a name for it, but immediately gives it a name drawn from its resemblance to some known object."

This natural propensity to apply an existing vocable to a new idea can be illustrated by the Sanskrit base previously cited (p. 26). *Gri*, to swallow with the throat, easily began to express the idea of eating in general; and as eating implies seizing with the mouth, as an animal does its prey, so this mouth-seizing would gradually come to include seizing of any kind. And this is undoubtedly the origin of the form *grabh*, "to seize," found in the Rig-Veda,[a] and which still lives in the vulgar English *grab*, to *grip*, or *grasp;* but which was softened into *grih*, "to take," and still further modified to *hri*, "to convey," in the later forms of Sanskrit. This word has even reversed its meaning, as is seen by the Gaelic *gabh*, "to take ;" the Gothic *giban*, the English *give* (Wedgwood). The vocable for seizing, after being applied to the idea of conveyance in general, gradually began to express every species of hauling and drawing, from the ploughed marks or furrows on the land to the lines

[a] A collection of 1017 hymns, in Sanskrit, addressed to the powers of nature. This is the oldest book in any Aryan language.

on a tablet or canvas, and so originated the Greek form γράφω, the Latin *graphicus*, English, *graphic;* Greek γραφίς, a drawing-pencil or pen ; γραφίον, a writing style ; whence the French *greffe*, stylet, and. *greffe*, an office where writings are engrossed and deposited ; also, in agriculture, the insertion of a small twig, like a stylet, in another tree is called *grafting*. Now the word *bio-graphy* would never suggest the idea of *eating* to modern ears ; but the above shows how simple is the process which has produced so artificial a word.

When *grabh* or *graph* assumes an initial sibilant, a very common change, it becomes *scribere*, in which the *crib* is clearly the Greek γραφ. From *scribere* proceed, of course, *scriba* and *scri-nium*, and such metaphorical terms as *de-scribe ;* also the English *scribble* and *write;* for *w* in this last word represents a guttural letter, just as *worm* is identical with the Hindî *kirm*, and the Sanskrit *krimi*.

As the evolution of γράφω from *grí* may, by some, be thought purely speculative, we will adduce one or two instances equally remarkable and more patent to the sceptic. When we *re-cover* our heads the term employed seems exactly to suit the action ; but when we *recover* lost property it is not so apparent that our intention is to bring the article again under the shelter of our protection ; and when we *recover* from sickness the last thread of connexion snaps. Here we have a common word, without the smallest change of form, assuming three very different meanings, caused solely by the operation of this law of Metaphor. But the word *re-cover* in any sense is now far removed from its basic signification. We get it from the French *re-couvrir*, *i.e.* re-*couvrir*, to cover again, the analogous Italian form being *coprire*, from the Latin *cooperire*, *i.e.* con-*operire*. And what is *operire?* It is an excellent instance to prove that French is not derived from Latin, but had an independent growth; because the French word is nearer to the older Sanskrit form than is the Latin, and it is inconceivable that a word having once been corrupted should, by further corruption, approach nearer to its original form. The Sanskrit form is *sam+vṛi*, meaning literally, " to surround with "; nor need we stop there, for *vṛi* itself, which by some would be called a primitive base, can be resolved into *vi+ṛi*, literally "to go about," a very natural and descriptive onomatop for the idea conveyed by " surround." But it may be asked how does the writer [F. P.] know that *operire* is at all connected with *vṛi?* The answer is that he has detected several other Latin words in which the same change manifests itself. For instance, *op-tare*, to choose,—in Sanskrit *vṛi* has also the sense of choosing ;—*op-erari* means " to operate, work, engage oneself in," and the Sanskrit base *vṛit* has precisely the same meaning; *op-es*, *op-imo*, *op-ulens*, &c., convey an idea of " riches," &c., and the Sanskrit *vṛidh* does the same ; *op-acus* means "shadowy" and the Sanskrit *vṛish*, to rain, whence *varsha*, " a cloud," shows the origin of the term ; *op-timus*,=" best, most to be chosen," is the equi-

E

valent of the Sanskrit *vrind-âraka*, "excellent," from
vri, "to choose." Some words show the alliance still
more plainly, such as *orbs*, *orbit*, in which the presence
of *vri*, to go round, is manifest   In the same way we
might ally the Latin *or-care*,[a] to shout, with the
Sanskrit *vrih* or *vrimh*, having a similar meaning;
or-dia, "first, principal," with *varh* or *valh*, "good,
pre-eminent," of (?) *vrish* "to be grand, powerful;"
and *or-are*, "to speak," seems to have been as active a
word in Sanskrit as it is in Latin, for a whole series of
bases exist presenting modified forms of *vri*, all having
the sense of "speaking:" thus, *vrimh*, *varh*, *valh*,
vridh, *vrit*, *vat*, *vad*, [?*vaj*], *vichh*, *vach*. The ima-
ginary base *vaj* is introduced merely to show the
phonetic link connecting *vach* with *vad*, the latter
being unquestionably derived, through *vat*, from the
form *vrit*. All these Sanskrit bases mean "speak,"
and again we find the sound *vri* modified to *or-o* in
Latin. A very little trouble would bring together
many more instances, but enough has been done to
show that *o-*, *op-*, *or-*, *orb-*, in certain Latin words
actually represent the *vri* of Sanskrit. It is contrary
to all the teaching of modern scholarship to suppose
that *sam-vri* having once degenerated into *co-operire*
could ever have gone back, by further corruption, to
the form *cou-vrir*; ergo the French word is independent of the Latin word. Furthermore, such words as
coupe, *cupidité*, *Cupidon*, &c., show that the French

---

[a] Auctor. Philom

would have found no difficulty in uttering the Latin *cooperire* had they tried to do so. There can, therefore, be no doubt that the exact meaning of *re-cover* is " to again surround with," and that it has acquired other meanings by metaphoric usage.

The word *box* is a most familiar instance of the many different ideas which metaphor will make a word represent.

In the foregoing instances (p. 47) we, incidentally, met one of the most pertinent objections to the theory of onomatops, which we advocate and maintain. Mr. Henry Sweet, in the course of a review in the " Academy,"[a] says, " The most primitive and indispensable words of language are just those which could not possibly have originated from imitation; the first object of language must have been to make known material wants such as *hunger* and *thirst*, not to call attention to the song of the nightingale, or discuss the ornithology of the cuckoo." We have seen above the simple guttural exclamation *gă*, giving birth to vocables expressive of the first wants of man (*grî*, to eat), and slowly enlarging in import with the growing exigencies of society, until ending in such words as *bio-graphy* and *graft-ing*. This is the process to which Mr. Sweet alludes, but does not rightly appreciate, when he says that, "as language increases in copiousness and precision, the imitation and gesture words drop out, and are replaced by legitimate non-imitation words." The real truth being that the

[a] Vol. iii. p. 219.

natural and animal utterances of man become consolidated into conventional symbols by advancing civilization, and afterwards assume new meanings by metaphoric usage.

Enough has now been said to define accurately our views on the development of onomatops; and of Onomatops themselves it may here be said that they are not sounds imitative of other animals, or of the powers of nature; they are not interjections, the exponents of transient passion; they are not innate bases with unalterable senses, created with man as an attribute of his being; but they are the simple sounds which man utters in common with the brute, but which the mental organization of man has wrought to the perfection of Homeric and Shakesperian verse.

We may say, in the words of J. S. Mill, when discussing universal law,[a] that we "have been enabled to see more clearly, in the progress of the investigation, the basis of all these logical operations is the law of causation. The validity of all the inductive methods depends on the assumption that every event, or the beginning of every phenomenon, must have some cause, some antecedent, on the existence of which it is invariably, and unconditionally consequent."

[a] Logic, ch xxi., Evidence of the Law of Universal Causation.

PRÆFAMEN.

FROM the Philosophy of Inductive Sciences, *Language* is called an instrument of thought;[*] but it is also the atmosphere for living thought. On the one side a medium essential to the activity of our speculative powers, invisible and imperceptible in its operations; and, on the other side, an element modifying by its quantity and changes the growth and complexion of the faculties which it feeds.

Onomatops are the primitive and original forms of the human language—the Ἐντελέχεια of Aristotle (De Animâ), or perfection coming from superior causes, pre-existent, and capable of receiving life and becoming finished vocables—the λόγος—what Geology is to the knowledge and science of our globe; or Astronomy to the study of the physical laws of the heavenly bodies; —or the representation of universe after its contemplation. Words exist from the very nature of man, springing from the faculties which enable him to obey the impulses of his being, urging him to express by sounds the wants and fears of his life, and the tempests of internal passion. All vocables become cognizable

---

[*] Words are the notes of thought, and nothing more;
Words are like sea shells on the shore,
    They show
Where the mind ends, and not how far it has been.
Bailey's Festus

through onomatops, because they are symbols of creation—*figmenta verborum*—the medium by which children learn all that they know, for the simple reason that that *fleur de rhétorique* is the *vox naturæ*, the corner-stone, from all antiquity, to the majestic edifice of language, and the very source of light from which flow the elements of strength and grace of the λόγος.

The word Onomatop, or more correctly Onomatopoïeia, is derived from the base of the oblique cases of ὄνομα and the verb ποιέω. It would have been more appropriate to have evoked a new term from τύπτω, since an Onomatopoïeia is a vocable coined, stamped to the effigy of the subject represented, of the nation where it is represented, and of the age in which it has been represented. The inconvenient length of the old term, on the one hand, and the desire to avoid the affectation of coining an altogether new word, on the other hand, have induced us to cut off boldly the latter portion of the word Onomatopoïeia, and to reduce it to the more wieldy proportions of Onomatop. The reader of this book will find that this is by no means the first time that a word has dwindled down to a single letter. This time the process is effected consciously, and for a practical purpose.

Onomatops have escaped the convulsions which have agitated the globe, and the revolutions which have again and again remodelled society, because they are fundamental and eternal principles. The ὄνομα once struck by the electric genius of man circulates among mankind for ever, carrying with it at all times the impress it has received; for, however much alloyed by foreign admixture, and disfigured by accumulated accretions, the pure and primitive elemental atom remains in every articulate word, awaiting the scientific analysis of the master of language.

The task of submitting the whole body of human speech to careful analysis, for the purpose of discovering the protean atoms from which it germinated, is beyond human power; but it is possible so to operate upon definite sections as to arrive at the real basement, and by occasional excursions into the general domain of speech to assure ourselves that our discoveries are universal facts. This we have in great part done, and have formed the onomatops we have discovered into a dictionary; but before publishing the matter so collected, we thought it advisable to make known our method of treatment, in order that, in the work itself, we might have the advantage of the criticisms of such scholars as might favour us with their notice.

The special object of writing this first Dictionary of Onomatops is to show, that we must look to nature only for the bonds uniting all languages together; and in adverting to the numerous affinities or analogies connecting languages, it is hoped that the proof of their true origin will be demonstrated. To do this we must go back to a period anterior to our civilization, although we do not pretend that civilization alone had the power to regulate the euphony of onomatops. *Eupho-*

nia, suprema lex est,—the consequent corollary is that letters or signs must submit and yield to the music of the word.

The only language we meet with in the long retrospect of the past by which the riddle of human speech can be solved, is the *Sanskrit,* the elaborately organized structure of which presents most highly finished forms, abounding with numberless inflexions and idioms of remarkable euphonic power; and, furthermore, a language susceptible of perfect analysis, exhibiting an incontestible and uncontested superiority over other idioms. This admirable language spread over India by virtue of its strongly marked vital force, and the children it has left, in such vernaculars as Bengalî, Mahratî, and Hindî, adapt themselves conspicuously to European languages, and elucidate them wonderfully by revealing the laws by which, in historic times, the monuments of Sanskrit phonology have crumbled to the dust.

As we have shown in the Introduction, man had much to do before he could arrive at the harmony of Homer's verse. Proceeding from simple unconnected utterances, passing on to a concatenation of monosyllables in the fashion of the ancient Chinese, developing an uncertain terminology, such as is seen in the hieroglyphs of Egypt, and finally reaching the fully inflexional phases of Semitic and Aryan languages,— such is an outline of the history of this remarkable acquisition; the whole affording a strong confirmation of Dr. Darwin's theory of continuous evolution.

The principles we announce, when fully developed, will lay the foundation for a new school of Philology, and do for Language and Philosophy what Dr. Darwin has done for the science of Physiology.

In this Præfamen we propose to give only some illustrations of our method of analysis, by which we shall seek to show a bond of union among large numbers of words hitherto supposed to have had independent origins. Some of these words we treat more fully and trace up to their onomatopic original; but a preliminary sketch such as the present would have extended beyond reasonable proportions had we done so in every case. We take a sentence and show that every word is but one of a series of words, all clearly pointing to some common original. The method of recovering that original we illustrate in some cases, which it will be seen is not guess-work, but is effected by a careful examination of both modern and ancient forms and by building upon a broad basis. It is not improbable that many of our alliances may prove faulty and may have to be rejected, but so long as our principles are not overthrown the value of our work remains untouched. These principles may be stated in a few sentences, as follows :—That every abstract in language is evolved from a more primitive concrete ;—that every concrete was, originally, expressive in all its parts ;—that each part (or pronounced letter) was a distinct expression of a separate material fact, or a phonetic modification of such an expression ;—that each expression had a distinctly recognizable relationship with the fact described; and that it originated in the natural vocal utterances arising from the fact itself.

But before placing the illustrations we have to adduce before our readers it is essential that we should very clearly explain what we mean when we speak of onomatops, and how we operate to discover them. To do these things more perfectly we shall discuss what we have to say in separate sections.

SECTION I.

ONOMATOPS ACCORDING TO FORMER WRITERS.

In the Introduction we have principally concerned ourselves with the laws which produce the most striking changes in language, and have only incidentally expressed our views on what onomatops really are. It is, however, evident that, to carry our readers with us through the wide field into which our method of treatment leads us, it is necessary to make very clear what we consider an onomatop to be, and how we deduce words from the elemental germ. To do this effectually we shall first of all place on record the opinions that have been advanced on this subject by previous writers, as far as they are known to us; and then enter more fully into the results of our own reflections.

Starting from Herodotus and Epicurus, we are astonished to find how accurately the old Greeks reasoned on such subjects. This is the more remarkable when we remember that the Greeks came to their conclusions without the aid of anything approaching to scientific examination, but solely by aid of philosophical speculations, and an intuitive sense of the fitness of things.

The Chaldean oracle of Zoroaster leads with a word on our subject:—

'Ονόματα βάρβαρα * μὴ ποτ' ἀλλάξῃς, εἰσὶ γὰρ ὀνόματα πάρ' ἑκάστοις θεόσδοτα δύναμιν ἐν τελεταῖς ἄρρητον ἔχοντα. —(Cozy, Anc. Frag., pag. 271). " There are *names* given by the Deity, and they are eternal ; others are variable which are made by mortals."

Herodotus says : ἤχοι ζῶον εἰσὶ ἁπλοικοί. " The *sounds* produced by animals are elementary."

Aristides, lib. i. p. 3, Ælii Adriensis (Oxonii, 1722):— Ἔργον εἶναι μουσικῆς οὐ τὰ ·φωνῆς μόνον μερὴ συνιστᾷν πρὸς ἀλλήλα, ἀλλὰ πάνθ' ὅσα φύσις ἐχεῖ, συνάγειν, τε καὶ συναρμόττειν.

Strabo, lib. xiv. :—Οἶμαι δὲ τὸ βάρβαρον κατ' ἀρχας ἐκπεφωνῆσθαι οὗτός, κατ' ὀνοματοποείαν ἐπὶ τῶν δυσεκφόρως καὶ σκληρῶς λαλούντων, ὡς τὸ βατταρίζειν καὶ τραυλίζειν καὶ ψεφαλίζειν. "*Barbar* is a word formed by an onomatop, signifying *murmur,* from that *sound,* as denoting a man who speaks with difficulty and *hardness.*" Ἐν βάρει εἶναι, " to be burdensome."

Epicurus ap. Dig Laert., x. 32 :—Περὶ τῶν ἀδήλων ἀπὸ τῶν φαινομένων χρὴ σημειοῦσθαι· καὶ γὰρ καὶ ἐπινοίαι πᾶσαι ἀπὸ τῶν αἰσθήσεων γεγόνασι, κατά τε περίπτωσιν καὶ ἀναλόγιαν, καὶ ὁμοιότητα, καὶ σύνθεσιν συμβαλλομένου τι καὶ λογισμοῦ. " Concerning things not manifest, *signs* must be taken from those which do appear; for all ideas (or thoughts) have arisen from the *senses,* according to circumstances or opportunities,—analogy, similarity, synthesis, and symbols also contributing something."

Orig. c. Cels. :—Ἐπίκουρος. Φύσει ἐστι τὰ ὀνόματα ἀπορ-

* " Barbarus hic ego sum quia non intelligor ulli."—Ovid in Pontus, Trist. v. 10, 37. " I am a *barbarian* here, because I am understood by no one."

ῥηξάντων τῶν πρώτων ἀνθρώπων τινὰς φωνὰς κατὰ τῶν πραγμάτων. "Language is the produce of man's instinct sharpened by the spur of necessity; or, *nouns* or *names* are by nature, the first men having *burst forth* certain *sounds* about things."

The remarks of Proclus not inaptly follow here. He says :—

Ὁ γὰρ Ἐπίκουρος ἔλεγεν ὅτι οὐχὶ ἐπιστημόνως οὗτοι ἔθεντο τὰ ὀνόματα, ἀλλὰ φυσικῶς κινούμενοι, ὡς οἱ βήσσοντες, καὶ πταίροντες, καὶ μυκώμενοι, καὶ ὑλακτοῦντες, καὶ στενάζοντες (p. 9). "For Epicurus said that these men did not put forth names scientifically, but *named naturally*, as those who cough, sneeze, bellow, bark, and groan." (See Laurenz Lersch, "Die Sprachphilosophie der Alten," p. 41; Bonn, 1839.)

This last writer is very precise in his enumeration of the processes by which words are formed. From his Cratylus we gather the following ideas :—

"Words are made (1) by imitation, κατὰ μίμησιν, as *to kiss*, σίζειν; (2) by reference to something, or by analogy; (3) by catachresis, as when one says that *sound is sweet;* (4) pseudonymously, or with a disregard of etymology, as when we talk of a *silver box*, or of a *brass looking-glass;* (5) by reference to history, as ὀβολός, *obol,* from βέλος, *ingot;* (6) by an extension of meaning, ἐπιδιαθητακόπα, as ζωγράφος, a painter of animals, to a painter of animals in any other subject; (7) by hyperbole, as when we talk of a man having no heart; (8) euphemistically, as when we call the Furies " gentle ones;" (9) analogically, as when we speak of the *head* of a mountain; (10) by resemblance, as when we say that a man's frame of mind was *crude;* (11) by a slight modification of an existing word; (12) elliptically, as τράπεξα; (13) by discovery, as when we call *wine,* "Bacchus;" (14) by naming the producer from the product, as " Vulcan" for *fire;* (15) by excess, κατὰ ὑπεροχὴν, a physician, a surgeon χειρουργὸς, &c. &c., figures of speech."

The following passages, culled from the writers indicated, will also satisfactorily attest that from the most ancient times to our own, a long succession of thoughtful men has felt that onomatopoieia formed the real basis of language.

Lucretius de N.D.,[a] lib. v., vv. 1027-1388 :—

At varios linguæ sonitus Natura subegit
  Mittere, et utilitas expressit nomina rerum :
Non alia longe ratione atque ipsa videtur
Protrahere 'ad gestum pueros infantia linguæ ;
Quom facit, ut digito, quæ sint præsentia, monstret :
Sentit enim vim quisque suam quod possit abuti.

    *   *   *   *   *

Proinde putare aliquem tum nomina distribuisse
Rebus, et inde homines didicisse vocabula prima,
Desipere est : nam quur hic posset cuncta notare
Vocibus, et varios sonitus emittere linguæ,
Tempore eodem aliei facere id non quisse putentur ?
Præterea, si non aliei quoque vocibus usei
Inter se fuerant, unde insita notities est ?
Utilitas etiam, unde data est huic prima potestas,
Quid vellet facere, ut sciret, animoque videret ?
Cogere item plureis unus, victosque domare
·Non poterat, rerum ut perdiscere nomina vellent :
Nec ratione docere ulla, suadereque surdeis,
Quid sit opus facto ; faciles neque enim paterentur,
Nec ratione ulla sibi ferrent amplius aureis
Vocis inauditos sonitus obtundere frustra.

  Postremo, quid in hac mirabile tantopere est re.
Si genus humanum, cui vox, et lingua vigeret,
Pro vario sensu varias res voce notaret ;—
Quom pecudes mutæ, quom denique secla ferarum,
Dissimileis soleant voces variasque ciere,

---

[a] The old orthography of some of the words has been preserved.

Quom metus, aut dolor est ; et quom jam gaudia gliscunt ?
Quippe etenim licet in rebus cognoscere apertis.
  Irritata canum quom primum magna Molossûm
Mollia ricta fremunt, duros nudantia denteis,
Longe alio sonitu rabies districta minatur,
Et quom jam latrant, et vocibus omnia complent.
At catulos blande quom lingua lambere tentant,
Aut ubi eos lactant pedibus morsuque petentes,
Suspensis teneros imitantur dentibus haustus,
Longe alio pacto gannitu vocis adulant,
Et quom desertei baubantur in ædibus, aut quom
Plorantes fugiunt, submisso corpore, plagas.
  Denique non hinnitus item differre videtur,
Inter equas ubi equus florenti ætate juvencus
Pinnigeri sævit calcaribus ictus Amoris ;
Et·fremitum patulis sub naribus edit ad arma ?
Et quom sic alias concussis artubus hinnit.
  Postremo, genus alituum variæque volucres,
Accipitres atque ossifragæ mergeique marinis
Fluctibus in salso victum vitamque petentes,
Longe alias alio jaciunt in tempore voces,
Et quom de victu certant prædaque repugnant.
Et partim mutant cum tempestatibus una
Raucisonos cantus cornicum secla vetusta
Corvorumque greges ; ubi aquam dicuntur et imbreis
Poscere, et interdum ventos aurasque vocare.
  Ergo, si variei sensus animalia cogunt,
Muta tamen quom sint, varias emittere voces ;
Quanto mortaleis magis æquum est tum potuisse———
Dissimileis alia atque alia res voce notare ?
  *   *   *   *   *   *
  At liquidas avium voces imitarier ore
Ante fuit multo, quam lævia carmina cantu
Concelebrare homines possent, aureisque juvare.
  *   *   *   *   *   *
  Sic unum quidquid paullatim protrahit ætas
In medium, ratioque in luminis eruit oras.

Varro, Lingua Latina, 1064, 20. 30 :—" Vocabula piscium, pleraq. translata et terrestribus ex quâ parte similibus rebus ut anguillas linguata sudis."

Quinctil. Instit. Orat. viii. :—"'Ονοματοποιΐα, id est fictio nominis, Græcis inter maximas habita virtutes, nobis vix permittitur; et sunt plurima ita posita ab iis, qui sermonem primi fecerunt, aptantes affectibus vocem."

Quinctil. Orat. viii. :—" Nomina aptare, non aliâ libertate quam quâ illi primi homines rebus appellationes dederunt."

Origen c. Cels. :—Λόγος βάθυς καὶ ἀπόρρητος ὁ περὶ φύσεως ὀνομάτων. " The nature of names is a deep and mysterious subject."

St. Augustin, A.D. 430 :—" In the case of things lifeless, and to carry with it an impression, a certain analogy was allowed to come into play, as that of the softness or hardness of things. The very words *levis* and *asper* have a lightness and asperity in their sound ; *voluptas,* pleasure, is a soft, as *crux,* cross, is a harsh word: *mel,* honey, is as sweet to the ear as honey is to the taste ; *acre,* sour, is bitter to both ; *lana,* wool, and *vepres,* a bramble, are as rough to the ear as the things they mean are to the touch. The Stoics considered a concord between sound and sense to be the very cradle of language."

Suidas, Lexicon :—'Ονοματοποιΐα δέ ἐστι φωνῆς μίμησις πρὸς τὴν ποιότητα τοῦ ὑποκειμένου ἤχου. " Onomatopoieia is an imitation of the voice, in reference to the quality of the sound which is the subject thereof."

Dionysius Halicarn. :—Μεγάλη τούτων ἀρχὴ καὶ διδάσκαλος ἡ φύσις, ἡ ποιοῦσα μιμητικοὺς ἡμᾶς καὶ θετικοὺς τῶν ὀνομάτων, οἷς δηλοῦται τὰ πράγματα. " A great principle and teacher of *these* (*onoma*) is nature, which makes us (to be) imitative and productive of nouns (*or* names) by which things are set forth."

Alex. Aphrodisiensis (Oxon. 1481, fol.) :—Τὰ ὀνόματα καὶ τὰ ῥήματα φωναί, αἱ δὲ φωναὶ φύσει, τὰ ἄρα ὀνόματα καὶ τὰ ῥήματα φύσει. "*Nouns* and *verbs* are *sounds;* therefore nouns and sounds are by nature." (See Dr. Laurenz Lersch, "Die Sprachphilosophie der Alten," i., p. 89 ; Bonn, 1838.)

Antonius, Epig. lxxvi. (edit. Lemaire) :—

Gallorum Cantus, et orantes gutture corvos,
Et vocum quidquid bellus et ales habet,
Omnia cum similes ita voce ut ficta negentur
Non potes humanæ vocis habere sonum.

Petrus Nigidius (the elder), *Commentariis :* — " Nomina verbaque non positu fortuito, sed quadam-vi ac ratione naturæ facta esse P. Nigidius in Grammaticis Commentariis docet; rem sane in philosophiæ dissertationibus celebrem. Quæri enim solitum apud philosophos, φύσει τὰ ὀνόματα sint, ἤ θέσει. In eam rem multa argumenta dicit, cur videri possent verba esse naturalia magis quam arbitraria."

IsaacVossius, De Poemat. Cantu (see "De Arte Grammaticæ,") p. 66 ; Oxford, 1676 ; and London, 1688 :—"Nunc vero ita comparatum est ut animalium quæ vulgo bruta creduntur, melior longe quam nostra, hâc in parte videatur conditio, utpote quæ promptius et forsan felicius sensus, et cogitationes suas sine interprete significant, quam illi que quando mortales, præsertim si peregrino utatur sermone."

The Indian commentator on *Yaska's Nirukta*, a Sanskrit work on Etymology dating 400 years B.C., remarking on the fact that among many qualities one only is chosen as the name of the object, says: "You may well ask why this is so. But, my friends, go and ask the world. Quarrel with the world, for it is not I who made this law. For although all nouns are derived from verbs, yet the choice of one action (which is to be predicated in preference to others) is beyond any control. . . . . *Words* are fixed in the world we cannot say how (*svabhávatah,* by nature)." (Quoted by Professor Max Müller, Anc. Sansk. Lit., p. 167.)

In. the Mahâbhâshya (B.C. 200) we are told that " A *word* is that through which, when uttered, there is cognition (of objects of sense) ; or, in the world, a noise (*dhwani*) [a] with a recognized sense is called a *word.*"

Among French authors the following are selected:—

Charles Nodier, Des Onomatopées, ed. 1828, Préface, p. 11:— " L'onomatopée est le type des langues prononcées, et l'hiéro- glyphe le type des langues écrites."

Ibid., p. 15 : — " Indépendamment des mots formés par *imitation,* il y a dans les langues un très grand nombre de mots qui, sans avoir la même.origine, n'en sont pas moins composés très naturellement et doivent être rapportés à l'onomatopée, ou fiction de nom."

Biondelli, Etudes linguistiques ·—" Lorsque nous considérons (*il ragguardevole numero*) le nombre remarquable d'onomatopées épars çà et là dans les langues, et surtout les onomatopées qui conservent encore les marques de leur formation première, nous ne saurions douter de la tendance naturelle chez l'homme à représenter les objets sous leurs formes les plus distinctes."

Pictet, Les Aryas Primitifs, Introduction, p. 12 :—"En thèse générale, lorsque deux mots de même son se trouvent pré- senter le même sens dans deux idiomes différents, il en résulte, tout d'abord, une propension à croire, soit à une transmission, soit à une commune origine, à l'exception de ce qu'on appelle les *onomatopées qui naissent d'une imitation directe.*"

Ibid., vol. ii., p. 347 :—" Il est certain que d'anciennes ono- matopées se conservent souvent à travers les siècles, et que retrouvées dans les diverses branches d'une même famille de langues, elles concourent à en démontrer l'unité primitive."

M. Littré, Hist. de la Langue Française (Paris, 1869), vol. i.

[a] This word *dhwani* is connected with the A.S. *dyn*, confused noise.

pp. 26, 27 :—" Sans doute l'*Etymologie* ne mène pas encore et, on en peut dire, ne mènera jamais à toucher les origines et les sons primordiaux d'où les langues sont sorties par un développement régulier. Mais, pourtant, elle a fait bien de chemin dans cette voie ascendante vers le passé de notre histoire, et elle en fera certainement bien davantage à mesure que le cercle de ses comparaisons s'étendra, et que, dans chacune des grandes familles d'idiomes, elle aura réussi à distinguer, avec une précision suffisante, les éléments radicaux. Les espaces intermédiaires lui sont ouverts, et le fait est, que la faculté qui transforme est de même nature que la faculté qui créa; les transformations étant dans tous les cas, une création pour une part."

E. Renan, Origine du Langage (Paris, 1858), pp. 136, 137 : —" La langue des premiers hommes ne fut donc, en quelque sorte, que l'écho de la nature dans la conscience humaine. . . Dans les langues sémitiques et dans l'Hébreu, en particulier, la formation par onomatopée est très-sensible pour un grand nombre de racines, et pour celles surtout qui portent un caractère marqué d'antiquité et de monosyllabisme."

Idem, ch. vi. p. 136 :—" L'onomatopée, ou l'imitation, parait avoir été le procédé d'après lequel l'humanité primitive forma les appellations. La voix humaine étant à la fois *signe* et *son*, il était naturel que l'on prit le *son* de la voix pour signe des *sons* de la nature. D'ailleurs, comme le choix de l'appellation n'est point arbitraire, et que jamais l'homme ne se décide à assembler des sons au hasard pour en faire les signes de la pensée, on peut affirmer que de tous les mots actuellement usités, il n'en est pas un seul qui n'ait eu sa raison suffisante, et ne se rattache à travers mille transformations à une élection primitive.

" Or, le motif déterminant pour le choix des mots a dû être, dans la plupart des cas, le désir d'imiter l'objet qu'on voulait exprimer. L'instinct de certains animaux suffit pour les porter à ce genre d'imitation, qui, faute de principe rationel, reste chez eux infécond."

German scholars[a] have written largely on onomatops; the following passages show the tendency of their thoughts.

Heyse, C. W L., System der Sprach-Wissenschaft, &c. (Berlin, 1856) p. 90.—(Translation.) "If we consider on the ope hand the different kinds of natural sounds, and, on the other, the stock of words which belong to intelligent speech, we shall find many close points of contact and transition between the two."

Herder (der Ursprung der Sprache) was a strenuous defender of onomatopoieia, but in later life he abandoned his belief.

Steinthal, der Ursprung der Sprache (Berlin, 1858).—"It is inconceivable that anyone should be hardy enough to deny that onomatopoieia was the primæval tendency of language which has furnished us with all elements of words."

Ibid.—"The *word* belongs not only to the speaker but also to the hearer. Comprehension and speech are only different effects of the power of language."

Bopp, Comparative Grammar (Trans. into English by E. B. Eastwick).—"Of every thing in nature, of every animal, of every plant, speech can seize one property to express the whole of it."

Pott, Etymologische Forschungen (Lemgo, 1833.)—"There is unquestionably a certain meaning, appropriateness, and *symbolic power* in sound."

Bunsen, Outlines.—"Language has all the distinctive peculiarities of vegetable nature."

[a] F. Wallner *Ueber den Ursprung der Sprache,* Munster, 1838; Woigtman, *Die Bau-wau Theorie,* Dresden, 1865; *Diez,* translated into English by Cayley, 1863, and his *Etymologisches* by T. R. Donkin, 1865; L. Wienborg, *Das Geheimniss des Worts,* Hamburg, 1852.

Idem.—"The imitative nature of Language consists in an artistic imitation, not of things, but of the rational expression which an object produces by its qualities."

Bunsen, Egypt's Place in Universal History, vol. iv. p. 485:—"Primitive language spoken with rising and falling cadences; elucidated by gesture; accompanied by pure picture writing; every syllable a word, every word a full substantive one, representable by a picture."

Professor Max Müller,[a] as is well known, is decidedly opposed to the theory of onomatopoieia, but still he makes admissions which tell in its favour. Thus he allows that "onomatopoeias are material for language—stepping-stones to it." This is all that the most advanced onomatopist desires to establish. Professor Max Müller also admits that "There is a vast stock of onomatopoeias in every language; some words originally expressive of *sounds* only, might be transferred to other things which have some analogy with sound."

Every thing that so excellent a scholar writes is valuable, we therefore cite, from his "Science of Language," two or three more ideas.

"Every thing in language, but the roots, is intelligible, and can be accounted for,"—p. 260. "They [the roots] are *phonetic types* produced by a power inherent in human nature."—p. 370. Language is built up by the mind of man, "guided only by *innate laws,* or by an *instinctive* power,"—p. 296. But at

[a] The Languages of the Seat of War in the East, second edition, London, 1855. Lectures on the Science of Language, First Series, 1861; Second Series, 1864, London.

p. 346 he says, " We cannot deny the possibility that
a language might have been formed on the principle
of imitation :" which is afterwards (p. 351) amusingly
modified by the remark that "though a language
might have been made out of the roaring, fizzing,
hissing, gobbling, twittering, cracking, banging, slam-
ming, and rattling sounds of nature, the tongues with
which we are acquainted, point to a different origin." ·

A few passages from English writers will end these
selections.

Horne Tooke, Diversions of Purley, vol. i. p. 62 :—" The ·
dominion of speech is erected upon the downfall of interjections. Without the artful contrivances of language, mankind
would have nothing but interjections with which to communicate,
orally, any of their feelings."

Campbell, Rhetoric :—" Onomatopœia is not a word invented
on the basis of sound-imitation, but the transformation of a
sound-name into a vocable."

Rev. R. Garnett, Essays on the Nature and Analysis of the Verb,
pp. 289 to 342 :—" We believe with Mr. Max Muller, that all
language is reducible to *roots,* which are either the bases of
abstract nouns, or are pronouns denoting relations of place,
which latter we believe to have arisen from interjectional or
onomatopic elements."

Trench, The Study of Words, 4th ed., p. 15 :—" He [man]
did not thus begin the world *with names,* but *with the power of
naming ;* for man is not a mere speaking machine ; God did
not teach him words, as one of us teaches a parrot, from
without ; but gave him a capacity, and then evoked the capacity which he gave."

*John Stuart Mill, System of Logic ratiocinative and induc-
tive,* vol. i., chap. ii., p. 23 :—" A *name,* says Hobbes (*Compu-
tation of Logic,* chap. ii.) is a word taken at pleasure to serve

for a mark which may raise in our mind a thought like to some thought we had before, and which being pronounced to others, may be to them a *sign* of what thought the speaker had (or had not). This simple definition of a name as a *word* (or set of words) serving the double purpose of a mark to recall to ourselves the likeness of a former thought, and a sign to make it known to others appears unexceptionable. But seeing names ordered in speech are signs of our conceptions, it is manifest they are not signs of the things themselves; for that the sound of this word *stone* should be the *sign* of a stone cannot be understood in any sense but this, that he that hears it collects that he who pronounces it thinks of a *stone.*"

Ibid., chap. v., on the Natural History of the Variations in the Meaning of Terms, p. 237 :—"The history of a word, by showing the causes which determine its use, is a better guide to its employment than any definition; for definitions can only show its meaning at the particular time, or at most, the series of its successive meanings, but its history may show the law by which the succession was produced."

Rev. Frederick William Farrar, Origin of Language, chap. viii. p. 88 :—"The theories of the *Interjectional* and *Onomato-poetic* origin of language are not in reality different, and both of them might, without impropriety, be classed under the better name Onomatopœia; for, in point of fact, the impulsive instinct to reproduce a sound is precisely analogous to that which gives vent to a sensation by an interjection."

Ibid., chap. iv., p. 39 :—"If language was a human inven-tion, and was due to a gradual development, there must have been a time in man's history when he was possessed of nothing but the merest rudiments of articulate speech, in which, there-fore, he must have occupied a lower grade than almost any existing tribe."

Wedgwood, Dictionary of English Etymology, Introduction, p. iii. :—After saying that a rational inquirer will not be satisfied until he meets with a principle adequate to give rise to the use of language, he goes on, " Now one such principle at least is universally admitted under the name of Onomatopoeia, when a word is made to imitate or represent a sound characteristic of the object.it is intended to designate, as *Bang, Crack,* *Purr, Whizz, Hum.* In uncivilized languages the consciousness of the imitative character of certain words is sometimes demonstrated by their composition with verbs like *say,* or *do,* to signify making a noise like that represented by the word in question."

The reader who has attentively considered the foregoing opinions (which could be much increased in number) cannot fail to have remarked their diversities and similitudes. The greatest diversity of opinion seems to prevail on what an onomatop is; while singular unanimity is manifest in the declaration that language had an onomatopic origin. Professor Max Muller is the important exception to this general unanimity, and even he confesses that a language might have been so formed. It is clear that these writers viewed the question more from a poetic and philosophic point of view than from a scientific and analytical one. Some of these scholars appear to think that words are the natural correlatives of form, that the sound is moulded on the form and being presented to the ear, as rays of light are presented to the eye; necessarily and inevitably occasion a perception of the object intended; others seem to believe that sound is, as it were, plastic, and is itself moulded by the will of the speaker into the verisimilitude of the object spoken of; others, again, deduce words from interjectional noises, and others from the imitative faculty of man

which led him to recognize objects by the sounds
emanating from them. It is not too harsh a judgment to pronounce on the majority of these unscho-
lastic opinions if we set them aside as mere poetry
and dreaming. Of course we do not mean that all the
eminent men from whom we have quoted are unprac-
tical dreamers, but that they, having discovered that
the beginnings of language must have been onomatopic,
instead of patiently analyzing facts so as to find what
onomatops really are, allowed themselves to speculate,
to argue, and theorize, as to what was or was not a
probable starting point for language. It forms, however, no part of our present purpose to descant upon
the views we have quoted. The object of this section
is to place before our readers an historical summary of
what has hitherto been said of onomatops. In the
next section our own views will be fully set forth.[a]

---

[a] This Section (Sect. I) is due to the researches of the Count
de G.-Liancourt.—F.P.

SECTION II.

WHAT ONOMATOPS REALLY ARE.

In the preceding section we have stated as succinctly as possible the views of preceding writers on the nature of onomatops, but have spent no time in discussing them. It seems to us that, with the exception of some of the more recent, their interest is mainly historical, enabling us to see that the general sentiment of philologists for thousands of years has tended towards the onomatopic origin of speech. The reason why this idea has never been consolidated into the basis of a real science of language is that it presents so tempting a subject for the poetic faculty of our species to dream over. No sooner does the mind realize the notion of an imitative origin for words than an impulse almost irresistible leads the speculator to ponder on the still and gentle, the sweet and soft, the hurrying and boisterous, the grand, terrifying, yea, horrifying sounds that alternately please and startle the ear of man. The lion's roar and the bulbul's song, the crash of bursting rocks, the howl of the eddying tempest, and the gentle ripple of the murmuring stream, are felt to be the monitors of man, imparting to him, with nature's untiring pertinacity, the mysterious art of inspiring sentiment and arousing thought by aid of sound alone. The poetic instincts within us are awakened by such reflections, and the imagination at once busies itself in framing theories and in explaining away facts. The judgment is fascinated by the pleasing vision.

There can be no doubt that many words owe their being to the imitation of natural sounds, and many more bear the semblance of such a genealogy; but still, as sceptics have repeatedly pointed out, though languages are enriched by such imitative vocables, they do not constitute the essential basis. They are tributaries, not the parent stream. After the excision of all words that can fairly be considered imitative, there always remains a small but important residuum that obstinately resists any reasonable effort to demonstrate its evolution from either the heavens or the earth.

Now this general concurrence of opinion as to the onomatopic origin of words, and the inability, at the same time, to explain the process of evolution, must be primarily occasioned, or at all events largely affected, by the want of a clear and rational definition of what an onomatop really is. It is for this reason that we think it of essential importance to explain in this section what we mean when we speak of *onomatops ;* so that we may not be confounded with poets and dreamers, who are charmed by a name to which they attach no proper sense.

And, first, we must remark that those who seek to deduce all our words from the sounds of animals and

the elements, do not seem to perceive that, by so
doing, they reduce man below the level of the brute.
We have nothing to object to that on sentimental
grounds ; but we do object to it on the score of
logical inconsistency. For in all historical time man
has been in advance of the brute, and the qualities
that have kept him in advance must have been those
that brought him to the front; and first among
these qualities is language itself. But were this not
so, it is surely unreasonable to argue that the animal
which has always shown the largest amount of intellectual capacity, should, in the beginning, have possessed the very least; insomuch as to have been
unable to express its passions by sounds until it had
acquired the art from other creatures. It must not
be forgotten that the purely imitative theory carried
to its logical conclusion brings mankind to a time of
absolute dumbness,—when the dog could bark and
the monkey could chatter, but the man could utter
never a word. This view of the argument is something like a *reductio ad absurdum*. Furthermore, if
we suppose our species to have acquired the power
of speech by nothing but imitation, we are at once
deprived of all spontaneity. Without going so far as
M. Renan, and asserting that " spontaneity is everything," we yet think it very certain that human-
beings are, at least, as capable of originating as the
inferior animals; and if a dog could bark untaught of
man, so man may be safely accorded the power of
speaking untaught of the dog. Again, there seems

something unaccountably contradictory in maintaining that the progenitors of our race were so hopelessly imbecile that they could not cry out if they were hurt, and yet were intelligent enough to perceive the advantages that would accrue from an interchange of ideas, and to set themselves to overcome their great natural defect. Did anyone ever hear of an idiot arguing within himself that idiotcy is folly, and re- solving to desist from foolish pranks and become a savant ? The two ideas seem utterly irreconcileable. There is yet another and unanswerable argument why human beings have as great a claim to spontaneity in their use of sound as other creatures, and that is the possession of the means of articulation. What process of imitation could have given to man his mouth, teeth, palate, tongue, and vocal cords ? Can we suppose a creature possessed of appropriate organs without the capacity for their use ? ·This argument requires no elaboration. As it is simply absurd to suppose that imitation could have conferred on human beings the *faculty* of speech, so is it altogether beyond credence that the organs of speech should exist without the capacity for their employment.[a]

Pure imitation, then, fails to account for language ;

[a] As it might be urged that parrots, magpies, &c., have the organs necessary for articulate speech, and yet do not talk unless specially instructed, we here remark that the wild-wood screams of the parrot, &c., form the natural language of those creatures. What the parrot is taught is the art of regulating his screams, and bringing them into conformity with a human standard. The bird, in fact, is not taught *to speak*, but to speak a new language.

and the recognition of this fact has led to the suggestion that all words grew out of emotional sounds,—
the sudden and uncontrollable ejaculations which express the transitory passions. It will be seen that
this theory goes to the other extreme; for, as the first
supposition reduces man to an incapable dummy, painfully imitating sound after sound of the more advanced
brute, so this theory, casting aside imitation, rests entirely on man's spontaneity. In the first case the
human animal originates nothing; in the second, blind
impulse originates everything. However convenient
such a theory might be, the words we now-a-days
use persistently refuse to be reduced to interjections.
Furthermore, under such an hypothesis our reason
·assures us that we should find one word only to express one idea all over the world, more especially those
primitive ideas that must have been among the very
first such a process called forth. Some form of "oh!"
should be the word for "woe" all over the world, and
it could never be subject to phonetic corruption from
its extreme simplicity, and its constant reference back
to nature. This we know is not the fact. Every man
of every race cries out "oh!" when he is hurt,—M.
Du Chaillu tells us that when the gorilla received his
death-blow he exclaimed, in the most terrific and
human-like voice, "ah!"—but man uses some widely
different sound when he speaks of the injury he has
received. So far from finding but one word to express
one emotion the very reverse is in reality the case.
Even the simplest and most barbarous language is

found to offer a choice of vocables for any idea the speaker may desire to express.[a] The alternative words, too, are as diverse in construction as can well be imagined. Take, for example, the English *sorrow* and *grief*, both of which are as hopelessly removed from any conceivable interjection as they are from each other; and comparing these with the Sanskrit *rodana* and *álápana*, we have at once four vocables radically distinct to represent one of the prime emotions.[b]

History is, furthermore, altogether against the interjectional theory. · Many instances occur of words passing into unmeaning exclamations; but we meet with very few undoubted interjections assuming the powers of ordinary vocables. Thus, *alas!* is derived from *lax-us*, *lass-itude*, the being *loose*, or *re-laxed;* so the Greek ἀγὲ, "quick!" "good!" "come on!" sprang from a base that is also found in the Latin *ago*, *age-dum* (for *agendum*), *agesis*, meaning " to set in motion," to *agi*-tate (Fr. *agir*). It is not improbable that these broken-down words may have deceived inquirers

---

[a] We mean, of course, the native speaker and his own ideas; not that a barbarous language can express civilized refinements.

[b] *Sorrow* is the Gothic *saurgan*, the Norse *sorg*, connected with the words *sough* and *to sigh*, the Sans. *śoka*, allied to *śwas*, to breathe, to heave *sighs*. *Grief*, Fr. *gréver*, Ital. *gravare*, to oppress; from Lat. *gravis*, heavy, Sans. *guru*, with which also is connected the Gothic *kauritha*, *kaurs*, A.S. *caru*, Eng. *care*, Lat. *cura*, and that which exhibits tokens of care or is *curious*. *Rodana* from *rud* and *ru*, to make a *row*, to *roar*. *Álápana*, from *lap*, to speak, to sound, to use the *lips*.

once penetrated with the notion that interjections
formed a rational base for language. The sounds
which human beings uttered from the promptings of
impulse only are very few, and what is more to the
point they are altogether wanting in descriptive power.
The necessity for finding both a descriptive and a plastic basis for language led the authors of this book to
the conviction that speech could only find its origin
among the sounds which are completely under the
control of man. A potter could never shape pots to
his wish out of clay that started spontaneously into
regular forms; neither could a speaker modulate into
descriptive vocables sounds that started forth impulsively only upon the awakening of the passions.
Such reflections seem to dispose finally of the interjectional theory, and to throw the inquirer of necessity
upon some other source. That other source, as we
have indicated in the "Introduction," is found in the
illimitable number of sounds, other than exclamatory,
which all creatures possessed of appropriate organs
can emit or not at pleasure. These sounds, it will be
remarked, are not necessarily imitative; for they are
peculiarly subjective, and can be occasioned by a thought
as well as by a fact. Not that we suppose for a moment that thought primarily suggested words; on the
contrary, we maintain that words occasioned thought.
The facts of life were the first monitors. Man in his
animal state bit, grasped, swallowed, snarled, licked,
fought, ran, and felt the emotions of fear and love;
and actions and impulses such as these being continu-

ally repeated and experienced by particular organs and in particulars ways, were gradually *felt* to be symbolized by the sounds and gestures with which they were constantly accompanied.

The important part which gesticulation played in early language must never be lost sight of. " Loqua-cissimæ manus, linguosi digiti, silentium clamosum." * All uncultivated languages supplement their defective vocabulary by gestures which are frequently as ex-pressive as words themselves. The language of the Kafirs of South Africa, for example, to the ear consists of a succession of *clicks*. Two, three, and many *clicks* are uttered, to which sense is given by expressive gestures ; insomuch that it is jokingly said Kafirs cannot talk at night without a fire. The same, to a lesser extent, is true of more advanced idioms. Everyone will recollect the following scene : When a high priest in Greece was celebrating, with pomp and solemnity, the services of the gods at Athens, a messenger entered the temple, and going straight to the altar, threw himself on his knees, and with extended arms exclaimed, " O Lord, thy son lost his life yesterday on the battle-field ! " .... The priest immediately took his tiara from his head, and deposited it upon the altar as a sign of mourning .... " but," continued the messenger, " he died while fighting the enemy ! " Then the father and priest instantly replaced his tiara on his head, and unconcernedly continued his sacrifice,

* Cassiodorus Varro, " De Linguâ Latinâ," iv. 51.

to the gods.. There is a marvellous depth of poetry in such gestures, they symbolize by a motion the most subtle impulses,—grief, humility, joy, content, glory, and all of them together.*

We have, however, not yet given our definition of an onomatop, or rather the sense in which we employ the word throughout this treatise; and one reason for not doing so is that it is no easy task to formulate what is nevertheless clear to the conception. What is foregone will, however, enable the reader to see the view we entertain of language itself, and will act as a gloss on the following, which we think the most apt words to describe an onomatop:—*A sound consciously uttered for a purpose.* Perhaps we could do without the word " consciously," for everything done with intent must be performed consciously; but we think it better to insert the word so that it may be unmistakeably apparent that we consider the will of the utterer an essential factor. When a pig screams it gives vent to interjections; when it murmurs over the trough it utters onomatops. So also the yell of

* Marsh, in his "Lectures on the English Language," pp. 487, 488, gives the following surprising instances of gesture.—"The language of gesture is so well understood in Italy, that when King Ferdinand returned to Naples, after the revolutionary movement of 1822, he made an address to the lazzaroni from the balcony of the palace, wholly by signs which, in the middle of the most tumultuous shouts, was perfectly understood by the public; and it is traditionally affirmed that the famous conspiracy of the Sicilian Vespers was organized wholly by facial signs, not even the hand being employed."

the lion is an interjection, but the roar is a genuine onomatop, uttered consciously for the purpose of terrifying the prey.

Few people are aware of the fact that the lion's roar is systematic. In proof that it is so, we give the following narrative from the experience of S. Gérard, the lion-killer. This undaunted hunter was once, early in the morning, at the foot of the Atlas, selecting a recess under a projection of a rock whence he could easily observe the plain, and be himself protected in the rear. When established and ready for work, with his two guns, his pipe, his biscuit and flask, he had his ingenious triangle displayed and planted in front on the sand of the desert. He then sat down, drew a telescope from his knapsack, and waited the arrival of an antagonist. Soon a clattering noise was heard, like horses' feet, as though a squad of Arabs were riding on the rocks hanging over his head, which inspired the single-handed man with serious reflections. Then there was a perfect silence : no Arab could be seen. At a quarter of a mile off, a monstrous bison-like animal was moving. It was a lion of gigantic stature, such as Gérard had never seen before. The animal now advanced in a right line toward the rock, sometimes crawling and beating the sand with fearful blows, his tail serving as a flail; sometimes erect,—his mane about four feet wide in front. When arrived within forty yards of Gérard, the lion excavated a hole in the sand, six feet in circumference and eighteen inches deep ; then putting

his mouth in the hole, he began to roar in so terrific a
manner that all animated creation within hearing
ought to have been transfixed and unable to move.
The most remarkable fact was that the lion turned
round and round the hole when roaring, so as to
deceive the hearer, who thus could not determine
from whence the sound proceeded. The strategy of
the noise being performed, the lion passed to mimicry
no less terrible. He made a new move in advance
toward Gérard, intending to frighten him with his
glaring, fiery eyes. Sometimes crawling, sometimes
erect, sometimes beating the sand, sometimes gnashing
the teeth in a savage manner. The space was now
considerably lessened, and the tragedy was nearing
the final bound. In one jump the monster could
reach his foe. Gérard raised his gun, and pointed at
the shoulder, where a ball would destroy the animal
at once. But the lion was stopped by the puzzling
triangle. Three small iron rods an inch in diameter,
six feet high, each forming a reversed pyramid.
Gérard was so struck with the magnificent form of the
creature, and with the ingenuity of his tactics, that he
was inwardly regretting the necessity of killing the
noble brute. Their four eyes were gazing at one
another with a seeming interrogation. The thunder
was calm, the animal was puzzled to the utmost at the
aspect of that other animal which had not been cowed
by the demonstrations made against him. The lion
was astonished, feeling himself in presence of a mystery. He stopped in his advance, turned back, tail

down, and went quietly off never to show himself again.

Why, then, do not all creatures talk, since they can and do utter the sounds from which language is elaborated ? The reply may take the form of a question— How do we know that they do not talk in a way sufficient for their needs ? When a hen finds a sprinkle of corn, she clucks with a peculiar sound that brings her chickens rapidly from every direction in the farmyard; but should a cat appear instead of corn, she lifts up her head and utters a sudden noise that puts all her brood on guard. This is certainly effective language. It will, however, be rejoined that as the hen clucks now, so there is every reason to believe she always did and always will cluck; the sound is impulsively and instinctively uttered, and so on. Human beings, on the other hand, do not now utter the same sounds they used to utter only a few hundred years ago, and we know that, in a few generations, the words we now use will cease to be understood. To this argument we reply, first, that the fact that language changes need not alter the nature of its origin ; and, secondly, that the reason for these changes in the use of sounds is to be found in the mental constitution of man. Granted that animals are purely instinctive,—man, we know, certainly is not. Man possesses a power of will to do, or not to do, and he is not slow to use his power, being ever pursued by an insatiable love of change. The spirit of Dissatisfaction with every state in which he may exist,

is a very characteristic difference between man and
brute. "Man never is, but always to be blest." How
low soever in the scale of civilization the human being
may be, we still find him bent on increasing his
gratifications. Even the most stationary nations are
always busy in devising new delights, from a constant
sense of dissatisfaction with those they already enjoy.
The civilized man is for ever striving to augment his
wealth; the semi-civilized seeks to gratify in new
ways his lusts; the uncivilized strives to increase his
food. The whole human family is divided among
these three classes, and in each the mainspring of
action is Dissatisfaction. As Mr. J. S. Mill wisely
pointed out, all the improvements in the world result
from the labour of "discontented" men. This dis-
satisfied yearning for something not yet attained
proceeds from cerebral peculiarity. It is man's
ἰδιοσύνχρασία. Every other creature is satisfied with
the food it eats and the natural functions it ordinarily
performs, and manifests no wish to change its accustomed course; hence they do to-day what they
did yesterday, for no other reason than because they
did it the day before; and this is instinct. How
man became possessed of his faculty for discontent,
that is, how man became man, forms no part of this
treatise to explain. Darwin, Wallace, and Huxley
have proved conclusively that existing animal natures
are the results of progressive developments. This is
a fact; and it is a fact that accounts perfectly for man's
possession of articulate speech. The gratification of

the gregarious instinct which the human animal shares
with the monkey, afforded opportunities for the interchange of cries[a]; and associated labour in procuring
food, &c., combined with the constant desire for
increased gratification, would gradually stamp upon
those cries more and more precision of meaning, as
the purposes to which they were applied became more
and more precise. Hence we see the reason for the
extreme plasticity of onomatopic bases. One simple
onomatop may underlie scores of words that grew out
of the primal idea, as will be abundantly illustrated
in the next section when discussing the word "Law."
Simple onomatops are susceptible of indefinite development, insomuch as to become the grand and expressive
vocables of the most polished languages. Human
speech is, indeed, a mass of onomatops. Language
does not consist of onomatops and something else, but
of nothing else than developed onomatops. Every
sound was at one time significative, save only those
produced by phonetic corruption. Onomatops are,
therefore, roots—the bases of words; but differ from
what are ordinarily understood by roots in that they
are the ονοματα struck by nature or natural processes,
whereas roots are the discoveries of the etymologist.

The word *root* has been hitherto misunderstood and
misapplied. What is termed a root is frequently
spoken of as a block, devoid of special signification;

---

[a] See what is said about those born deaf in Introd. p. 10.

that it bears the same relation to a word that a block
of marble does to a statue. It is said to be a mass
of crude material which acquires sense and dynamic
power only upon the performance of certain grammatical operations. As long as these operations are
unperformed, the root remains inert and lifeless. A
root, however, cannot be an *inutile lignum*, a *truncus*,
but the very reverse; it is a plastic force existing in
every animal being. It is altogether a misnomer to
speak of *roots* at all. We shall see this more clearly
by reflecting on the manner in which we came by
our knowledge of roots. The Semitic languages first
familiarized us with the term, because in those languages nearly all the words they contain are palpably
deduced from sets of articulations, each of which comprises three letters. These three fundamental letters,
by the operation of certain definite changes in the
vowels by which they are vocalized, and by the addition of particular auxiliary letters, produce large numbers of words, each of which words bears a definite
relationship to the three primitive letters on which it
is based. The identical changes that produce any
particular word from one triliteral cluster, would produce an exactly similar word from any other cluster,*
—the form of the two words would be alike, and they
would differ only in the idea conveyed, which depends,
of course, upon the meaning of the root operated upon.
But these triliteral roots are never devoid of sense;

---

* This is true theoretically; in practice every root is not subject
to every possible grammatical change

on the contrary, they are as perfectly apprehendible as
the most developed vocable educed from them;—they
are, indeed, used as the third person singular of the
past tense, and so have a constant place in spoken
language. The word *root* is only a poetic description
of the basis of a set of words, which grow from it as
naturally, and apparently as irresistibly, as do the stem
and branches from the root of a herb. The study of
Sanskrit-grammar, however, revealed another kind of
root which appeared to have no definite relationship to
the words educed from it, and which was never employed in language without some grammatical adjunct,
the addition of which not only modified the sense ascribed to the root, but also gave the vitality necessary
to make it into a real word. What, then, are these
roots, and how did we come by them? The answer
is, that they are mere grammatical abstractions, and
that we get them from ancient Indian grammarians,
who subjected their old idiom to an exhaustive process
of analysis, and by patiently stripping off fragment
after fragment from the word in common use, ultimately
arrived at a monosyllabic residuum to less than which
the word could not be reduced without destroying its
individuality. This final residuum was called by the
Indians a *dhátu*, which literally means an "ore" or
"mineral,"—the crude material from which the finished vocable was wrought. It will, therefore, be
evident that there is nothing sacred and inviolable in
Sanskrit roots, nothing connected with them that need
be spoken of with awe, or wrought into any poetry;

they are nothing more nor less than the smallest fragments to which Indian grammarians, according to the
lights they possessed, were able to reduce the words of
their language.　This consideration will, we think,
modify somewhat the superstitious reverence with
which Sanskrit roots are generally regarded.　"It is
a Sanskrit root" is, apparently, held by many to be a
conclusive argument—the *ultima Thule*—the last ap-
peal.　Any doubt upon the finality of a root is regarded
as a kind of profanation, or a mania, akin to disbelief
in the rotundity of the earth or the motion of the
celestial bodies.　Mr. Wedgwood makes the following
very sensible observations on roots, which we quote
entire, as they cannot be repeated too often until the
present practice of philologists is abandoned :—

"Etymology is still at the stage where an arbitrary theory
is accepted as the basis of scientific explanation.　It is supposed that all language is developed from roots or skeletons
of articulate sound, endowed with distinct and often very abstract meaning, but incapable of being actually used in speech
until properly clothed in grammatical forms.　And this
theory of roots takes the place of the elementary powers which
form the basis of other sciences.　The etymologist, who suc-
ceeds in tracing a word to a Sanskrit root, is as well satisfied
with the account he has rendered of his problem, as the astro-
nomer who traces an irregularity in the orbit of a comet to
the attraction of a planet, within whose influence it has been
brought in its last revolution.　Now in what condition is it
possible that roots could have existed, before they were actually
used in speech?　If it be suggested that they were implanted
by nature in the mind of man, as some people have supposed
that the bones of mammoths were created, at the same stroke
with the other materials of the *strata* in which they are buried

—we can only say that it is directly opposed to anything we observe in infants of the present day. But if it be said that no one supposes that the roots, as such, ever had independent existence; that they are merely fictions of the grammarians to indicate the core of a group of related words having similar significations, ... or if they are regarded as the remains of some former condition of language, then they cease to afford a solid resting-place, and the origin of the roots themselves becomes as fit an object of inquiry, as of the words in actual use at the present day. Nor will the curiosity of a rational inquirer be satisfied until he meets with a principle adequate to give rise to the use of language in a being with a mental constitution, such as he is conscious of in himself, or observes in the course of development in the infants growing up around him."—(Introduction, pp. ii. iii.)

We ourselves are anxious to be counted among the most devoted admirers of the wonderful scholarship enshrined in the noble language of the Brahmans, but we have not brought ourselves to the conviction that those ancient scholars were possessed of all linguistic knowledge, insomuch that their deductions are beyond all doubt the last words on the subject. On the contrary, we are rash enough to think that their conclusions are still open to the criticisms of scholars; but at the same time we are prepared to receive their dicta with much reverence, from the conviction that the grammatical system of the Hindûs represents the accumulated wisdom of generations of patient and pains-taking workers, who laboured with unprecedented and, as yet, unrivalled zeal to elucidate the facts of their marvellous idiom. With thoughts and feelings such as these, and with a knowledge of the way in

which Sanskrit roots were educed, we do not hesitate
to deal with these roots as we should deal with any
other abstractions of former writers.

As we have before said, it is a misnomer to speak
of roots at all. The attentive reader of this book
will find the clearest evidence that what are ordinarily considered roots are in reality developed forms
of yet earlier roots. Let us take as an illustration the
root *krit*, meaning " cut." The bases *kut*, *kutt*, *kash*,
and *karn* are certainly developed from *krit* by mere
phonetic corruption. The form *kut*, with the guttural
softened to a palatal gives birth to *chut*, *chatt*, *chunt*,
chund, and *chun*. When the cerebral *t* passes into *r*,
as is frequently the case, from *kut* we also get *kshur*,
and from this last *khur*, and *chhur*, *chho*, *chhut*, and
with a reappearance of the dental, as in *krit*,—*chhid*,
chhidr, and *chhed*. The roots *kshad*, *khad*, *khand*,
khud, *khund*, *khan*, are parallel forms closely related
to *krit*. These many roots, all of which have the
same meaning, " cut," must have been developed the
one from the other. Again, the base *klis*, " to be
distressed," exists also in the forms *khid*, *kut*, *kunt*,
kutt, *kund*, *kath*, *kút*. The word for " give " is found
under the following forms : *dá*, *dáy*, *day*, *dás*, *dás*,
dad, *dadh*, *dhá* ; and the word " grind " is expressed
by the bases *mrid*, *mrad*, *mut*, *munt*, *math*, *mud*,
mund. Such instances might be indefinitely multiplied, and they prove conclusively that by far the
greater number of the Aryan roots we possess are
developments from yet earlier roots. It is, however,

absurd to speak of the root of a root, and we, therefore, eschew the term altogether. We call them *bases ;*
and when our investigation reaches beyond them to
yet earlier forms, we find no inconsistency in speaking
of the base of a base.

In the Introduction (pp. 23, 27, 39), we have shown
how primitive descriptive sounds became consolidated
into words. In this section we have endeavoured to
make clear the sense in which we employ the term
onomatop, because in that consists the essential difference between our views and those of former writers.
The sense in which we employ that term permits us
to answer the most difficult problem in the Science of
Language, viz. the natural construction of bases or
roots. - The root is the *ultima Thule*, or *ratio*, of all
preceding writers, even of Mr. Wedgwood; for he only
seeks to explain roots by referring them to some natural
action which he believes to be graphically depicted by
the sound that expresses it. Professor Max Müller
does not attempt an explanation,—"Every thing in
language, except the roots, is intelligible," he says.[a]
The disciples of that excellent scholar have not yet
advanced beyond their master, as witnesses the following from the *Saturday Review* of May 31, 1873 [b]:—
" Let us take any Aryan root, say the root *vid*, When
we have traced all the various cognate forms up to
the root, there we stick ; we can get no further. We
see that *vid* means to *see*, and therefore to *know*, but

---

[a] Science of Language, I. p. 260.   [b] S. R. vol. 35, p. 720.

we cannot say why it should mean to *see*. If Mr.
Wedgwood can tell us, we shall sincerely thank him.
If he can show us how *vid* came to have the meaning
of seeing whether by onomatopoeia or by any other
process, we shall not have to give up one tittle of
what we have already made out by the Comparative
method; we shall only have learned something else
into the bargain:" Our definition of an onomatop will,
we think, materially aid in the elucidation of such
questions, by permitting bases to be dismembered and
resolved into elemental fragments, as will be illustrated further on in this Præfamen.

The filling up of lexicons is a mere question of time
and endeavour; the process once begun the result
became inevitable. Sounds expressive of the simplest
actions, a ·*g*·, gullet, swallow, ·*l*·, lick, tongue, ·*p*·
lip, suck, &c., gradually lost their spontaneous character by constant repetition, and so became the symbols of ideas. At first they were mere noises, produced
by a particular organ, naturally calling attention to
that organ and its functions; and as long as they re-
mained so they would be in what we might call the
" spontaneous " stage of language, in which any noise
could be used by any being to serve any purpose
desired. Gradually one complexion of sound, from its
more expressive character, would gain the predomi-
nance over others, and it would then cease to be spontaneous ; it would have become a recognized name, a
word, the symbol of an idea. These symbols of ideas

acquired intensity by doubling, as *g·g·*, *gar-gle,* Fr. *gor-ge,* &c., and, losing their intensiveness by familiarity, were revivified by fresh duplication, or modified and distinguished from each other by the addition of other sounds as the humanizing process proceeded. These added sounds need not all of them have previously existed as separate onomatops with special meanings of their own; analogy would rather lead to the conclusion that many of them must have been added by way of stress or accent, or as descriptive of particular states or actions. As Mr. Wedgwood has pointed out, sounds such as *posh, blob, gob,* &c., are highly descriptive; they need no interpreter; it is impossible to differ as to the ideas their utterance awakens. The cerebral sibilant is a sound of this character, and it seems to have been added to many Aryan words as a kind of intensifier. Instances are found in the words *rush, crash, crush, dash, splash, smash,* with which may be contrasted *run, creak, crack, dab, smack.* The latter are clearly not so forcible as the former. The following Aryan bases all mean "strike," "injure," and in each case the cerebral sibilant seems added solely for the purpose of exaggerating the sound, because simpler forms exist for most of them :—*ísh, ush, kash, kishk, khash, ghush, chash, jash, just, júsh, jhash, jhúsh, dhúsh, dhṛish, pash, pish, pṛish, bash, brúsh, yúsh, rish, rush, lúsh, vash, vṛish, núsh, mush, śash, śish, hishk.*

A sharp dental, also, would give an idea of finality and decision to any onomatop,—an idea covered by

such words as *down, done* with, *there*, there's an end.
The following bases are offered in illustration:—*at*
or *it*, to bind up; *krit*, to wrap up; *kṛit*, to cut up;
kit (from *ki*), to know; *chit*, to wake up; *chrit*, to blaze
up; *dyut, jyut, jut, yut*, to sparkle; *nṛit*, to lead forth,
dance (*nṛi*, to lead); *pat*, to fall down; *yat*, to knock
about; and *yat*, to strive after (*yá*, to go for). This sharp
dental *t* by the air of decision it imparts to bases, is a
rather apt exponent of the ideas intended by *there,*
that, and is what may be called "the remote definite."
Considering it to have this sense the results are not a
little curious when we seek to analyse old bases. For
example the Sanskrit *sad* is the same as the English
sit, set, which may be resolved into *s·t·*, the *s·* = "exist"
(Sans. *as,* English *is,* Lat. *s*-um), and the *t·* = "there."
Sit is then the equivalent of "exist there," which is
by no means an unreasonable explanation. The base
sthá, "stand," (Lat. *sto, stare*) admits of a similar
rendering; but here the dental *t* or *th* has more the
force of "down," so that *sthá* may mean "exist down,"
"be placed." The word "down" itself will be seen
to be based upon a dental, which in Sanskrit takes the
asper under the form *adhas,* and the preposition *adhi*
= super, upon, which may also come from the notion
of placing down one thing upon another.

　　The letter *s,* besides its sense of "being," is also
commonly used to define that which is near, whether
the nearness be of likeness or of vicinity. In this
sense we find it in the Sanskrit *sah,* "he," "this;"
sa and *saha,* "along with," in the preposition *sam,*

"with," and as the sign of the nominative case in
Sanskrit and Latin. The Hindî ablative *se*, "with,
through, by means of," is another instance. The
letter *s* most clearly marks the difference between *this*
and *that* in English; *this* meaning "the defined which
is near," and *that*, "the defined which is remote."
For this reason we call *s* "the proximate definite."
Abundant illustrations are readily found for its sense
of nearness of likeness in such words as *same*, *similar*,
such, *thu-s*, *as*, *so*, the Sanskrit *sama*, "like," the
Hindî *sá*, "like," "similar;" and, in composition, in
such words as *aisá*, "this-like," *waisá*, "that-like,"
&c., &c. The letter *s* in the form *sam* was frequently
used in Sanskrit grammar as a verbal prefix to indicate
proximity; as *samgam* = "to go with," *samjná* = "to
be conversant with;" but this prefix was felt to be
an addition to the base, insomuch that the verbal
augment was inserted between it and the base; thus
in the preterite we say *sam-a-gachchhat*, "he went
with," *sam-a-jánita*, "he was conversant with," and
not *a-sangachchhat*, *a-sanjánita*. The more recent
Sanskrit books, as for example the Mahâbhârata, do,
however, frequently place the augment in a position
that shows a disposition on the part of these prepositions to become welded on to the verbal stems. The
very preposition of which we are now speaking is
treated thus in Mahâbh. i. 5515, where we meet the
word *anwasancharat*, "he traversed" (*anu-a-sam-
char-at*), instead of the regular form *anusam-a-charat*.
Here the preposition *sam* has lost its independence,

H

and is become welded on to the base *char*, which thus
becomes *sanchar*, and then takes the augment as a
simple verb (*asancharat*).   This process accounts
fully for the presence of the letter *s* as an initial in
many Aryan bases.   *Sam*, as Professor Th. Benfey
points out, is the accusative singular of *sa*, and is
frequently employed without the inflexional mark in
such words as *saphala*, "fruitful," "with fruit." Just
on this model we find the base *sabháj*, meaning "to
serve," and also the base *bhaj*, "to serve," the former
being clearly a developed form of the latter; and it is,
therefore, not unfair to suppose that *sanj*, "to be
attached," really grew out of *sam-ga*, "to go with," ·
or that such a base as *say*, "to go," is deduced from
sa + i, "to accompany." That the prefix *sa* or *sam*
can dwindle down to *s* only, we have positive proof,
in the case of *sarj*, "to acquire," which is clearly
arj, "to acquire," with the addition of an *s* prefix, as
both Westergaard[a] and Benfey[b] properly state.

This long argument on the prefix *s* will, we hope,
strengthen our conjectures as to the origin of some
Aryan bases.   To apply this notion to the analysis of ·
a base we will select *strí*, to "stretch," every letter of
which appears to be significative.   To *stretch* is to
extend from here to there connectedly ; and the sound
strí exactly represents that complex idea.   Thus, as
we have just been arguing, *s* = "with," "likeness,"
"connection," "alliance," so removing the *s* from the
base we are examining, *trí* remains.   Now *trí* is also

---

[a] Radices Sanscritæ.   [b] Sansk Dict *s. v.*

a base, meaning "to cross over," "to go *there*," the *t* being the remote definite. When the *t* is removed *ṛi* is left, also a Sanskrit base meaning "go," "move;" and as the trill of the *r* most frequently imparts nothing else than a sense of rapidity to bases, that also may be removed and we find the vowel *i* finally remaining, which is the well known Aryan base, the *i-re* of Latin; Greek, *ἰ-έναι*; "to go," "to move." Synthetically we have,—*i* = go; *ṛi* = go quickly, and after losing its intensive character, simply "go;" *tṛi* = "go there," "cross over;" *stṛi* = "go there connectedly," "to stretch." Each of the four letters composing *stṛi* is thus, not improbably, a separate onomatop; and if this is thus shown to be the case in one instance, the probability that it is generally true is much strengthened. That the letter *s* is only accessory to Sanskrit bases, admits of ready proof from the following set of double bases:—*sri* and *ri* both mean "go;" *svri* and *vri* = "go;" *srip* and *ri* or *rep* = "move;" *svart* and *vrit* = "turn;" *sphal* and *phal* = "expand;" *sphul* and *phul* = "expand"; *skhad* and *khad* = "be firm;" *spas* and *pas* = "injure;" and *sagh*, "strike," formed of *sa* + *han*, *han* standing for an original *ghan*, as shown by the 3rd pers. plu. pres. *ghnanti*, "they strike," and by the redupl. pret. *jaghána*, "he struck."

These illustrations are sufficient for our present purpose, which is to make it clear that bases as they now exist are in reality composite factors, and so establish the conclusion that we must look beyond

them for the onomatopic bases of language. Onomatops are thus reduced to the simplest proportions, to
the elemental articulations upon which modern words
are based. These elementary sounds will be found
to be related to, and to be expressive of, the natural
functions of animal nature, and to be destitute of all
that is miraculous on the one hand, or poetic on the
other.

SECTION III.

COLLECTIVE ANALYSIS.

It will be evident to the reader that we are not
guided entirely by the ordinary rules of comparative
philology. Some words of explanation are, therefore,
necessary so that it should not be thought that we
recognize no restraints whatever. The present school
of philologists lays great stress on the difference between base and termination, and we quite agree with
them in maintaining this intrinsic difference. We
agree also with other philologists in separating prefixes from the base; so that, being agreed on these
fundamentals, it is evident that we work by method,
and are not mere dreamers. Where we differ from
philologists is in the treatment of the residual base.
After the separation of prefix and termination, the
remaining portion of a word is generally considered
irresolvable into simpler elements. So much is this
the case that every philologist seeks to carry a word
up to its most antique form before eliminating the
radical, and when he has done this he thinks that he
has the word in its purest form and can do no more.
Here we differ; for it is our opinion that the bases

themselves show marks of alliance and divergence
sufficient to allow the inquirer to detect bonds of
union among classes of bases, leading to the conviction
that many of the oldest bases we possess are themselves compounds, formed by the aggregating or weld-
ing on of more ancient formatives. This fact, for we
think ourselves entitled to speak of it as a fact, has
been noticed by Professor Max Muller. In discussing
some roots in his work on the Science of Language,
that scholar points to the undoubted connection between *tud, tup, tuph, tuj, tur, túr, turv, tuh, tuç,* and
between *yu, yuj, yudh,* &c. In these instances we
find a general idea of " striking " expressed by the
letter *t·* with varying adjuncts, which have the effect
of defining to some extent the particular kind of
striking each base is intended to express. In the other
case the letter *y·*, with a primary sense of junction, is
combined with other letters which discriminate between
many ways of associating things together. Now we
maintain that it is very unscientific to hold that each
of the words *yu, yuj, yudh,* had an independent origin,
and that the presence of the same initial is due to
accident or chance ; on the contrary, we think it more
conformable to reason to believe that the initial is one
and the same primitive base modified by certain adjuncts, which in course of time and by certain repetition in a particular sense, have ultimately lost all trace
of independence, and so are become indissolubly welded
on to the parent stock. This indeed seems to be the
opinion of Professor Max Muller with regard to these

particular bases, and he considers that a large number
of other Aryan roots came to their present forms by a
similar process. That eminent scholar does not, however, say how far he would be prepared to allow the
operation of this law; and it is very apparent that
the philologists who think they follow his teaching will
not allow it any operation whatever. The oldest form
preserved in literature is treated as the oldest possible
form of a base, and any attempt to apply inductive
reasoning to the elimination of the earliest forms of
words is looked upon as idle dreaming.

A little reflection will convince the reader that for
the purpose of reaching the ultimate base of a word
the more modern forms are in some respects as useful
as the more ancient. If sense naturally attaches itself to particular sounds, it is evident that as soon as
those sounds were entirely eliminated the word would
become senseless; hence it follows that the most
modern words, which we know by experience to possess
sense, must contain within themselves the primitive
bases upon which they are built. It is the task of
the philologist to point out that central and vital
spot around which successive strata of modificatory
sounds have clustered, and too frequently almost ob-
literated.

A necessary preliminary to this inquiry is an examination of the phonetic changes which words have
undergone independently of accretions of sense-modi-
fying adjuncts. We have before (p. 37) alluded to
this in the Introduction, as one of the laws of change

to which words are subject, and we recur to it here in order to show to how great an extent it transforms the appearance of words. The instances we shall shortly cite will be such as are undoubtedly known to have been evolved from each other; and it will, we believe, be admitted that the words among which we seek to establish a relationship are in no case so diverse in appearance.

Let us take the common word *am*, which is only another way of pronouncing the French word *suis*. The two words are identical in both base and inflexion, and one is merely a phonetic corruption of the other. The French *suis* and Italian *sono*[a] represent the Latin *sum*, in which the letter *m* of the Anglo-Saxon *eom* makes its appearance. The Latin *sum*[b] is the equivalent of the Greek εἰμί, the Lithuanian *esmi*, and the Sanskrit *asmi*, the last being a compound of *as*, "the existing," *mi* "(of) me," *i.e.*, I exist. Here we have unanswerable evidence that *am* and *suis* are only phonetic varieties of the same word.

Further instances of identical words strangely differing in appearance are found in the French *guépe*, the representative of the English *wasp*; the Sanskrit *yakrit*, Greek, ἧπαρ, Latin, *jecur* (liver); Sanskrit *yájya*, Greek ἄγιος (holy); Sanskrit *udra*, Greek ἐνυδ-ρις (other); Sanskrit *yatas*, Greek ὅθεν (whence). From

[a] L. Delâtre, La Langue Française dans ses Rapports avec le Sanscrit, Introduction, page 6.

[b] *E-sum* was the old form for *sum*, *simus* for *sumus*, subj. present was *siem*, *sies*, *siet*, &c., for *sim*, *sis*, *sit*.

an analogous cause words passing from one people to another are, at times, completely changed into other words of somewhat similar sound; thus the apple known in France as *belle et bonne*, "beautiful and good," appears in English as *belly-bound;* and, as is well known, the ship *Bellerophon* is called by our English tars the *Bully-ruffian.* In a similar way *Sandy-acre*, a parish in Derbyshire, is meant for *Saint Diacre*, "the holy deacon;" and the hill in Oxfordshire called *Shotover* was named from the *Château vert*, or "green castle." *Sparrow-grass* is as near as some people can approach the pronunciation of *asparagus*, and *Beef-eater* has completely supplanted the old *buffetier*, "side-board attendant." *Filibusters* is from the French *Flibustiers*, a corruption of the English *freebooters*. The signs of public-houses afford familiar instances of phonetic corruption, changing "God encompasses us" into the "Goat and Compasses," and the "Bacchanals" of Chelsea into a "Bag o' Nails."

The Greek language furnishes us with a set of almost systematic changes; such as a Prothesis, which prefixes a letter or a syllable to the beginning of a word, as τε-τάγων for ταγών from τάξω;—an Aphæresis, which, on the contrary, takes away a letter or syllable from the beginning of a vocable, as ὄρτη (Ionic) for ἑορτὴ;—a Syncope, which takes away a letter or syllable from the middle of a word, as ἔγεντο for ἐγένετο;—an Epenthesis, or the insertion of a letter or syllable in the middle of a vocable, as ἔλλαβε for ἔλαβε;—an Apocope, which cuts off a letter or syllable from the end of a word, as δω for δῶμα;—or a Paragoge, which occurs when an addition is made to the last syllable of a word, as ἦσθα for ἦς, ἐτύπτεσκε for ἔτυπτε.

The singular disfigurement noticeable in these words is produced mainly by phonetic corruption; and when we see such striking divergences developing in historic times we are prepared to believe that analogous changes took place at a yet earlier period.

Indian grammarians have not overlooked these modulations in the sounds of words, and have embodied some of their conclusions in the following rule :—

RYor ḍLos tadvaj JYor BVor api—
śsor MNoś chánte savisargávisargayoḥ ‖
Savindukávindukayoḥ syád abhedénakalpanam |

"The letters R and L, D and L, J and Y, B and V, ś and s; M and N; a final visarga [ḥ] or its omission; and a final nasal mark or its omission, are always optional, there being no difference between them." [a]

Here it will be remarked that some of the permutations which we point out, and which, we suspect, will meet with much scepticism among European scholars, are looked upon as well known and established facts that admit of no controversy. It is upon the mutual

[a] Wilson's Sanskrit Dictionary, Preface, p. xli.

convertibility of R, L, and D,[a] and the optional insertion or rejection of a nasal, that we base our belief in the unity of the words *flower* and *expand* (in Sect. IV.), and the more we examine that matter the more are we convinced of the truth of the alliance.

The foregoing examples of phonetic change, which, we think, will not be disputed, afford sufficient evidence that the corruptions to which words are liable are practically limitless. With such instances before one's face, it seems mere idle quibbling to object to a derivation because *s* has unaccountably become *k*, or *p* has been replaced by *m*, or because vowels have been interchanged or elided. Mr. Wedgwood says very truly that the only rule for palæographic permutation is that any letter may interchange with any other letter; and it is almost labour thrown away to attempt a systematic classification of anything so capricious. It is notorious that no two districts in any country pronounce the words of their common language alike; it is even questionable whether any two people can be found who can give to any word exactly the same phonetic power. Nature has endowed us with boundless diversity in this as in all other things, and we must expect that this diversity in the

---

[a] Scholars will find European examples ready to hand in—

Δάκρυ	.	.	.	Lacryma.
ὁ Δυσσευς	.	.	.	uLysses.
oDor	.	.	.	oLeo.
cicaDa	.	.	.	cicaLa, *Ital.*, cigaLe, *Fr.*
ægiDius	.	.	.	giLles, &c., &c., &c.

appreciation of sound and in the capacity to imitate it, will also show itself in the symbols intended to present sounds to the eye. In Somersetshire the sound given to the word *this* is, to a Londoner's ear, exactly like *thik*. We know that the two words are identical in construction, and are supposèd to be identical in sound by their respective utterers.[a] The same change is to be remarked in India, where the word for " language" is both written and pronounced *bháshá* and *bhákhá* indifferently. So identical are the sounds *kh* and *sh* thought to be in India, that the writers of many manuscripts employ one or other of these letters throughout, to do duty for both sounds in any words in which they may occur. The Sanskrit *śwan*, a dog, which reappears in the Greek word κύων, κυνός, then in Lat. *canis*, *catulus*, French, *chien*, Ital. *can*, O. H. G. *hunon*, Saxon, German and Swedish, *hund*, Esthon. *hunt*, Scotch and English, *hound*,—shows us that, as an initial also, a guttural, palatal, or asper, may supplant a sibilant. If we, now, only imagine a word having an initial, medial, and final sibilant converted, on the principle of these examples, in each case into a letter of another class, such a word, though a mere phonetic corruption, would be unrecognizable, and would be treated by all philologists as an independent creation.

Instances of *s* becoming *k* acknowledged by scholars, are found in the following:—

[a] These provincialisms are very numerous in all languages.

Sanskrit.	*Greek.*	*English.*
s'was'ura	. . ἐκυρός	. . father-in-law.
s'was'rû	. . ἐκυρὰ	. . mother-in-law.
paras'u	. . πέλεκυς	. . an axe.
s'ankha	. . κόνχη	. . a shell.
âs'u	. . ὠκύς	. . swift.
as'man	. . ἄκμων	. . stone.[a]
s'ringa	. . κέρας	. . cornu, Lat., horn.

Another remarkable instance of phonetic corruption is the interchange of L with N, two letters which appear to have nothing in common. The following will, nevertheless, show that they have been used as equivalents of each other :—

Lat. Lympha	. . .	*Gr.* Νύμφὴ.
Gr. Λιτρον (νίτρον)	.	*Lat.* Nitrum.
Lat. L-utra	. . .	*Span.* Nutria.
Lat. Lamella	. . .	*Prov.* Namela.
Lat. Lib-ella	. . .	*Fr.* Niv-eau.
Ital. veLeno	. . .	*Lat.* veNenum.
Span. ca-Lange	. . .	*Lat.* caNonicus.
Span. comuLgar	. . .	*Lat.* commuNicare.
Fr. orpheLin	. . .	*Lat.* orphaNus.
Sans. Lânghana	. . .	*Hindí* Nânghnâ (trespass).
Sans. Lângala	. . .	*Hindí* Nângar (plough).

Doubtless a very useful work is accomplished when any scholar discovers the laws by which letters interchange when passing from one particular language

---

[a] ἄκμων, used by Homer, is an anvil.

into another.　Such discoveries clear away many
mists of uncertainty, and, as in the case of Grimm's
law for the convertibility of tenues into aspers, in
Sanskrit, Latin, and German, give at times a secure
base of operations from which to advance to future
conquests.　Indeed one such demonstration of regular
action, like the law of universal gravitation, evolves
harmony out of discord, and conducts almost of necessity to conclusions akin to those sought to be established in this work.

Here the question as to what is to be considered the
real base of a word naturally suggests itself.　If any
letter may interchange with any other letter at the
beginning, middle, and end of a word, what *point
d'appui* remains on which to rest our confidence that
any word is certainly the *confrère* of any other word?
To this we would reply that, in our opinion, the
result of former attempts to connect particular words
together has proved that there is no certain means
of recognizing congenital characteristics.　It is notorious that very absurd mistakes have been made by
allying words somewhat similar in form; so absurd
indeed have been the results that philologists now-a-
days very properly pay no attention whatever to accidental resemblances or differences, but rely entirely
on historical evidence and the operation of such phonetic
laws as have hitherto been discovered.　But, as has
just been shown, the φώνη is so capricious a manifestation of the λόγος that the very cautious method now
pursued by philologists prevents their tracking vocables

through more than a fractional part of their wanderings, and allows their deductions to culminate in only vague generalities about the possible development of language from a few hundreds of primitive bases. It is this state of the science which has led us to suggest the system of Collective Analysis, illustrated in this book, and which promises to unlock many of the sphinx-like riddles that have hitherto teazed inquirers. It is by the simultaneous examination of collections of words in one and the same language, which are more or less indefinitely related to each other in meaning, that we hope to arrive at some unchanging or recognizable central point which may be taken as the sense-giving element, and therefore the base of the whole congeries. It is true that at last we can give no more definite shape to the base we eliminate than a single letter; but this is so because we wish to keep ourselves clear of assertions which it is impossible to verify. The consentient opinion of all scholars is that modern words arose from monosyllabic bases; and it would therefore follow that all words are resolvable into some simple sound, the vocalizing element of which must ever remain a moot point, and which we represent by a dot both before and after a consonant to indicate uncertainty as to whether the vowel preceded or followed the letter. It must not, however, be supposed that we promise to reduce every word to such modest proportions. It forms no part of our programme to reduce the Greek language to the letter *i*, or the whole speech of mankind to seven

primitives, as has been seriously attempted in times
past; neither do we suppose that this will be the last
book ever written on the subject, and that it will
for ever set at rest all doubts and scruples connected
with etymology.   Our ambition has more reasonable
bounds; as we only seek to lead the way in a
new method of investigation, which promises, by the
combined labours of such scholars as think our method
worthy of elaboration, to establish relationship among
large classes of words hitherto thought to be distinct,
and in this way to reduce materially the number of
necessary bases, and finally to prove that each arose
as the natural expression of a common want,—natural,
as the imitative expression *not* of the sound of bird
and beast, but of the *very idea* intended to be conveyed. The bases resulting from our exhaustive
system of analysis are undoubtedly genuine onomatops,
and, when discovered, commend themselves to our
intelligence; as in the identification of the letter *l*
as the phonetic exponent of the tongue's action (p. 141),
in that of *g* as the representative of the throat
(Introd. p. 27), and in that of *p* as the puffing symbol
(*see* Sect. IV.).

What we mean by "collective analysis" can only
be explained by an example ; and we therefore append
the following examination of the word "Law." Here
we may as well add the general remark that in seeking
to probe language down to its ultimate bases, we
would be understood as laying no great stress on the
alliances which we endeavour to show to be subsisting

between particular words. What we mainly seek to establish is the recognition of new principles in the treatment of bases. If we succeed in proving the ultimate connexion and positive affiliation of numbers of words hitherto supposed to be distinct one from the other, it will matter little that particular alliances may afterwards be shown to be doubtful or erroneous.

It will be remarked that we do not deal with letters so much as with phonic or syllabic instants, pulsations of sound which do not change letter by letter, but sound by sound. To give an example, *vri* becomes *wri*, *whor*, *wel*, &c., by phonetic, not palæographic transmutation. The modulations of syllabic instants may be well illustrated by this sound, *vri*, which is a Sanskrit base, meaning " go round," " surround." It presents us with the following among other changes :—*wrea-th* (to go round the head), *wri-the* (to turn round about), *wri-ng*, and *wre-nch* (to twist anything round), *wri-ggle* (to twist round), *wri-nkle* (that which is so twisted), *wel-ter* (to roll about), *wel-t* (a small roll or crease), *wel-kin* (that which surrounds) the *worl-d* or *e-or-th*, both of which are forms of *or-bs*, Latin. To *wra-p* is to inclose anything, a *wal-l* is an enclosure; to *ware* is to make a ship turn away from its course, to make it go *a-wry;* and to be *war-y* is to circumvent, to make any one subservient to your *wil-l* (see p. 49), to get them into your *wiles* or toils. A *wheel* is so called from its circular and revolving character, and a *whor-l* is a circular arrange-

I

ment of any kind; to *wiel-d* a sword is to make to go
round, to *whir-l* it about, so as to over*whel-m* the foe
or co-*ver* him with confusion. A *whel-k* is a curly
shell-fish; a *wire* is a flexible object that will turn
to-ward-s any point; and a *wil-d* or *weir-d* creature
is one that wanders round about according to its own
will. The fact that these words have reached us
through different Aryan channels in no wise affects
their utility for the present purpose, as they all come
from one primitive base, which appears in Sanskrit as
vṛi. Here, then, we have the idea of circular motion
expressed by *vṛi, wri, wry, wre, wrea, weir, wir,
war, ver, or, wel, wal, wil, wiel, whel, whil, whor,
worl,* and *wheel,* all of which are clearly but different
forms of each other. The greater part of such transmutations were wrought by people innocent of alpha-
bets, who repeated the sounds they heard uttered.
in the best way they were able, without any regard
to the appearance their words would present upon
paper.

It is also proper to remark that in our opinion too
much stress is at times laid upon the differences
between what are called vowels. It should be re-
membered that vowels have, in reality, no substantive
existence in language,—the Semitic languages entirely
ignore them. Vowels are merely vocalizations of the
consonants, and they differ from each other solely
according to the place in the mouth at which the
emission of sound is permitted, and the more or less
degree of relaxation of the throat. They pass into

each other in the following order :—*i, e, a, o, u ;*[*]—*i* being the sharpest and most guttural, the rest opening out one after the other as the muscles of the throat are relaxed, and the vibration approaches nearer and nearer to the front of the mouth. Hence it follows that *ki* differs from *ka* solely from the fact that in pronouncing the *k* in the latter case the throat is somewhat more relaxed; and so of any other vocalization. With these preparatory explanations, we proceed to discuss the word "Law."

"LAW."

A word is used in the title of this book which has sorely puzzled etymologists, and given rise to much curious speculation. The word "law" is, as it were, "Nobody's child"; no parent has, as yet, been found for it; its *raison d'être* is still undemonstrated. It is, therefore, an excellent subject on which to operate by our method of collective analysis, for the purpose of arriving at some definite result.

As soon as we bring together the congeners of *law* we see that they agree in only one particular, which is, in containing the letter *l*, and this of itself is *primâ facie* evidence that the sense of the word attaches, in an especial degree, to that part of the word. It is true that, at times, the sense-giving element in a word entirely disappears; but though this takes place in a few words in each language, it is incredible that many

---

[*] Continental pronunciation.

different languages could all have dropped the essential sound, and could all have united in preserving some merely adventitious adjunct. The letter *l* may, therefore, be fairly held to represent the base of the word *law* (*lah*, *laga*, Anglo-Saxon ; *lag*, Old Norse ; *lex*, Latin ; λέγω, Greek ; *laie*, Norman French ; *loi*, French ; *legge*, Italian ; *lége*, Wallach.; *lēge*, Russian; *lage*, Swedish ; *ley*, Spanish ; *lauwe*, Dutch).

Now the *x* of the Latin *lex* we know stands for a simple guttural, which comes to light in the genitive *legis*, exactly presenting the shape of the Anglo-Saxon *laga*, and Icelandic *lag*. In Old English the sound of *g* or ȝ was frequently softened into *y ;* hence the word *laga* passed by phonetic change into *ley*, and its use in this form directs us to the sense attaching to the word. Thus while *ley* meant simply *law*, a *ley-gager*, was a gage deposited or laid down to abide an issue ; it was a gager in law. While the word *ley-gager*, from its nature, preserved a technical sense, the same form in *ley-land* (*lea*, *ley*, Norm. Fr.), or fallow land, —land lying dormant, — never lost a general, and therefore original import. The base, then, of *laga*, a law, is to be found also in *ligan*, A.S., to *lay* or place; which is further illustrated by the Old English word *leke*, lawful, closely allied to *league*,—the Fr. *ligue*, Ital. *legua*, Lat. *ligare*, to bind.

Norman French is a language which had a considerable effect in moulding the forms which words in English ultimately assumed, and the remarkable changes which the word we are discussing undergoes in Nor-

man French will help the reader to understand how
such forms as the Latin *ligo, lego,* and *lex,* passed into
each other. The word *law* in Norm. Fr. is written
lai, laydé, laie, leye, lee, ly; and in the plural *lez*
and *lous.* Here we have the vowels *a, e, y, o,*
used indifferently, which are certainly more violent
changes than the conversion of *i* into *e* (*ligo* into *lego*).
The adjective *lawful* undergoes the following transformations in Norm. Fr.:—*loiastes, luist, lyst, leust,
laust, licette, liat, leux, leus, leu, loyse, lyse, list, lise,
leise;* under another form *loisible, lisible, leisible,
leissie,* or *loial, laiel, lealment.* Each of the vowels
is used indifferently in these words, and it will be
perceived that the only fixed point in all these words
is the letter *l.* When we find a word undergoing such
transmutations in one language, without any change
of meaning, we shall be less surprised at the changes
to which bases are subject when they assume new and
technical significations.

The connection between *law* and *ligan,* to lay, was
pointed out by Horne Tooke a hundred years ago, yet
his explanation is not generally accepted, and the
Latin *licere,* to permit, to allow, has been thought, by
some, a more probable source of the word. It will be
shown in the sequel that *licére* itself, and all such
words, originate in the idea of *laying, leaving;* and
therefore the ultimate base of *law* through either channel would be the same. Still there can be no doubt
that *ligare,* to bind, is a nearer relative to *lex, legis,*

than *licere*, to allow; and we, therefore, agree with
Mr. Wedgwood in thinking that by *law* is meant
" what is *laid* down." In corroboration that author
says, " so Lat. *statutum*, statute, from *statuere*, to lay
down; Ger. *gesetz*, law, from *setzen*, to set; Gr.
θεσμος, law, from τιθημι, to lay;" and we may
add the Sanskrit *dharma*, law, from *dhṛi*, to place
or lay.

The kinship between *law* and bondage is further
illustrated by the Norm. Fr. *ly*, law, and *lyance* or
ligesse, allegiance, the duty of the *liche*, *lige*, or *liege*,
the subject, one under the law of a particular ruler;
that is, one bound to conform to what is laid down for
his guidance; a meaning which receives further elucidation from the term *liege-man*, a feudal tenant who
owes absolute fidelity, one bound to unquestioning ser-
vitude, in fact, a *bond-man*. The word *lige* or *liguie*
is the Norm. Fr. for a bond; *liers* = prisoners, *lyer* =
to bind, *liaz* or *lyaz* = bundles, and *loiens* = bonds,
presenting forms closely analogous to those which
represent the fetters of the law.[a] In the same language those who bound themselves for a term, or who
were hired, were called *loians* or *loueez*, and the act
of hiring *lowance*, *lowange* or *lovage* (Fr. *louer*, to
let a house), while that which was paid for the service
was known as *lower*, *luer*, *lowir*, *loos*, or *alegance*,
that is, an al-*low*-ance, obviously allied to *louer*, *al-*

---

[a] In modern French *re-lier* means ' to bind' (a book); and *re-lieur*
is a binder.

louier, Fr., to assign; *alogar,* Prov.; *allogare,* Ital., to settle; *locare allocare,* Lat., to place, *i.e.,* lay down (*locare argentum,* Lat., to *lend* money on a rental).

To Lay a thing down is really to place it in contact with something else, as is proved to demonstration by the Sanskrit form of the same word. Lag, in Sanskrit, means both to *lie* and to *ally;* and in its derivative Lagná, in Hindî, it comprises every kind of application both mental and physical. The Latin word Ligare, to attach, to bind, gives the nearest rendering of the word *law, lex,* the Lig-*ament,* the agreement or League binding well-ordered societies of men, without which there can be no *alliance,* no Lock-*ing* together of numerous interests into a compact bLock or Log. The Law is a Link which, like the Lainers or Lanyards of a ship, Laces, Lashes, or Latches together the elements of a common polity, in the same way that a Leam or Leash binds dogs, a Linch-pin binds the axle of a cart, and a Langot or Latchet binds the two sides of a shoe.[a]

The above instances show some of the changes which the base ·*l·* undergoes while retaining its older sense of attachment. It will, we think, be acknowledged that the passage of *ligan* into *law* is trifling in comparison. The original identity of the words above given is shown more clearly in their older forms: thus,

[a] Cf. the Persian Langar, a rope for steadying a tent; and the Sanskrit Labhasa, a rope for tying horses, in French *longe.*

to *latch* is in A. S. *leccan, gelæccan,* to *lock* is *beluc-can,* Loc is a shut-in place, the Icel. Loka; and a *leash* finds its representatives in the Norm. Fr. Lease, a leash, Laces, snares, and the Old Fr. Lacs, the Prov. Lac, *latz, laz;* the Spanish Lazo; Fr. Lacet, a string for stays ; Bavarian geLass, the Lat. Laqueus (snare) ; and the modern Dutch Laschen or Lassen, the Danish Laske, the Bavarian geLassen, to join things together,—show how commonly the guttural passes into a sibilant (see p. 108).

There are, however, very many other words in which the same base ·*l*· enters to impart a ligamentous sense ; such as Leetch-lines on board ship, Lime (another form of *leam,* the coupling of dogs), Loam, the adhesive kind of earth, and Lime (*leim,* G. ; *lijm,* Du.; *lim,* Icel.; *limus,* Lat. ; *lym,* Nor. F. ; *beliman,* A. S. ; *leimen,* G.), a sticky substance, the ag-*glu*-tinative property of which is its distinctive feature. So also the Sanskrit words Laguḍa, a club; Laḍḍu, an ag-*glo*-merated sweetmeat ; Lákshá (*lacca,* Lat. ; *lacca,* Ital. ; *laca,* Sp. and Port.; *lack,* Dan. ; *lak,* Dutch ; *lack,* Swedish ; *laka,* Pol. and Russ.), "gum-lac;" Leshṭu, Loshṭu, Loshṭra, Loshta, "a clod of earth."

From *lime* we naturally pass to sLime, the *s* of which is adventitious, and changes to a guttural· in cLeam (*clæman,* A. S.), "to glue or fasten," and so passes into cLew (*clywe,* A. S. ; *knauL,* G.), the Teutonic form of gLue, *glu,* Fr., "birdlime ;" gLus, gLu-*tinum,* coLLer, Lat. ; gLud, Welsh ; γλοιός, Gr. ;

"nasty, clammy;" the Scotch ɢʟair, glar, glaur,
"slime, saliver;" and the French ɢʟaire, "slimy soil,"
or "the white of an egg." The obsolete word
ɢʟaimous is a bond of union with cʟammy, sticky,
adhesive, and a word which at once puts us into communication with cʟam, "to glue or daub;" A. S. cʟam,
a bandage, clasp; kʟamm, G., viscous; kʟam or
kʟamp, Du., sticky. The last Dutch word shows the
form the base assumed on taking a new sense; for
kʟamme or kʟampe is also the Dutch for a hook,
cʀamp, or cʟamp, used for the purpose of holding
things together,—the German kʟamme, kʀampf, Fr.
cʀampe.

The following batch of words from Hindî will show
how adhesiveness is expressed in that language:—
ʟagân, holding fast; ʟamḍor, leash for catching
game, ʟoknâ, to catch; ʟachchhâ, a bundle, ball;
ʟaṭ, tangled hair; ʟuj-ʟuja, clammy, viscous; ʟach-
ʟachânâ, to be clammy; ʟas, tenacity, viscosity;
ʟasaknâ, to become viscid; ʟasnâ, to embrace,
adhere; ʟasorâ, name of a glutinous fruit; ʟâsâ,
anything clammy; ʟâhjâ, viscosity, ʟâkh or ʟâh,
gum-lac; ʟâgú, adhering to, desirous of; ʟânk, bird-
lime; ʟabʟabâ, clammy, glutinous; ʟipaṭnâ, to cling,
adhere: ʟaptî or ʟapsí, glutinous food. In all these
words (and many more might be added) the constant
phenomenon is the presence of the letter *l*.

The form *cʀamp* above mentioned has congeners in
cʀump-led, to be pressed together, to have the *cʀamp*

(*crampe*, Fr.), to be cʀushed, made cʟose, stuffed, cʀam-med (A.S. *cramman*); and when meaning simply "bent together" the nasal is dropped, as in the form cʀub-ach, Gaelic, a cʀip-ple, one cʀab-bed, or cʀooked. That cʀab (a cʀaw-ling cʀeep-er) has the sense of adhesion is shown by the tool of that name used for clamping boards together, and also as applied to the animal, *crabba*, A. S.; *carabus*, Lat.; *krabbe*, Dan.; *krab* or *krank*, Breton; *krebs*, G.; *krabbi*, Icel.; *cancro*, gʀanchio, Ital.; *kaʀkaṭa*, Sans.; καPκίνος, Gr.; *cancer*, Lat., in which *l* (or *r*) is entirely suppressed; but as it appears in the Italian word, we have an instance to prove that modern European languages are not *derived* from the classical tongues, but had an independent growth.

Closely allied to the *crab* is the cʀayfish or cʀaw-fish, the *kʀebiz* of O. H. G.; *kʀevisse* or *kʀevitse*, Du.; *écʀevisse*, Fr.; *escaʀbot*, a beetle (cʀap-aud, a cʀawling toad) *escaʀabot*, Langue d'Oc; σκαPάβειου = σκαράβος, Gr.; *scaʀa-bœus*, Lat.; the creature with cʟaws, or cʟeyes (Sax. and G. *klave*), by which it can cʟutch, cʟip, cʟasp, or cʟeave to anything. The A. S. cʟeowan, to close, is clearly allied to such other forms as cʟeofan, A. S.; *kʟeben*, Germ.; *kʟeeven*, *kʟijven*, Du.; *kʟœbe*, Dan., all of which mean "to cleave," "to adhere;" and the Somersetshire cʟytty, sticky, is near akin to cʟeat, a piece of wood on which ropes are fastened, approaching the word cʟaut, which Chaucer uses as synonymous with cʟaw. It is, furthermore, the *claw* with which we cʟing to-anything, enabling

us to cLimb or cLamber, i. e. to scRamb-le up, Fr.
gRimp-er, gRiffe, akin to gRip, to gRasp; Gr. γPιπί-
ζω γPίπos, Fr. agRaffe, gRippé; cLeik or cLek,
Scotch, to seize; kLupe, Swiss, claws; kLænga,
Swedish, to climb.

Very similar to the form cleye, a claw, that by
which we adhere, is the word cLay (Gr. ἄργιΛλos,
Lat. argiLla) the adhesive kind of earth, Fr. argiLe,
Ital. argiLla, Luto, Span. arciLla, Russ. and Pol.
gLiua, A. S. cLæg, Du. kLey, Dan. kLæg or kLeg,
clammy, kLag, mud. The adventitious character of
the initial of clay is well shown by the German Letten,
Lehm, the Italian Luto, the Russian Letiŏ, the Wallachian Letiu, the Danish and Saxon Leer, and the
Swedish Lera, all of which are deprived of the
guttural. In Sanskrit clay is termed çiLindhrî,
basically identical with çiLí-pada, çLí-pada, çLí-padin,
cLub-footed; analogous to çLesha, union; çLeshman
or çLeshmaka, mucus; and çiLá, a Rock [a] or bLock of
matter. The final g of the A. S. cLæg is softened in
the word cling, and yet further changed in cLench or
cLinch, though it is again hardened upon dropping
the non-basic initial, as in Link (cf. the Hindî words
Lag, Lagbhag, and Loṇ, meaning " near to," " close
to "). The link (Langa, Sans.) which unites two
objects is nearly related to cLink-er, matter linked or
clenched together; kLinken, Du., fasten or clench a
nail; kLanken, Bav., to knot together; kLynge, Dan.,

---

[a] Rock = log, by change of r to l.

a knot or *cluster*. The word *cluster* is itself expressive of aggregation or joining together of many units, *cluÿster*, A. S.; *klister*, *kluster*, Du.; *klissen*, Du., to *close*, to be *close*, *clÿsan*, A. S.; *schliessen*, Germ.; akin to *cloister*, what is en*closed*, *kloster*, Germ.; *cloître*, *cloture*, Fr.; κλείω, κλίθρον, Gr.; *claustrum*, *claudo*, Lat.

, What is *close* is *crush-ed* or *crowd-ed* together, and *crowd* (*cruð*, A. S.), which was at one time written *curd* or *crud*, and lost its dental in *crew*, is traceable in such words as *curdle*, to *cruddle*, c·*ower*,* *crouch*, as is shown by the Dutch *kruyd-en* or *kruyen*, to hustle together; similar to the Polish *gruda* or *grud-ka*, a lump or *clod;* Fr. *crottes;* Eng. *crottles,* *cruttles*, or *crums*. Closely akin to *crowd* is the word *cloud* (*clote*, Du., αχλὺς, Gr., *caligo*, Lat.) which has long been known as a companion form to *clot* or *clod*, which may be strikingly illustrated by the expression *clouted* or *clotted* cream. To the word *clod* (*clud*, A.S.) must be allied *clog*, the changes of the final letter being illustrated by the Dan. *klods*, the Swed. *klots*, the Du. *klot* and the Germ. *kloss*. *Clog*, by loss of its adventitious initial, becomes *log*, expressive of an aggregated mass, a *block*. *Log* is found in the Hindî *laggí*, a staff or club, to which the following words are allied: *lakuṭ* or *lakaṛ*, a club or cudgel; *lakṛá*, a lump of wood; *lothrá*, a lump of flesh; *labedá*, a club; and *loprí*, a lump of anything moist.

---

* The dot in this word marks the absence of the base.

The word *clod* takes a nasal in the Dutch form *klonte*, and Danish *klunt*, so bringing about a not uncommon result, that is, the change of the letter following the nasal into a labial. Hence arises *klompe*, Du.; *klumpen*, G.; *klumbu*, Icel.; *klump*, Dan.; *clump*, Eng. The last word is, as Mr. Wedgwood says, "related to *club* as *stump* is to *stub*, *bump* to *bob*, *hump* to *hob*." A *club* is clearly a *log* or *lump*, an aggregation of matter, as the Swedish *klabb*, a log; *clava*, Lat., a bundle of sticks; the Russian *klub'*, a ball; the Polish *klqb*, a ball; the Welsh *clob*, a boss or knob; the Dutch *kluppel*, a cudgel, the German *kloben*, *kolbe;* the Latin *gleba*, a clod; and the English *club*-footed, abundantly attest.

The elision of a labial following a nasal is, also, a common occurrence, as was shown above by the change of *clamp* into *clammy*, *clam*, and *cram*; and so in the form of the base we are now discussing we find that the word *clump* or *cloud* passed not unnaturally into *clown*, to express one who is agglomerated in intellect, and who is also called a *clod* or *clot-pole*, a lumpish, stupid boor, a *log-gerhead* (Lat. *colonus*, stupid) ;—just as we find in German the word *klotz*, meaning a log, and *klotzig*, for that which is boorish or rustic. When the word *clown* loses its initial, it produces the form *loon* (*lawand*, Pers., foolish) or *lout*, applied to any *lub-ber* (*ligu*, Sans., a fool), in which last the labial reappears, bringing us back to *lump*, anastomosing with *clump*, *clamp*, and all that have preceded.

While mentioning *clump*, we must not forget *cLumsy*, which Mr. Wedgwood prefers to derive from *comelyd, cumbled, clommed, clomsid,* "stiffened with cold," without perceiving that all such vocables arise from the onomatop expressive of closing together, or aggregating, whether it be by application, agglutination, or by meteoric or other causes. The very word *coLd* (*ceaLd,* A. S.; *geLidus,* Lat.; *kuhL,* Germ.; *chiLl,* Eng.; *ceLe, cyL,* A. S.), that which con-*geals* or *gel*atinates, is a pertinent instance of the use of the base ·*l·* in a ligamentous sense.

From *cloud*, by mere change in pronunciation, we educe *gLout, gLowt,* and so *gLum, gLoomy* (*glomung,* A. S.), words expressive of a *cloudy* or frowning countenance, the looking *gRim,*—to *gLombe* (Chaucer); *gLupna,* Norse; *gLomme,* Dan.; *gLoeren, gLuyeren,* Dut.

Among the forms above given as near of kin to *clog*, we mentioned the word *block;* but this is by no means the only vocable in which a labial occurs as initial to our base. The continental equivalents of this word lead us into regions as yet untrod; the Swed. *bLack,* Dut. *bLucken,* Ital. *b·uzzelli,* Germ. *bLock* or *kLoss,* Fr. *bLoc* or *bLot;* Prov. *bLoca* or *bocLa,* the boss of a shield, that which is *bLunt;* Dut. *pLukk,* which in Somersetshire is also pronounced *pLock;* leading to the Danish *pLet,* Eng. *pLot,* and ultimately to *bLot;* which last is, in German, expressed by the three words, *bLosse, kLeck,* and *fLeck,* the last of which conducts us to a *fLake* or knot of snow, and a *fLock* of wool (*flocc*, A. S.; *flocke*, Germ.; *floc, flocon*, Fr.; *pʟecta*, Lat.), a *fʟock* of sheep, and a *fʟeece* or bunch of wool (*fʟyse*, A. S.; *vʟiess, woʟle*, Germ.; *vʟies* or *woʟ*, Dut.; *uʟd*, Dan.; *uʟl*, Swed.; *ʟaine*, Fr.; *ʟana*, Ital.; *ʟa*, Sp.; *ʟàa*, for *ʟagna*, Port.; *Λανω*, Doric), and at last we arrive at *fʟax* (*fʟeax*, A. S.; *vʟas, vʟasch*, Dut.; *wʟakno*, Bohem.; *ʟinum*, Lat.; *ʟin*, Fr.), which the Russian words *wʟas, woʟos'*, hair, enable us to recognize as a form of the word *wool*. The demonstration of this alliance is furnished by the following paragraph, simply copied from the first edition of Mr. Wedgwood's "Dictionary of English Etymology":—

"Wooʟ. Goth. *wulla*, ON. *ull*, Fris. *wille*, Fin. *willa*, Russ. *wolna*, W. *gwlan*, Gael. *olana*, wool. Lith. *wilna*, Let. *willa, wilna*, Illyr. *vuna*, Lat. *villus*, a lock; *vellus*, a fleece; Gr. ουλος, woolly; Esthon. *wil*, wool; *willane, wildne*, woollen, woolly."

These words are given by that gentleman without comment of any kind; but they at once suggest how the *w* passed into *v*, and then into *f*, and finally coalescing with the letter *l*, transformed *wool* into *fl-eece* (? the old Aryan genitive, *wool-is, vl-is*) and gave a name to that which has a *fʟossy* appearance, *i. e. flax*. The Norman French *lins, laisnes*, or *leignes*, wool; *lanuz*, woollen; *linge, lenge*, or *leignes*, linen, are additional evidence.

The kind of *block* with which we stop a hole is called a *pʟug*, a word which retains the *k* in the Finnish form *puʟkka*, and the Esthonian *puʟk*, as indeed is the case in the Pl. Du. *pʟukk*, which means

both a block and a plug ; while the words *pLugge*,
Pl. Du.; *pLug*, Du.; *pLigg*, Swed.; offer forms which
balance the initial surd by a final sonant. The French
en-cLoyer, to stop with a plug, to *cLog*, or *cLoy*, gives
a parallel form, in which the final melts into a vowel,
the not uncommon end of a guttural. That the letter
l in *plug* is radical may be shown by the word *peg*;
which, however closely it approaches to *plug* in both
form and sense, is nevertheless derived from a quite
different base, as will be shown in the Dictionary.

The word *block*, besides changing its initial to the
spiritus asper in *flock*, *fleece*, &c., at times loses it
altogether, so that we meet with the alternative forms
flocke and *locke* in German ; *vlocke* and *locke* in
Dutch ; *lockr* in Icelandic ; *locca* in Anglo-Saxon,
and *lock* (of hair) in English. The word *lock* is
applied to an aggregation of hair just as *log* is to an
aggregation of woody matter, and *rock* or *block* is to
a mass of stone. In every case the idea is that of
associated units forming a common *buLk*.

Having thus followed the base ·*l*· through so many
changes arising out of its sense of attachment, agglutination, and aggregation, we will return to the forms
link, *clench*, *cling*, and follow the base through a
different channel among a series of words which
adhere in meaning more closely to the idea of simple
alliance, the bringing, laying, or placing together.
For the word *cling* so naturally suggests the form
Linger, that it would require more reasoning to prove
they were not akin than to establish their relationship.

Linger suggests Loiter, Lounge, Lurch, Lurk (Luk-ná, Hindî) and Langour,[a] to remain attached to a particular place or state (Lirka or Lurka, Norse, Lauern, Germ., to lie hid), to be slow (slaw, Sax., slov, Du., Lent, Fr.) as a slug or a sluggard (*i.e. slow*-ard), to lag behind, be loth, and, with a nasal accent, to be Long. There does not, at first sight, seem much connexion between the ideas expressed by *long* and *loitering*, yet in their Hindî forms (*vi*-lamb, procrastination, de-Lay, and Lamba, long, tall) the identity of the two is rather strongly marked. Such is also the tendency of the Walloon Lon=*slow*, the Limousin Loung, Loun=tedious; the Italian Lungi, French Loin=far, Old French esLonger, éLoigner, to put at a distance; and the Old Norse Langr, Goth. Laggs. Very near of kin to *langour* is the French Languir, to Languish; to *linger* in confinement; and Long (Scotch *lang*) passes readily into Lank, (to be long or Lean,) by the mere sharpening of the final. He who lingers behind becomes Late, he may even be the Last to move, or he may not move at all, but continue or Last in the hypothetical condition an indefinite time. Lagna, "attached," the past participle of the Sanskrit base *lag*, also means "left," "remaining." To express continuance our Saxon ancestors would have employed the word Lestan, but the Germans would now say bLeiben (*af* Lifnan, Goth.; bLifwa, Swed.), which seems

---

[a] Cf. the Sanskrit Langúla, Lanja, LaLáma, Lángula, Lúma, all of which mean "tail," or vertebral lengthening.

K

to be as near to ʟeben (Goth., ʟiban, Nor. Fr., ʟib,
ʟibe, Eng. to ʟive) as *give* is to the Gothic *giban*,
Sanskrit *grabh*, "to take." To *live* is, in fact, to ,
remain, to continue, to *last*, and the letter *l* has in
this word the same sense of abstract attachment to
existence as it has of concrete attachment in the words
ʟine and ʟigament.

A ʟane is an opening aʟong a line (Λογχὸς, a
lance) and so is a gʟen (*glyn*, Nor. Fr.), showing
how small is the effect of these fickle initials upon the
sense. A ʟawn is very similar to a *lane*, it is a ʟevel,
and is one form of ʟand, just as *clown* is a form of
clod, or *tun* of *tub*. A *level* or *lawn* is a place *laid*
out flat, as is proved by the way in which we always
speak of producing one ; for we build a house, but *lay
out* a lawn. The same may be said of ʟake (*lac*, Fr.,
lacus, Lat., λάκκος Gr.,) which is a smooth sheet of
water. But this word may be more nearly allied to
the Saxon *loc*, an inclosed space (Scotch *loch*),
though, as we have formerly shown that *lock* and *close*
both originate from the idea of binding or attaching inherent in all forms of ·*l*·, to ally, this circumstance will
have no effect on the propriety of the insertion of *lake* in
the present series. Perhaps a ʟath exhibits the
singular metamorphoses of this base in an equally
striking manner ; for a *lath* is a piece of wood that
has been *dis*pʟayed, spʟayed, or ʟaid open. A ʟattice
(*lattiz*, Nor. Fr.) is a window formed of laths.

The idea of laying as associated with the letter *l* is
clearly seen when we speak of ʟoading a cart, or the

bill of Lading (A. S. *hlàd*, Hindî Ladânâ, to load, Lâd or Ladâ-o, a load); but we forget this radical meaning when we use the noun and speak of a Load, or a Last of corn; so also when we speak of our Lodging, that is, our Lair, where we lay, last, or abide. When we Lodge anything under certain circumstance it is called a pLedge (*plegg*, Nor. Fr.), the thing is pLaced or *laid* down to abide a certain contingency; and when we *pledge* or pLight our words, we bind or attach ourselves to something in a way analogous to that in which a sailor spLices the two ends of a rope, or an artilleryman Lashes a gun to the lifting gear.

The letter *l* in the word pLaint (*plaindre*, Fr.) points to a similar origin. It is a complaint, or pLea in legal phraseology, an *al-Leg-ation*, that which is *lodged*. In Norman French a *plea* was called *pleintie*, *plaint*, *pleit*, *plet*, *plait*, *plaid*, and *lai* or *laie*, leading directly to the forms *alaier*, *lier*, *lyer*, to allege, the last identical with *lyer*, to bind; and the word *aliaunce* or *alience* was used indifferently to express either alliances or allegations.

This word causes us to notice the radical difference between the French *plaindre* and *pleurer*. The latter is the equivalent of the Latin *plorare*, to weep, the English *flow*, Fr. *fleuve*, a river, Sans. *plu*, &c. This last sentence is enough to show that we use discrimination in the alliance of vocables.

In all these numerous instances we find a ligamentous sense attaching to the words in which the letter *l*, or its correlative *r*, is a constant accompaniment, and it would require the faith of a Buddhist to suppose that all occurred by chance. An exact study of the physical phenomena of the universe is establishing with accumu-lating force the conviction that chance has no place in the realm of matter; and we may rest assured that the same is true of the phenomena of language. A scientific study of language will tend more and more towards a demonstration that language is the out-come of definite laws, which await only the patient and comprehensive analysis of existent facts to reveal themselves to the diligent student. But our present duty is to argue not to perorate, and we, therefore, proceed to cite other examples, such as *pLait*, to intertwine or lay together, to *bRaid* (deadening the sound of the consonants), to *bLend* or associate together, to *foLd,* to *pLeat*, to *pLy* or cause to lie in a particular direction, with a pair of *pLiers* (*plier*, Fr.). The word *ply* has a secondary sense, for we speak of those who *ply* an occupation (Ger. *pflegen*, Swed. *plaga*, Dan. *pleger*). This must mean, apply themselves to it, expressed in German by the word *obliegen*, which can be at times divided so as to show that the latter part of the word really means to *tie;* thus, *es liegt mir ob*, " I am ob*liged* to it," " it is my duty."

That which hangs or lies about is properly said to be Loose, to hang in Loops (Sans. *lab* or *lamb*, to hang down, dangle ; Lat. *labi*, *delabi*) to be Lithe, supple, or Limp; and Lither is an old word for Lazy, *idLe* (*jedeL*, Du., loose, Ger. *lassig*, Gal. *lesg*,

Fr. *lasse, languissant*), one who is *di-La-tory*, a Lozel, Loll-ard, who Lolls about, who Leans (*laners*, Nor. Fr., idle, sluggish) on others for support, in short, a sLoven (*slaw*, A. S., *slove*, Dan.), sLattern, a sLut, one whose garments are sLack (*śLatha*, Sans., loose, Latá, a creeping plant) or sLouchy, who is addicted to sLumber or sLeep (*slumerian*, A. S.; *slummer*, Dan.; *sommeil*, Fr.; *sonno*, Ital. ; *sueno*, Span. ; soná, Hindî ; *swap*, Sans.) ; *i. e.*, to lay down and rest. So in Hindî, the connexion between these various ideas is manifest in such words as *Liṭáná*, to lay, cause to lie; Laṭthar, slack ; Lithárná, to draggle ; Laṭaknâ, to dangle ; Latárna, to be fatigued. *Loose* (*leosan*, A. S.; *losen*, Germ.; *loser*, Du.; *losa*, Swed.; λύω, Gr.; *láche*, Fr.; *laus*, Goth.; *las*, Dan.), lax, laxity, Lat. *laxus, laxare*, to unloose, to re-lax, to re-lieve; Ital. *lasciare*, Fr. *re-lacher, laisser*, Prov. *laissar*, educed from a base that gave birth to *lex, league, lien*, &c., afford an instance of diametrically opposite meanings being expressed by the same base.

In connexion with the word *sloven* must be mentioned sLobber and sLur (sLet, Du.; schLostern, Germ.; sLog, Sax.; sLyk, Du.; sLush or sLudge) to smear or daub over anything, and the Dutch word sLobbern, to bag, hang loose, or fLag ; the last word leading on to such words as *faiL*, to sink down, to *faLl* (*fallere, lapsus*, Lat., be faLse; σφάλλω, σφάλμα, Gr.; *fallire*, Ital.; *faillir*, Fr.); and *fooL*, one known for his *failings*. For fear the last etymology should be thought far-fetched, we hasten to add that in Sanskrit a precisely analogous change has certainly taken place: thus the base *mṛi*, to die, to sink down, a parallel form to *mlai*, to be weary or *fail*, has passed into *mlechh*, to be obfuscated, *mûrchhâ*, fainting, a swoon, and *mûrkha*, a fool. Before leaving *fail* we notice *ail-ment*, a failing or *ill-ness;* the word *ill* being akin to the Gothic *ubils*, Germ. *übel*, Eng. *evil, fal-libility*, which is, therefore, no worse than a failing or falling short of a prescribed standard. The vocable *evil* brings us into communication with the primitive base in an unlooked-for way; for *eviL* is merely the Teutonic form of *viLe*, the congeners of which are *defiLe, fouL, fiLth,*[a] *guiLe, guiLt*. The direct parent of *vile* is the Latin *vilis*, the Fr. *vil*, Ital. *vigliacco*, that which is base or *Low*, closely akin to *vaLlis*, Lat., *vaLlé*, Fr. *vaLley*, *vaLe*, Eng., the depressed or *low*-lying ground between two mountains. *Vile* is not allied to *villain*. The latter word has a curious meaning when traced to its origin; for the ancient *villein, villanus*, was the servant of the *villa*, which last is undoubtedly a form of *villus* or *vellus*, the skin of a sheep, akin to *pellis,*[b] the skin of any beast, *velamen*, a covering in general, and *vallum*, an enclosure, a *wall*,—the *v* passing into *b* in the word *buil*-ding,—all of which meet in a point in the Sanskrit base *vṛi*, to surround, co-*ver*. Thus a *villain* is, etymologically, "the servant of a covering."

[a] Thus there is no connexion between these words and *fy! fo!* as suggested by Mr. Wedgwood.
[b] By change of *v* into *f*, then into *p*.

We return to the vocables meaning "lay," "ally." To sLing anything (Sans. *śLath*, be relaxed) is to cause it to hang *loose* (Dut. *slingern*, to dangle; Germ. *schlingeln*, to loiter); to sLay is to lay low, to cast down (Swed. *sLaga*, a sword, a slayer); and the sLain are to a battle what the sLag is to a furnace, the dross, that which is Left behind (cf. Sans. *lagna*, laid, left), by which last word the senses of continuance and attachment become manifest. The verb to Leave (*linquer*, Nor. Fr.; *re-linquere*, Lat.) fits into the series containing *linger*, *late*, and *last*, previously mentioned; but we did not then instance the word Let (*lait*, Nor. Fr., *laissar*, Prov.), to al-Low, permit, Leave remaining, with a secondary sense of hindering. Mr. Wedgwood so clearly shows the connexion between *let* and *loose* that we cannot do better than quote his short argument,—

"The idea of slackening lies at the root of both applications of the term. When we speak of letting one go, letting him do something, we conceive him as previously restrained by a band, the loosening or slackening of which will permit the execution of the act in question. Thus Lat. *laxare*, to slacken, was used in later times in the sense of its modern derivatives, It. *lasciare*, Fr. *laisser*, to let. *Laxas desiccare*, let it dry, *modicum laxa stare*, let it stand a little while.—Muratori. Diss. 24, p. 365. So from Bav. *lass*, loose, slack, slow, G. *lassen*, to permit, to let. The analogue of Bav. *lass* is ON. *latr*, lazy, torpid, slow, the original meaning of which (as observed under Late) was doubtless slack, whence E. *let*, to slacken (some restraining agency), to permit."

There are hundreds of other words containing the base ·*l*· which we must pass over with only a hasty

allusion, such as Lull (*luller*, Du., *lullen*, Ger., *loisir*,
Fr., *loire*, Old Fr., and *lolo* for the nursery), Lure
(*leurre*, Fr.), to allay apprehension; a bRaiL or bRace;
to pLaister, to Lute, different modes of applying sub-
stances; and such possible forms as Lug, Luggage,
to pLuck, puLl, to Lead, the Load-stone, &c., &c.; for
the idea of application or attachment soon assumes the
meaning of seizing or arresting, as is shown by the
legal phrase of "*attaching* a prisoner," the Ital. *at-
taccare*, to fasten. There are other words of like origin,
such as Lot, a share, portion, one appropriation which
the recipient takes to himself, what indeed be-*longs*
or appertains to him. *Lot* (*hlot*, A. S., *lott*, Swed., *lot*,
Fr.) also means an aggregation or collection. The
word Lift (*hlifian*, A. S., *lüften*, Pl. Du., *löfte*, Dan.,
lever, en-lever, Fr.) means "to lay hold of," "appropriate,"[a] to gLean; and that which is readily lift-able
is Light (*laghu*, Sans., *levis*, Lat., *léger*, Fr., *licht*, Du.,
leicht, Ger.) or sLight, sLender. A Leech is a creature
that lays hold and attaches itself with vigour, remind-
ing one of a *leash* or thong. Mr. Wedgwood thinks
"it is more likely that the radical idea is the application of medicinal herbs," which gave a name first to
the physician, or healer, and then to the blood-sucking
mollusc. He associates with it the words house*leek*,

---

[a] The *f* in *lift* is almost certainly the remains of *up, upper,
over*, by the change of *p* into *v* and *f*. The meaning of *li-f-t* is to
attach upwards, to *lay-up*, to make *aloft*, to heave, to have, to
appropriate. The last two words being based on the Sanskrit
dhṛi or *dhá* joined to the same word *up, over*.

leeks, &c., " whence in all probability the *lock* or *lick,*
Ger. *luege,* which forms the termination of many of our
names for plants ; *hemlock, charlock, garlick,* Swiss
wegleuge, wild endive; *kornleuge,* galeopsis ladanum."[a]
All this is very possible, and as the physician or *leech*
was named from the poultices or applications he ad-
ministered, his name and its derivatives are good
examples of the sense of laying or applying imparted
by the base which we consider to underlie all such
words.

Now it will not be uninteresting if we show that
in the Semitic languages also the letter *l* is pursued
by its ligamentous sense. To do this it will be
enough to cite a few instances from Arabic, because
the Semitic languages are radically so similar, that
what is true of one is roughly true of all. The words
we shall choose are such as, according to the laws of
Arabic grammar, are radically distinct from each
other; we are, however, aware that all Arabic triliteral roots have been traced to biliteral stems. This
fact does not detract from their value for our purpose;
because, in the mouth of an Arab, they are as much
apart as *block* and *plug* and *clump* are to an ordinary
Englishman. The following will, no doubt, suffice :—
'*aʟṣ,* sticking ; '*iʟq,* being attached (mentally); *siʟqá,*
lying flat ; *saʟf,* levelling ; *ʟaykat,* clay; *ʟazab,* ad-

---

[a] Is not this termination allied to that in such words as *wed-lock, know-ledge ?*

hering, also clay; 'aʟfaṭaṭ, mixing; ʟamm, assembling; ʟamʟûm, a crowd; ʟawṭ, bedaubing, luteing; ʟayf, fibres, filaments; ʟafq, sewing two things together ; ʟafm, binding, fastening ; ʟaḥq, adhering ; ʟaqṭ, gathering together ; ʟaqs, mixing; ʟaqs, inclining towards, laying; ʟaqy, meeting; ʟakk, mixture; ʟaka or ʟaṭab, adhering; ʟaṭs, collecting; ʟath, laying on the ground; ʟaṭf, drawing near; ʟaṭm, joining, glueing together; ʟaṭy, cleaving to the ground; ʟa'áb viscosity; ʟa'z, lying with; ʟaghís, a mixture; ʟaff, joining; ʟazaj, viscous, being glued together; ʟazaz, fastening, joining; ʟizaq and ʟisaq, adjoining, close; ʟazak, coalescence; ʟazm, sticking close to anything; ʟasb or ʟaṣab, adhering; ʟaṣf, joining together; ʟaṣúgh, cleaving to the bones; ʟaṣúq, conjunction; ʟaṭṭ, fastening; and ʟazy, attached.

Nearly all the foregoing words are simple bases giving rise to a whole vocabulary of derivatives expressive of every species of adhering and placing together; and when we further remark that, while differing from each other in every other respect, they all agree in containing the letter *l*, it is impossible not to believe that the meaning common to all is imparted by some ultimate base represented by that letter.

The resemblance between the Arabic words ʟafík, foolish, and ʟafíf, a crowd (akin to ʟayf, filaments, and lifáfat, any kind of bandages) shows that the Semites also recognized the likeness between a *clown* and a *clod;* and littikh, a fool (cf. ʟaṭy, cleaving to the ground) tends in the same direction. The word laghúb, foolish, from *laghb*, to become weary, tired, exactly tallies with our derivation of *fool* from *fail*, and the Sans. *múrkha*, a blockhead, from *mlai*, to fade (p. 133).

Returning to the Aryan family, the writers would remark that a careful examination of the Sanskrit language has convinced them that the number of bases might be materially reduced. The majority are of a secondary, tertiary, or yet more developed form, very few having any pretence to a primitive character. The real ultimate bases of that language will form the subject of a separate treatise; here it will be enough to state that the germs of all the vocables that have illustrated this exposition of the congeners of the word *law*, are to be found among the Sanskrit bases, and that the process of development is not altogether hidden from sight. Thus starting from the simple sound *iL*, to lie down, we get *eL*, to place, and the secondary bases *Lí* and *Lag*, to place, to adhere. From *lí* arises the series *Lyí*, *Lwí*, *vLí*, *bLí*, *Lpí*, *Lud*, *Las*, all of which mean "to join together," "to embrace." The change of *lwí* into *vlí*, *blí*, and *lpí*, may be purely phonetic; but *lud* and *las* originate from the addition of a sibilant, meaning "to seek," "to wish," "*souhaiter*," Fr. *Las* in its sense of "clinging" gave rise to *Losht*, to collect; and *blí* naturally developes into *pLaiṇ*, *pRaiṇ*, *paiṇ*, *peṇ*, all meaning "to embrace." These last forms show that we must expect to meet vocables of ligamentous sense which have lost the dis-

tinguishing liquid. The form *las*, by accession of a
strengthening initial, becomes *ślish*,[*] to *clench*, to
embrace, and also *śil* or *sil*, *ślon*, *śron*, to collect;
ślok, to compose verses. By *ś* becoming *k*, *śil* passes
into *kíl*, to attach; *kul*, *kshal*, and *khal*, to aggregate, or bring together. The base *kíl*, to attach, to
lay with, introduces the forms *klam* and *glai*, to lay
down, fade; and *klív* or *klíb*, to fail, or be weak.
More directly from *ślish* come the bases *ślath*, *śrath*,
and *śar*, to fade, fail, be weak; and from *lpí*, or one
of its sisters mentioned above, we may not improbably
deduce *pul* and *púl*, to aggregate; and *píl*, to be
agglomerated in intellect. At times the letter *p* is
supplanted by the letter *m*, which enables us to understand the origin of *mil*, to unite, embrace; and its
congeners *mlai*, *murchh*, to lay about, to fade (phonetically corrupted into *muh*, be faint); and *mlaid*, *mraid*,
med, *mlait*, *mrait*, *met*, different forms meaning " to
be foolish " Even the bases *nil* and *sthúl*, to be
thick, gross, contain the letter *l* with a sense of aggregation; but it would be venturesome to include these
in the series. Omitting these two, we have here forty-
six Sanskrit bases which may not unfairly be referred
to the primitive sound *il*, the venerable parent of so
many thousands of vocables preserved to us in this
perhaps its simplest form.

But beyond the large family of vocables containing

---

[*] In Sanskrit *s* generally becomes *sh* after any vowel but *a;* the
change in the vowel sound would, therefore, produce the change in
the final letter of *ślish*.

the base ·*l*· in a sense of physical attachment, we find
it applied, as indeed we might expect, to every kind
of mental or sentimental attachment. Thus we are
said to Like that upon which we fix our minds—*us ne
us par dil* LAG-*áyá*, " he set his heart upon her," is
the Urdú idiom for " he loved her," or was attached
to her. The word Love itself (*leof*, A. S.) is a modification of Lief (*lefe, leve*, Chaucer, "loving;" *lief*,
Du., dear, pleasing), seen also in Leaman or Leman
for Lefman, one to whom we are attached sentimentally
or carnally. Still more evident is this in Sanskrit, in
which language from the base *lag*, attach, directly
arises *langa*, union, a lover; *langiman*, union; *langaka*, a lover; and *lagnaka*, a surety, one bound for
another. In Hindî also the chain is complete; thus,
lagná, to adjoin; *lagáná*, to apply, place; *lág, lágút*,
or *laggá*, attachment; and *lagú-á*, a paramour.

    Mr. Wedgwood very reasonably connects the voca-
bles *love, lust, like, luck*, &c., with such words as *lick*,
γλῶσσα; and *the application of the tongue* may really
be the idea underlying all the preceding derivatives.
If so the origin of the connexion between sound and
sense is patent, as the action of the tongue necessarily
produces the sound which is represented by the lingual *l*. This liquid is clearly the onomatop on which
thousands of words suggestive of the tongue and its
operations are built; and the great probability that
licking suggested the ideas of clamminess, adhesiveness, smearing, and other methods of applying, and so
passed on to allying, binding, and aggregating, is not

by aný means so improbable as many of the changes of sense which words are. known to have undoubtedly undergone.

The Sanskrit bases *lih*, to lick ; *lag* or *lak*, to taste; *likh*, to write; and *ling*, to paint, reveal some part of the process. In the form *lag*, to taste, we have perfect coalescence with *lag*, to adhere ; and the French *le-s-cher* or *lécher*, to lick, may be juxtaposed to *leash* and *lash ;* while the Gothic *laigon*, *bi-laigón*, to lick, shows a bond of union with *laga*, the law ; as does also the Saxon *liccian*, and the Gaelic *ligh*.. That the letter *l* is the natural exponent of licking may be readily shown by the Aryan forms found in the German *lecken*, Fr. *lécher*, Ital. *leccare*, Persian *lisídan*, Armenian *lezal*, lick, *luzw*, the tongue, Russian *lokat'*, Lithuanian *lakti*, Latin *lingere*, Gr. λείχω, λιχανός, λειχήν, and the Sans. *lih*, Eng. *lick*. Arabic, a Semitic language, abounds in similar instances, such as ʟass, ʟasb, ʟasd, ʟasn, ʟaḟ, ʟaʿz, ʟaʿq, all meaning "licking," and, indeed, nearly all the Arabic words formerly given as expressing "adhesion," have also this sense of "licking." The same language, furthermore, contains such words as ʟasm, tasting ; ẓaʟq, ʟughat, ʟahja, or ʟisân, the tongue ; and ʟaʿáb, spittle, from the base *la'ab*, to play, sport, be addicted to, showing the connexion between de-*light* and re-*lish*. The complete onomatopic origin of the sense ascribed to the letter *l*. is demonstrated by the Finnish[a] word

─────

[a] " Les langues finnoises contiennent beaucoup de mots ariens."— *Pictet, Les Aryas Primitifs*, vol. ii. p. 846.

Lakkia, to lick, and by the following words of Cochin-Chinese, taken from the Dictionary of that language by the missionary Josepho Maria Morrone. These words are the more remarkable as they present the letter *l* in all the senses which we have already ascribed to it, and in those which will be given further on. *Lai* and *luoi*=the tongue ; *lanh*=tongue and voice; *la*, to call; *lap*, to be loquacious. *Loi*=to shine. *Lao*, to hang loose; *la*, fatigue, lassitude ; and *lay* and *lat* have the opposite meaning of "bond" or "ligament," while *lap* means "to tie," and *loi* is the name of little strings; finally, *loi*, *la*, and *luot* are the words used to express "law," in singular conformity with what we are endeavouring to show is the universal practice. These words show that Aryans, Semites, and Turanians universally recognize the letter *l* as the fitting exponent of lingual action.*

The Latin *lingua* certainly gave rise to *lingere*, *delingere*, *diligo*, and *loquor*, to speak, *lingula*, a chatter-box, *loquax*, loquacious; and from the base of λείχω spring λέξις, λόγος, a word, λέξικον, a dictionary, also λύω, *lux*, *luxuria*, luxury, and λάω, to desire, analogous to λῆμα, λῆμμα, the O. H. G. *liuban*, Lat. *lubet*, Goth. *liubs* (dear), Sans. *lubh*, Eng. *love*, that which is worthy of praise, Laus, Lat., Lob, O. H. G., what makes us "*lick* our chaps," or *lust* after, *lustus*,

---

* Though employing a different phonic symbol, the Chinese also recognize the connectedness of the ideas illustrated under the word *law*: thus, *she*, the tongue ; *she*, to lick ; *shin*, the lip ; and *she cho*, to place, set down.

Goth.; *laska*, Bohem.; *las*, Sans. From the licking of the tongue, also, naturally arises *lubricare*, and γλίσ- χρος, a smooth surface; λεία, an instrument to polish stones; whence Gr. κρύσαλλος, Lat. *glacies* (*lubrica*), Fr. *glisser*, to *glide* or *slide* over; also *lino*, to spread, *liniment*, what is spread, *oleum*, *oil* (*huile*, Fr.), *oliva*, ἐλεία, from its *slimy*, or *saliva*-like appearance. A single smear was called *linea*, a streak, or *line*, the Hindî *lekhá* or *lakír*, Sans. *likh*, to write, from *lih*, to smear; whence *col-limate*, direct line, and *col-limata- neus*, common boundaries, or *limits*.

The application of the tongue to objects would be the most natural source of the idea of smearing, which is clearly shown in Sanskrit; for in that language the base *lih*, to lick, reappears in *lip*, to smear, and from this latter proceed *ling*, to paint (obviously akin to *lag*, to apply), and *likh*, to write. It is worthy of re- mark that the letter *h* at the end of *lih* is not radical,[*] but the remains of a guttural affix, which is seen in the *g* of *ling*, and the *kh* of *likh*. *Linga* is a deriva- tive, meaning "a mark," or sign of any kind; and hence applied to the phallus as *the* mark par excel- lence; and from *likh* we get *lekha*, a line, or writing; while *lih* is repeated to produce *leliha*, a serpent, from its resemblance to a smear or streak, and *lálá*, "spittle." The *p* of *lip*, to smear, is also significative; for it re- minds us of the *labia*, Lat.; *lèvres*, Fr.; *lips*, Eng.;

---

[*] Prof. Th. Benfey is of opinion that *h* is never radical in Sans- krit

which assisted in the primitive *lepana*, Sans., smearing ; whence arose *lepaka*, Sans., a bricklayer or *plas-*
terer, and *lepa*, Sans., a spot or stain. That *lip* com-
bines two onomatops : *l·* and ·*p·*, which respectively
signify "tongue" and "lips," may be inferred from
the simpler base *li* or *ri*, to be viscous, or moist, in
which the tongue only is concerned, and therefore the
p is wanting. The base *lap*, to speak, gives another
instance in which the action of tongue and lips are
expressed by one vocable. *Lap* gives, as a derivative,
lapana, the "mouth;" and also appears under the
forms *rap* and *riph*, to speak, showing how constantly
l tends towards *r*. *Lap*, furthermore, is the parent of
lubh, to covet, to lick the chaps (Lat. *lubet*) ; and *labh*,
to enjoy, get, obtain. The intimate relationship of
these bases is shown by the Sanskrit derivatives *lam-*
paṭa, covetous, a libertine, *limpaṭa*, a lecher, and *lipsá*,
a wish. In the sense of "wishing" we find the
onomatop ·*l·* assuming such forms as *lal*, *lash*, *lubh*,
luh, and also *rabh*, the last base affording the best
assurance that *labh*, though generally used to express
" obtain," proceeded from a base signifying " desire to
obtain," to hanker after, the appropriate gesture indicative of coveting being the licking of the tongue round
the mouth. In direct descent from *lih*, to lick, and
likh, to write, we get *laksh*, to make marks of any
kind, to distinguish one thing from another, a base
which, by phonetic corruption, passed into *lachh* and
lánchh, both of which retain the same meaning. The
form *mraksh* or *mṛiksh*, to anoint, brings us back to

L

the original sense of the word ; *m* being a prefix, and *r*, as usual, representing *l*. By transference of the qualities of the object to the subject, a very common manifestation of the Law of Metaphor, *laksh*, to mark, passed into *laksh*, to see, perceive, just as the English word *mark* (S. *mraksh*, above) is used in both senses in the phrases "*mark* those goods" and "*mark* what I say." With the help of a prefix, *laksh* becomes *vleksh* or, by corruption, *veksh*, and may ultimately have dwindled into *iksh*, all of which mean "see," "perceive." However this may be, *laksh*, to see, is certainly allied to *lok* or *loch*, to perceive, which only differs by rejecting the sibilant ;—and to *linkh*, to perceive,[a] which actually brings us back to the form *likh*, to write, or make marks, whence the series started.

Now when the tongue is applied to an object, not only is there engendered an idea of smearing, but a particular kind of smearing is always apparent. The tongue invariably leaves behind it a slimy or shiny mark, which soon evaporates, it is true, but while it continues gLazes or gLosses the surface completely; and the similarity between *gloss* and γλόσσα is not a little remarkable. But we have no occasion to compare ancient and modern languages together, for we have positive identity in the Sanskrit bases *lok* and *loch*, which mean, not only "see," "remark," but also "shine." The idea of "shining" is, of course, deduced directly from the mark of licking, and not

---

[a] Benfey's Sanskrit Dictionary, 1866.

through "seeing," so that the bases are parallel and not derivative. The bases *likh* and *laksh*, to mark, underlie those expressive of "shining," as might be inferred from the base *las*, to shine, which is clearly a corruption of such a form as *laksh*. The guttural is preserved in the word *langh*, to shine, which is also spelled *rangh;* and is modified to a palatal in *lanj* or *laj*, to shine, which last, through the base *ranj*, "to paint," or "smear," again places us *en rapport* with the primal idea from whence all these words arose. The identity of *lanj*, shine, and *ranj*, paint, is strikingly illustrated by the words *rub*, Gael., *rubba*, Old Norse, *ruobbet*, Lappish, *rhwbio*, Welsh, all of which mean to smear, stroke, or, as we say, to *rub*, which last appears in Latin as *lub-rico*, to render po*lish*ed or shiny. The identity of origin of the English *rub* (Pers. *rúf-tan*) and the Lat. *lubrico*, to po-*lish*, *lub-et*, to re-*lish*, to *lick* the tongue, and *lucere*, *luxi*, light, shine, cannot be doubted.

Returning again to our Sanskrit bases we find that *laksh*, *lok*, exist under the form *lut*, which changes its initial in *rut*, and regains the palatal form of its final in *ruch*, to shine. *Ruch* is an important base; but before tracing its derivatives, it is as well to give its immediate congeners. These are *runs*, *rej* or *bhrej*; *ráj* or *bhráj*, which reassume the final sibilant in the forms *bhráś* or *bhrás*, and regain the *l* in *bhláś* or *bhlás*, but modify it in *bhṛinś*, and lose it entirely in *bhás*, *bhas*, and *bhá*. Every one of these bases means "shine," and some elucidation is certainly needed to

L 2

show how *bhá* could be eliminated from *·l·*. The order in which the bases are given is designed to illustrate, in some way, the changes; none of which, taken singly, appear very violent. The greatest difficulty is to explain the prefix *bh*, which, for want of a better reason, may be supposed to be the remnants of the preposition *abhi*, "on," "over" (Arabic *fí*), a very common prefix in Sanskrit, though at the early stage of language at which these bases were formed, the *bh* might with equal propriety be deduced from *vi*, "about," or even *pra*, "forth," "per." If this conjecture be correct *abhi + ráj* would give *bhráj*, and *abhi + lás* would give *bhlás* or *bhrás*, &c. Whether this be so or not, it is clear that no great emphasis can be laid on the unchanging character of the initials of bases. (Cf. *pidhána* for *apidhána*, p. 20, &c., &c.)

Let us now turn to Semitic languages, and see whether similar words were evolved from this onomatop in that family. In Arabic we have seen that the vocable for "tongue" is *lisán*, and this is obviously based on the simpler form *lass*, "licking." When the medial vowel is changed it becomes *laws*, "tasting;" the *w* melting into *ú* produces *lús*, "meat," "food," that which is tasted. The addition of a final *m* makes *lasam* or *lisám*, meaning "tasting;" the medial *s* passing into *'ain* leaves *la'm* = "saliva;" and when the final *m* is replaced by a *d* we get *lasd*, "sucking," "licking." The connection of all these words with the action of the tongue is too obvious to require comment. Many more Arabic words could easily be

adduced, but the following will suffice for our present
purpose, which is to show that the licking of the
tongue gave a name to the tongue itself, and to its
actions, and metaphorically to other kinds of smearing,
marking, and applying. The words we shall adduce
are: *la'z* or *laṭ*, licking; *la'áb* or *lu'áb*, viscosity,
sliminess; *la'w*, lecherous, lusting; *lu'áq* or *lamẓ*,
licking the lips; *lamq*, writing, smearing out writing,
obliterating; *lawṭ*, bedaubing. Here we have precisely the same phenomenon that was presented in
Sanskrit, that words expressing "licking" develop in
two channels, one conveying an idea of "lusting after,"
the other of "smearing," or "writing." Still more
strikingly is this parallel. shown in *lafẓ*, "a word,"
etymologically identical with the Sanskrit *lap*, "to
speak," which we have before shown produced the
derivative *lapana*, "the mouth;" and we may here
add *lapita*, "the voice," and *vilápa*, "lamentation."

In Arabic, as in Sanskrit, the letter *l* at times passes
into *r*, and so from *lasm*, "tasting," "licking," we get
rasm, "writing," "drawing," and *rashm*, expressive
of any kind of "marking" (S. *laksh*, *mraksh*). So
also *laf*, "licking," reappears as *raf*, to express
"rheum" or anything similar; and such forms as
la'áb, "sliminess," seem closely akin to *razab*, "sucking," and *ruẓáb*, "spittle." These changes prepare
us for forms very similar to *laf-ẓ*, "a word," such as
laflafat, a repeated base to express rapid action of the
mouth, "eating voraciously" (Johnson's Dict.); and
lafaf, imperfect action of the mouth, "stammering;"

and these suggest the parallel form *raff*, which means "*sucking, saliva*, and *shining*," whence comes the derivative *ràfif*, " shining," " glittering." *Rafif*, *raff*, and *lafaf* bring to mind *laff, lafm*, &c., formerly given (p. 138), with a sense of "allying, joining," lending probability to the suggestion that the application of the tongue suggested vocables indicative of other methods of applying one thing to another. In these instances from the Arabic we have, again, something like direct evidence that the action of the tongue gave birth to words expressive of sliminess, gloss, sheen, shine, brilliance, splendour, glare. The simplest process of natural development, would thus lead on from *laws*, " licking," to *lawá-ih*, "light and splendour."

Returning to the Aryan family of languages, we will trace the onomatop ·*l*· through a similar course in Persian, and then passing into Greek, will show its existence in many of the commonest words of the vernaculars of Europe.

There are two verbs in Persian for licking, *lishtan* and *lisídan*, both being near akin to the Sans. *likh*. Deprived of grammatical termination, we get at the nominal base *lis*, " licking," which passes into *ler*, " slaver," and into *liz*, to express anything soft and slippery. From *liz* we pass to *lush* and *loshan*, the name of slimy mud at the bottom of ponds, slush, and *lajam*, a general name for " slime." The sound of *j* in this last word approaches that of *sh* in *lush*, or is like the French *j* in *jamais*. That the vocable for "licking" passed on to express that which was

" luscious" we may infer from the word *lot*, "a
de-*li*-cious morsel;" but its slimy, shiny sense seems
to have found expression through the *r* form of the
base (cf. ʀau*ghan*, oil, butter). Thus it is indu-
bitable that in *ra*khshidan, "to shine," *ra*khshá,
"shining," and *ra*khsh, "lightning," we meet the
Sanskrit word *laksh*, "to mark, make manifest, see,"
in a slightly disguised form. Other Persian words
which help us here are *rusht*, "bright," "light,"
rosh, "light," "splendour," and *roz* or *roj*, "the
day." The connection between *rusht*, *rosh*, and *roz*,
is very apparent.

Here also we have reasonable proof that the vocable
for licking, lapping, came from the noise made by the
tongue, and that, by the action of the Law of Metaphor,
it ultimately came to express what had been licked,
and so appeared slimy, shiny, or bright. It requires
no stretch of imagination to see in the Persian word
rosh, "bright," the Sanskrit base *ruch*, of precisely
similar import, to which we have already called
marked attention at the end of our examination of
the Sanskrit series. As this base is one of the
furthest removed from the more primitive ·*l*·, *lih*,
likh, *laksh*, we may safely conclude that it was
posterior to those forms in date ; and as a necessary
corollary, it is the form most likely to be met with
in derivatives. In this expectation we are not dis-
appointed, as the following from Sanskrit will prove:—
rochaka, "what brightens," "pleases;" *rochana*,
"splendid ;" *rochishṇu*, "gaily attired ;" and *rochis*,

" flame ;" and, subjectively, *loch*, " to see," and
lochaka or *lochana*, " the eye." Professor Th. Benfey,
in his Sanskrit Dictionary, says, " *loch* = *ruch*, the
initial *r* is changed to *l*, as in the kindred languages,"
and then makes reference to *ruch*, under which vocable
we find ourselves in communication with the Greek,
λευκός, λεύσσω, ἀμφι-λύκη, &c., and λύχνος. These
words naturally suggest the ideas λείχω, Latin *lingere*,
and the other words to express licking already given
on p. 142. That shining is intimately associated with
smearing in Greek may be inferred from the words
λίπος, " grease," λάμπω, " to shine," and λάμψις,
" splendour ;" words which reappear in the Latin
lux, *lumen*, *luceo*, *lychnis*. In this sense the base
·*l*· is found all over Europe as the idea of brilliance,
or " light," is represented by ʟumière, ʟampe, ʟuire,
in French, by ʟucerna in Italian, by ʟamparas in
Spanish, by aʟampados in Portuguese, by ʟampor in
Swedish, by ʟamper in Danish, by ʟampen in Dutch,
by ʟampadii in Russian, by ʟampy in Polish, by
ʟeuchten, ʟicht, in German, by ʟiuchan, ʟuchjan, in
Old High German, by ʟiuhath in Gothic, by ʟios in
Norse, by ʟeus in Gaelic, by ʟuc'ha, ʟuia, in Breton,
by ʟlúg in Welsh, and by ʟight in English. The
English *light* is found in the Anglo-Saxon words
leoht, lioht, leóma (flame), *ge-lihtan*, and *lócian*, the
last word meaning " to see," and being the Sanskrit
base *loch* (= *ruch*, Benfey), in, almost, purity. When
to the Anglo-Saxon *leóma* we add the Gothic *lauhmuni*
and *liuhtjan*, we think we have satisfactorily de-

monstrated the European domestication of this base.

It must not be thought that the base ·*l*·, "lick," "shine," is found in European languages only in the case of a solitary word, that may have been passed from one to the other until all acquired the use of it. On the contrary, each language will be found to possess numerous words into which this base enters as an inalienable and integral element. To establish this point, we will cite some words to prove how firmly the base is imbedded in English; and if we succeed in that object the reader will, no doubt, credit the assertion that the same could be done in other languages, without the wearisome detail necessary to establish the fact in each case.

Lamp (*lampe*, Fr., *lampas*, Lat.) is a kind of light or *lantern* (*lanterne*, Fr., *lanterna*, Lat.), which sends forth a *flame* (*flamme*, Fr., *flamma*, Lat.) or *flash*; as does also a *flambeau* (Fr.), which burns with a *flare*, or, as it was also written, *blare* (*blaren*, Du.), that is, a *blaze* (*blæse*, A.S.) or *bright* (*beorht*, A.S.) light. Closely allied to *flare* is *glare*, to dazzle; to *glaze*, to put a *gloss* on anything, and *glass* (*glæs*, A.S.), that which is trans-*lu*-cent, through which a *glance* can penetrate, or a *gleam* of light. *Gleam* is certainly the congener of *glitter* (*glitenan*, A. S.), *glisten* (*glisteren*, Du.), *glimpse* and *glimmer*, the Pl. Du. *glimmen*, *glimmern*, to shine; Swed. *glimma*, to glitter; Norse *glima*, to shine brightly, to dazzle; Old Norse *lioma*, splendour; A. S. *leoman*, to shine;

Old English *leem, liom*, a gleam. Chaucer uses Lowe for a *flame* of *light*, which suggests such words as Lightning, anciently called Levin; and the words Link, a torch, and Lin-stock, i. e. a stick for holding the match for a gun.

. In this way we see that the derivatives of ·*l*·, "lick," "smear," "shine," anastomose with those given under "Gloriam" (p. 168). One series helps to explain the other, for it is impossible to conjecture why *śri* and *ślish* should have ever come by their sense of "shining," unless we discover the ultimate onomatop on which they are erected.

We leave it to the patient scholar to say whether our long argument does not afford reasonable ground for believing that ·*l*·, as the exponent of lingual action, is really the parent of the diverse ideas which we have indicated.

At p. 147 we have connected another series with the same base by introducing the word *ráj*, the immediate parent of *rájaka*, "splendid," found under what we have said of "Regnare" at p. 165. We lay no great emphasis on this alliance, and would be understood as leaving it an open question whether or not two separate bases have here passed into one identical shape. If so *ráj*, as connected with *raksh*, "to preserve," and with *laksh* or *ruch*, "to be bright," will have two independent origins. It is, however, noticeable that *raksh*, "to preserve," through its derivative *rakshika*, "a watchman," &c., seems to convey an idea of "looking after" (*laksh*), and if so *light* and *right* are etymologically identical, and a *rule* or *regulation* (*regula,* Lat.) brings us directly to *regalis* as another form of the word *legalis*. The ease with which these words arrange themselves lends much probability to the suggestion. However this may be, we think we have proved to demonstration that many vocables expressing "shining" took their origin from the glossy appearance of a "licked" surface; and that the smearing of the tongue gave names to other kinds of smearing, marking, writing, applying, laying on, and so developed, with the growing wants of man, into the exponents of placing together, attaching, fastening, and binding. The best proof of the truth of these affiliations is found in their extreme simplicity, and the eminently inartificial way in which one grows, as it were, out of another. In the course of our argument we are never reduced to the necessity of talking about Nature's harmonics, or the mysterious correlation of sound and form, and such-like wonderful things. The whole affair is very simple. An inevitable sound accompanied, and therefore expressed, a natural action, which we can as well recognize at the present day as could the first human being who uttered it. This simple sound was applied to other cognate ideas, as ideas multiplied with the gradual dawn of civilization; and these new ideas were distinguished from each other by gestures and equally expressive modifying intonations; until at last, the sounds became substantive vocables, the onomatopic origin of which was completely lost, and they had to be passed mechanically from father to son in the manner with which we are all familiar.

This long examination of the word *law* and its associates is an illustration of what we call Collective Analysis, which it will be seen differs totally from the process of former etymologists, who take a single word with its meaning, and then seek its origin by help of other words of similar import from other languages ; whereas by our method of analysis large numbers of words in the same language of similar, but not necessarily of identical import, are collected together, and the feature common to all is eliminated. This common bond of union is taken to be the base, and if an identical phonic symbol with like import is found in any considerable number of words in other languages, we then feel sure that we have discovered a natural onomatop, more especially when some common action, as the licking of the tongue, the puffing of the lips, &c., is found to correspond in both sound and sense with the derivatives that have led up to it.

SECTION IV.

GENERAL ILLUSTRATIONS.

In this section we shall apply our method to a variety of words, in order that its general applicability may be apparent; and to make this still more evident, we shall take two whole sentences and examine each word they contain.

An idea prevails over the globe we inhabit, among civilized and uncivilized nations,—an idea not to be contested,—that of a *Supreme Ruler* of the natural phenomena of all eternity, and of which man is, or seems to be, the only interpreter. In a telling verse, written 2000 years ago, by the prince of Roman lyrics, touching the wonderful dramas that pass in heavenly regions, we shall detect as many grand onomatops as words. *Cœlo tonantem credidimus Jovem regnare* (Ode v. 1. 3, Carm.).

Cœlum, this vast source of onomatopic vocables (called *cœlus* by Ennius) was, by the Greeks, made κοῖλ-ον, concave and round, *con-cavus, curvus, cav-us = cuve*, Fr., *cir-cul-us*. From these descriptive vocables a large family has been produced, as, for instance, *ceil, ciel, cielo, cir-col-o, cin-gul-a, ceinture, cer-cle, coil, san-gle, cin-golo, en-ceinte*, urbs *cinc-ta*, κορ-ώνη, *cor-ona, crown, chaîne, gir-dle, gir-th, char-kh*, Pers., a wheel, *chakra*, Sans.

The onomatop on which these words are built is found in every class of language, as is shown by Dr. P. Bœtticher. On the Latin word *curvus*, Gr. σ-κολ-ιος, Slavonic *kol-o*, a wheel, that scholar remarks that:—

"The root means *to become crooked*, and is identical with the Hebrew '*q-l*, where '*ain* is as well a prefix, as sigma in σ-κολιός. Hence we have:—

Sanscrit	. .	krimi *for* kar-mi, *worm*.
Chaldæan	. .	qal-ma.
Coptic	. .	kri-mi.
Lithuanian	. .	kir-mi-nis.
Irish	. .	crui-mh.
Russian	. .	cher-vy.
even *Finnish*	. .	kar-me."[a]

He adds that the English word *crimson* = Sans. *krimi-ja*, what is born of a worm.

Among the principal derivatives from this onomatop is *circum*, L. (possibly an accusative of *circus* as its adverbial use might seem to indicate: "Hostilibus circum litoribus"—*Tacitus*); from *circum* arise numerous derivatives, as *circumference*, *circumlocution*, *circonférence*, Fr., &c. &c., *circuitus* and the *circuit* of a judge, *circem*, Lat., to encompass, deceive; *circulator*, L., a mountebank, one who wanders round about; *cir-ratus*, L., what is *curled*, *cur-rus*, a ringlet; *cir-cul-us*, L., κίρ-κος, a "top" which revolves, *cir-cus*, L., *cir-chio*, It., κοιλιακὸς, the abdomen, *col-ique*, Fr.; κόλ-ον, Gr., a flexure, Χορ-

---

[a] Bunsen's Christianity and Mankind, vol. iv. p. 356.

δή, the gut, Lat. *chor-da*, whence Eng. *cor-d*. Other examples of the onomatop readily suggest themselves in the Lat. *cur-rus*, *char*-iot or *car*, *cur-sio*, running, *cur-sorius*, pertaining to a race, *cur-sitore*, to run about, *cur-sus*, a running on foot (Ital. *cor-so*, Fr. *cour-s*, *cour-se*), *cur-vus*, Fr. *cour-be*, Eng. *cur-l*, a *coil* of rope, Gr. κόρη the circular pupil of the eye, κοίλη, the *keel*, because *curl-ed*. When-expressive of circumference it assumes the form *s-cor-tum*, Lat. *cuir*, Fr., the skin or rind; Lat. *cor-tex*, Fr. *é-cor-ce*, *es-cor-te*, Ital. *s-cor-za*, Span. *cor-tesa*, *cor-chos*, Dan. and Swed. *cor-k*, Du. *cor-ke*, *kor-k*, Swed. *kor-k*, Russ. *kor-kovoe*, Eng. *cor-k*.

Upon this vocable Mr. Wedgwood remarks (Dictionary of English Etymology, vol. i. p. 378) :—

" The root *cor* is widely spread in the Slavonic and Fin. class of languages in the sense of rind, skin, shell, uniting the Lat. *corium*, skin, with *cortex*, bark. Fin. *kuori*, bark, shell; crust, cream; Lap. *karr*, bark, shell; *karra*, hard, rough; Esthon. *koor*, rind, shell, bark, cream; *korik*, crust. Hung. *kereg*, rind, crust, bark; *keregdugó* (*dugó*=stopper), a stopper of bark, a cork; *kereg-fa*, a cork tree, *kérges*, barky, hard. Bohem. *kûra*, *kûrka*, bark, crust; Pol. *kora*, bark of a tree; *korek*, *koreczek*, cork, *korek-z-kory* (a stopper of bark), cork; — *drewniany*, a stopper of wood, — *szklanny*, of glass."

Tonantem.—This most descriptive onomatop arises from the simple articulation *u* (*ukti*, Sans., " speech"), meaning " to sound." *ululo*, Lat., *hurler*, Fr., *howl*, Eng., *úlf*, Norse, *wolf*, Eng., *lupus*, Lat., *loupe*, Fr., the howling animal. The base is found in its simplest form *u* in Sanskrit ; and as an instance of its use

Durgadâsa, an old Indian grammarian, gives the phrase, Av*ate gauh*, "the cow moos" (*u* becomes *av* in this case by Sanskrit euphonic laws). The ono-matop is produced by the mere expulsion of air through the nearly closed lips, so commonly and so naturally done, when, sitting in the shelter of our homes, we hear the wind howl around, and seek to describe its gusts. Strengthened in various ways by peculiarities of utterance and by the addition of particles, this sound animates the following series of Sanskrit bases:—*k*U, *kû*, *kh*U, *g*U, *gh*U, *ṇ*U, *t*US, *di*W (pron. *di-u*), *r*U, *śul* (c.f. *śr*U, to hear a sound), *sw*ṛ*i*, *swan*, *dh*w*an*, *dh·an*, *t·an*, *st·an*,[a] all of which mean "sound," "make a noise." The growing wants of man, and his love of exaggeration, caused the primitive

[a] The dot in the last three bases indicates the elision of the *u* ; *dhwan* passing into *dhan* by phonetic corruption, the *dh* sharpening into *t*, and finally assuming the *s* prefixed to the last.

The letter T is by no means so unchangeable as its sharp, clear dental sound would lead us to expect.

T changes to—

D, thus	*pater*	becomes	*padre*	(Ital.).
TT, ,,	*totus*	,,	*tutto*	(,,).
Z, ,,	*acutus*	,,	*aguezzo*	(,,).
SC, ,,	*angustia*	,,	*angoscia*	(,,).
SS, ,,	,,	,,	{ *angoissa* / *angoisse*	(Prov.). / (French).
X, ,,	,,	,,	{ *quexar* / *queixar*	(Span.). / (Port.).
TZ, ,,	*terra*	,,	*tzearë*	{ (Walla-chian).
S, ,,	{ *titionem, stationem,* / *justicia, otiosus*	,,	{ *tison, saison, jus-* / *tesse, oiseau, oisif*	(French).
C, ,,	*negotium, nuptiæ*	,,	*négoce, noces*	(,,).

bases to become rapidly obsolete, and in their places
the more developed and intensified forms are those
which are most frequently employed in modern speech.
Nevertheless, the former activity of the first five of
the above bases is attested by such words as γοαυ,
Gr., *gaunón*, Goth.; and, possibly, also by the Sanskrit *go;* Gothic *gavi, gauja;* Old High German
kô; A.-S. *cû;* English *cow*, the low-ing moo-ing
creature; an alliance much strengthened by the other
name of the cow, *i.e. ox* (*oxa* A.-S., *oxe* Dan.) in
which the *u* comes first, and is strongly aspirated in
the word *fox* (*vixen*, fem.), a kind of *ûlf* or *wolf*, a
howling animal, one with a *vox* or *voice*. The connection between *voveo*, to *vow*, Gr. βόω, to cry out,
vulpes and *vowel*, has never before been pointed out;
but their certain affinity shows, in a remarkable
manner, how the words that make up language are
linked together. The later forms of the bases above
given (*swan, dhwan, dhan, tan, stan,**) are those
which move in historic times, giving rise to the
Sanskrit *stanana*, groaning; *stanita, stanayitnu*,
thunder; Icelandic, *stynja;* New High German,
stôhnen; Anglo-Saxon, *gestun;* French, *étonner;*
English, *stun;* Italian, *stordire;* Latin, *at-ton-itus;*
French, *é-tour-dir;* Latin, *ob-tun-dere aures;* French,
? *é-tou-ffer.* The same idea is found in the Greek

---

* These dentals need cause no astonishment, they are frequently
prefixed to bases. A familiar example is found in *t-urn, t-our* and
t-urris, all from the Sans. *vri*, "to go round," the parent of both
wire and *tower*

τείνω, p. m. τέταται (τονθορύξω), στένω, τόνος; the
Latin, *tono, tonare, tonitrus, tonitruum;* the French,
tonnerre; Old High German, *donar;* New High German, *donner;* Anglo-Saxon, *thunor;* the terrible
thunder of to-day—the *thunder*-bolt. In milder accents we encounter *tone,* the French and Danish *ton;*
Latin *tonus,* Spanish *tono, tonidro,* Italian *tuono,*
English *tin-kle, tin-gle;* and by parallel derivation from
the form *swan,* the Gr. συ-ρίττω, the Latin *sonitus, sonare, susurrus,* murmuring; *susurramen,* muttering;
Italian *suono;* French *son;* English *sound.* In direct
descent from *dhwan* come the Sanskrit *dhwani,* the
Hindî *dhuni,* a noise, the A.-S. *dynan, dyne,* Eng.
din or uproar, meeting again the German *donner,* the
Eng. *thunder.* But of all the forms which the onomatop *u* assumed, perhaps the most prolific in derivatives is *ru,* the parent of the German *rûnên,* to
speak low ; *runa,* mystery ; *roar, rout, rave, raucus,
rumour, row, brook* (murmuring stream), *rook,* a kind
of c-*row,* raven (A.-S. *hrafn;* Ger. *rabe;* O. H. G.
hraben; Sans. *kârava;* Gr. κορώνη; Lat. *corvus;* Fr.
corbeau). From *ru* were likewise evolved the Sanskrit *rud, rodana,* weeping *rue*-fully ; *rodas,* the
heavens (the abode of roaring storms) ; besides the
base *ran* (A.-S. *ryn*), and after the addition of the
preposition *abhi* (*abhiran*), it gradually sank into the
form *bhran* or *vran,* whence arose the Greek βροντὴ,
βράγχος; French *bruit, brouiller;* English *brawl;*
French *é-branler,* that which shakes the canopy of
heaven—Latin *ful*-men.

Credidimus is a very old verb, which we find pure in Sanskrit, under the form *śrat, śrad-dhâ*, perfectly corresponding to the Latin *cred-o, cred-e me, croy-ez moi*. We have made out of it *creed*, a symbol, French *croyance, croire, cred-ibilité, créd-it* (a sale on promise to be paid, an obligation), *créd-itor, créd-ule, créd-ulité*. In many languages *credidimus* implies *faith* (res habere fid-em, *Ovid; croire* la chose) Gr. ϝείδ-ω, Lat. *vid-eo*, Sans. *vid*, Fr. *voir*, Eng. *view*. To believe is to have con-*fid*-ence, to have confidence is to see with one's own eyes the reality of a thing actually existing or manifested. Out of light, out of faith and confidence : *mihi cred-e*, ἐμοὶ πιθοῦ. Molière says, "Je l'ai *vu;* dis-je *vu* ; de mes propres yeux *vu*, ce que l'on appelle *vu*."

Jovem is another most interesting onomatop, which means Supreme Ruler, the *light* and *splendour*, luminous and resplendent : *Deva* = δειϝός = δεϝός = Θεός, adj. θεῖος=Sans. *daiva, divya*=*divine ;* διο, *div-inus, div-us*, δαί-μων, *de-mon, dia-ble, dev-il*, all arising from the base *div*, to shine, to *twi*-nkle. In Lettonian *deus=daeva, diewas, desos ;* Celtic *dia*, Gael. *duw*, God, the heavens, the light, δῆ-λος, *day*-light, (Eng. *day*=Goth. *dags*) ; Ital. *di-o*, Span. *di-os*, Fr. *di-eu*, Jove, the electric spark,—the modification of the initial of the base being shown in the Sanskrit forms *dyu, dyut, ɉyut, ɉut* (*jiv-a*, Sans. life ; *zi-stan*, Per. to live), *Ju*-piter, *Jov-is*=the Father of *joy*, of the day, *jour*, Fr. (Sans. *dyo, dyota*, lustre, *jyotish*, light ; *adya*

M 2

(*i.e. i-dyu,* this light), to-day, *ho-di-e* (*i.e. hoc die,*) Lat.; *og-gi,* Ital.; *ho-y,* Span.; *au-jour-d'hui,* Fr.),—the Father of *ju-*bility, re-*joi-*cing (*je-cus, jo-cus, jo-cor, u-vo, ju-bar,* Lat.).

In the "Saturday Review," vol. xxxiv. p. 830 (Dec. 1872), a writer remarks:—

"As to *Janus* we have the forms *Januspater, Dianus, Diana,* and with these *Διός, ΔίFα,* leading to the Latin *divinus;* and again with the Greek *Zeus,* we have the Vedic *Dyaus,* from *dyu,* to shine, and by the side of these we have *dy* passing into *j, Jupiter, Janus, Juno,* or *dj,* as in the *Djovis* of Oscan inscriptions, and the old Italian deity *Vedjovis, Vejovis.*"

The bases *jyut, jut,* cited above, show that Indian grammarians were familiar with this change of *d* into *j*.

Div, to shine, is clearly a metaphoric word; it is an idea betraying a large amount of discrimination in the speaker, and a state of society when such things as the shining objects of the sky could be contemplated, talked about, and required a name. In naming them the speaking animal would seek a characteristic mark, and would find it in their *di-*verse nature, in their *du-*plication, their fickleness, tricksiness, or, as we still say, their *du-*plicity. Such must have been the origin of the parent of *twi-*nkle, —the being *twi-*co, *twi-*sting, *twi-*ning, *dou-*bling, or changing. Hence it follows that the word *two* (Latin *duo,* Sanskrit *dwi,* &c.,) was the fore-runner of *div;* "to *twi-*nkle;" and, therefore, to reach the onomatop we must trace the numeral. And this is not very difficult, for it is obviously based upon the pronominal demonstrative base *t·,* "there," &c., which may be

called "the remote definite." As *i* betokens that
which is "here" (see p. 183), so *t·* designates what
is "there," or away from the speaker. The one
describes the speaker, the other the spoken to, or, as
we still say, the *second* person, the duplicate of the *I*.
As we show on p. 184, the word *I* is the universal
exponent of unity, and *thou* is, perhaps, equally wide-
spread as the sign of *du*-ality. Certain it is that in
a vast assemblage of words, two numerous to cite,
and which will readily suggest themselves to the
reader, forms importing duality and demonstration
are, basically, obviously allied to the second personal
pronoun. The result we deduce is that such words
as *that, there, thou,* and *two* have a common origin;
and that the *doubling* or uncertain light of the stars
caused the term to be applied to them. It is marvellous that such utterly dissimilar ideas as those of *deity*
and *duplicity*, should spring from the same base.

Regnare.—Genere regio natus, says Cicero in his
Republic—the action of *reign*-ing, of having power.
Regnare is to be *rex; roi,* μόνος-αρχὴ, p-*rinc-eps, ruler,*
taking the name from the Sanskrit *rij*, to stand firm,
the Greek ὀρέγω, ὀρέγνυμι; Lat. *reg-ere, rec-tus;*
Gothic *rak-jan, raihts;* A.-S. *rec-can;* Eng. *righ-t.*
In a secondary sense we have in Sanskrit *rich*, to
honour, whence *arch* or *arj*, to honour, to *shine*, the
Lat. *arg*-entum; further development produces *ráj*,
to illuminate, to govern, the parent of the Sanskrit
rájan, a king; *rájaka*, splendid; *rájya*, government;

and *rájanya,* a soldier;—descendants of which are
found in the Hindî *ráj,* a king; *ráná,* a prince; *ráj-
pút,* a warrior; and *ráj-pútí,* courage. The last form
in Sanskrit seems to have been *raksh,* to govern,
protect, the Latin *rex,* prolific source of the Sanskrit
rakshana, protecting; *rakshika,* a watchman; *raksh-
in,* a policeman; and even euphemistically, *rakshas,*
a demon;—in Hindî, *rakh-ná,* to keep or guard; *rakh-
wárá,* a shepherd; *rakhaiyá,* a keeper; *ráchh-as,* a
demon; and *rak-ásí,* devilish. Even the Persian
lash-kar, an army (for protection), and *lash-an,* a
prop or support, arise from the same base, by the
common change of *r* to *l.*[a]

Onomatops are very diversified in character; some
are proper, natural, primitive; others figurative,
metaphoric, analogic, abstract. Some reflect the
brightness of the diamond, others are priceless
pearls, all being of more or less value;—and, like
gems, they differ in their associations, and are produced in different latitudes, under different circumstances. But Man is the Vulcan that finds, cuts,
polishes, and harmonizes them; and, for that very
reason, a vast number of the gems preserve for ever
the stamp and mark of his workmanship. When
circulating in society each of these coins of language

---

[a] It is noteworthy that in Arabic, also, traces of this onomatop
are seen in *ráfi',* one who raises or exalts; *ráff,* a preserver; *rá'd,*
guarding, a prince, *rájih,* excelling: *ra-ab,* a chieftain; *rabb,* ruling, governing; *ribábat,* lordship, dominion. Also in the Armenian
rab-bud, a chief.

bears on its face the stamp of its own value; and the different parts of the world—kingdoms, capitals, towns, villages, hamlets—vary only in the manipulation of these natural and eternal symbols.

Ovid, Met. I. v. 84:—

"Prona que cùm spectent animalia cætera terram,
Os homini sublime dedit, cœlumque tueri
Jussit, et erectos ad sidera tollere vultus."

. We will give a last quotation, a truly royal inversion of Cicero's: "quis est tam vecors, qui, cùm suspexerit in cœlum, non sentiat Deum esse?"

David in the Psalms is made to say: *Cœli enarrant gloriam Dei*—a perfect fountain of descriptive vocables.

Cœli, as was said before; represents the great orb, τύρος, the majestic canopy of heaven, that endless *circle* that binds up our globe, for ever and ever effulgent with myriads of fires, most glorious and of all colours.

E-nar-rant, a beautiful and prolific expression, akin to the Sanskrit *jan*, Gr. γῆ=γί(γ)νομα, γυ-νὴ, γονὴ, γῶ=γάω Lat. *gi-gno, ge-no, ge-ro, ge-rato, ge-mius, ge-rmius, ge-stio, ge-sco, na-sco, na-scor, na-tus, na-rrare, gn-arigare, gn-aritas,* γί-νωρίξει, γινώσκω, γνώ-σομαι=*know*-ledge, judgment, thought. The bond of alliance being found in the expression "I *conceive*"—I give birth to—I think—shown also in the change of the Sanskrit *jan*, to con-*ceive*, into *jnâ*, to per-*ceive*, recognize, to *kn*-ow, γιγνώσκω, γνῶσις, ἄγνοια, νοῦς, &c., Lat. *nosco, co-gnosco, gn-arus, n-arro;* Pers. *dán-istan* (*j* becoming *d, see* p. 163); Gothic *kun-nan, kun-ths;* O.H.G. *kna-jan;* A.S. *cná-wan;* Eng. to *kn-ow, cun-*ning, to *con* over.

Gloriam—that which is glorious, celebrated, illustrious. Found in the Sanskrit *śrí,* light, splendour, beauty, fortune, prosperity,—the Latin *Cer-es;* it also means to heat, burn, make to *glow,*—Lat. *per-cer-pere, per-ci-pio, cre-mare, car-bo;* Gr. κρίβανος, κρά-μβος, καρ-πός, κάρ-φω, κίρ-νημι, κερ-άω, κερ-άννυμι, κλί-ος=*gloria,* κλε-ος κλέ-ομαι, κλέ-ιω, *cel-ebro.* In Sanskrit *śrí* assumed the form *'ri-sh* or *śli-sh,* to burn, to *glis-*ten, the congeners of which are *gli-tter, gla-ze, gla-ss, glo-se* (*glesan,* A.S.), *glo-ss* (*gleissen, glanz,* Germ., *gloser,* Fr.; *glossare,* Lat.), to *glo-w* (*glóa,* Old Norse; *glowan,* A.S.; *glühen,* Germ.), *glo-ria, glo-riola,* γλα-φυρὸς; *glo-ra,* Norse, to shine, to stare. Besides these we find *gla-re,* to over-dazzle, (*cla-rus,* Lat.), *gle-am,* a beam of light, *gla-nce, gle-nt, gli-mpse,* the ray of light from the eye; *gli-m,* a light or candle, and *gli-mmer,* to *glow,* or shine. Extremes do, indeed, meet here in *glim-mer* and *glo-ry.*

Dei, as we before observed, the Sanskrit *Deva,* effulgens; the Divine electric spark, the Δαίμων, διάσια, πάνδια-δείπολια, *Jovialia,* festivals in honour of Jupiter.

Marvellous are, indeed, the changes which most onomatops have undergone. Let us examine the word *flower,* and see where it will lead us.

"Flower."

It is scarcely necessary to remind the reader of this disquisition, of the laws discovered by Grimm, Burnouf, &c., regulating the permutations of certain letters. To these well established laws, by which a tenuis changes to its corresponding media or spiritus asper, must be added others, familiar enough to Sanskrit scholars, by which the liquids interchange and frequently, also, pass into *ḍ* or *ṭ*. Besides the foregoing, some of the changes here exhibited are produced by the addition of separate words, which are become absorbed into the body of the leading word by the efflux of time. This is the case with the Hindî word *pṭh*, derived from the Sanskrit *prishṭha*, which itself is formed of *pri + sthâ*, "to stand forth." The Urdû *pahup*, represents the Sanskrit *pushpa*, i. e. *push + pâ*, to increase by drinking, a flower. *Push*, again, is not improbably formed of *pṛi + s*, *s* being a Sanskrit desiderative adjunct (the verb *ish*, to wish), which, by Indian laws of euphony, became *pṛish*, *pûsh*, *push*;—and so on of other instances.

Flower, φύλλ-ον for φύλ-ιον (*fol*-ium, mono-*phyl*), *flora*, *flos*, *fleur*, *floraison*, changing to *blume* in German (the Eng. *bloom* or *blossom;* Du. *bloem;* Swed. *blomme;* A.S. *bloma;* Gothic *bloma*, *blostma;* Gr. βρύ-ω, to grow; βρύος,* a herb), exists in Hindî under the form *phûl*, and this last is from the Sanskrit

---

* Cf. the Fr. *brouter* l'herbe, Eng. *browse*.

base *phull.* Now the problem before us is, How came *phull* to express what we call a *flower?* To answer this question we must examine some of its congeners. In Sanskrit, besides *phull, blossom,* we meet with *phala,* a *fr*-uit, and *phal-ya,* a *fl*-ower, showing an alliance between these two phenomena, which leads us directly to the base *pul,* to enlarge; other forms of this base being *push, púsh,* whence come the common Sanskrit words *pushṭi,* increase (*pushta,* Pers., a heap), *posha,* prosperity, and *pushpa* a flower. The word still lives in the Hindî *posh-ná, pos-ná, pokh-ná,*[a] to breed, rear, foster.

Returning to our base *phal,* we find that it receives a strengthening *s* in the forms *sphal, sphar, sphul, sphur,* all of which are common bases in Sanskrit in the sense of "increase," "expand." *L* and *r* are, as we remarked above, interchangeable in Aryan languages, and frequently pass into the cerebral or dull sound of *ḍ* or *ṭ ;* this causes our bases to re-appear under the forms *sphaṭ* and *sphaṇḍ,* to break forth, *sphur-chh, svur-chh, sphuṭ, sphuṇḍ,*[b] to expand. These bases originate a host of words, such as ὄ-φελ-ος, ὀ-φέλ-λω, Gr.; *split,* Eng.; *spal-tan,* Old H. G.; *ex-pañse, ex-pansion, spar-go, di-sper-gere* (difflat ventus folia, *Plaut.*), Span. *spar-cir,* Ital. *spar-pagliar,* Fr. *éparpiller les feuilles; ré-pand-re,* Fr.; *aus-span-nen,* Ger.; *spend* money; *dé-pen-ser,* Fr.; the *span* of an arch,

---

[a] See p. 108, about this change of *sh* into *kh.*

[b] The insertion or omission of a nasal being optional, *see* p. 106.

" G. *spanne*, It. *spanna*, Fr. *espan*, *empan*, the length
of the outstretched thumb and finger."—*Wedgwood*.

The base *sphand*, to expand, is also found in the
Latin *frons*, *frond-eo*, *frond-escere*, *frond-osus*, *frondifer*, *frond-icamus*; and in its form *phull* gives meaning
to *fru-x*, *fru-ctus*, *fru-ctificare*, *fru-ctuosus*, *fru-ctifer*,
and even in *fru-cteta*, bushes, and *fru-ticare*, to become
bu-shy.

The word *bushy* suggests a new series, based upon
a phonetic corruption similar to that which produced
the Sanskrit *push* out of *pul*. *Bush*, formerly spelled
busk, is found in the Icelandic *buskr*, a tuft of hair,
a bush, a thicket; and in the French *bouche*, a
tuft or *bunch*, whence *bouchon de paille*, a wisp of
straw, a *bouchet*, a bush or bramble. Similar forms
are found in the Fr. *bosse*, a bunch, hump; the
Breton *bouch*, a tuft or wisp; the Frisian *bosc*, a
lump or cluster, the Ger. *bausch*, a projection,
bundle, bunch; and the Dutch *bos*, a bunch, knot,
bussel, a bundle. *Bushel* and the *bush* of a wheel
derive their names from their hollow, swollen out,
expanded nature, as is seen from the Provençal form
of the word " *boistia*, *boissa*, whence the diminutives
O. Fr. *boisteau*, *boisseau*, Lat. (A.D. 1214) *bustellus*,
a box for measuring, a bushel."—*Wedgwood*. The
Du. *busse*, a box, Pl. Du. *büsse*, *büske*, Ger. *büchse*,
lead to the A. S. *box*, the name of the tree and also of
a receptacle, akin to the Gr. πύξος, the box-tree, and
πύξις, a box, Lat. *buxus*, " Ital. *bosso*, box-tree, *bossola*,
a box, hollow place; Fr. *buis*, Bret. *beuz*, Bohem.

pusspan, box-tree, *pusska,* a box."—*Wedgwood.* Other receptacles are also derived from this base, as is shown further on.

Longitudinal extension is expressed by *spin,*[a] to lengthen out (*spinnan,* A. S., *spinnen,* Ger., *spinder,* Danish), whence arise *spindle, spindel* or *spille,* Ger., and a *spill,* or spindle-like twist for lighting the pipe, "N[orse], *spila spile,* a splinter, chip, peg; *spila,* Pl. D. *spilen,* to stretch out, to fix open."—*Wedgwood.* The verb *spill,* to *spri*-nkle, or spread out, seems to follow (Pl. Du. *spillen,* to shed, waste, spoil; Norse *spilla,* to gush, spill, waste), and so, metaphorically, to *spill,* to *spoil,* corrupt or *foil.* The last word brings us to the French *fil,* a thread, *fil*-ament, *fil*-ature; Eng. *fl*-oss, the Latin *pil, pila,* Fr. *poil,* a hair, the *pile* of velvet,—a striking anastomosis affording a remarkable confirmation of the genuineness of these alliances. Anyhow the Danish *spinder,* to spin, leads us to *spider,* the spinner; and so we advance to *spine,* a lengthening out; *spina,* Lat.

Returning to the form *sphaṇḍ, sphuṭ,* &c., with a sense of "spreading" we have in Sanskrit *sphuṭ-á,* perspicuity; *sphuṭ-a,* manifest; *sphuṭ-ana,* opening; *sphuṭ-ártha,* intelligible, *i.e.* opened meaning; *sphuṭ-i* or *sphur-a,* a swelling; *sphoṭ-a,* bursting; *sphaṭ-a, phaṭ-a, phaṇ-a, phuṭ-a,* the expanding hood of a snake; *sphir-a, sphár-a,* large, spreading; and *phal-gu,* the spring time, when nature expands. Other

---

[a] The short vowel conveying an idea of tenuity, as in *thin,* &c.

derivatives, deprived of the asper (allied to *phal*), are found in *pal-áṇḍu*, an onion, a *bul-b*, or *pl*-ump root; *pal-áśa*, *fol*-iage, leaf; *pall-ava*, a SPROUT or what is SPREAD ;—(allied to *sphaṇḍ*) *piḍ-aka*, a small *pimp*-le or swelling ; *piṇḍ-a* or *piṇḍ-aka*, a lump or ball.

In Hindî the words depart still further from their original. Thus we have *phúl*, a flower ; *phal*, a fruit ; *phúl-ná*, to blossom ; *phúl-á*, swelled ; *phúl-á-o*, a swelling; *phoṛ-á*, a BOIL or sore; *phoṛ-ná*, to break, SPLIT; *phúṭ-ná*, to be broken ; *phuṭ*, *phuṭ-í*, *phúṭ-an*, disagreement, *i.e.* breaking apart; *phail-áná*, to spread; *phail-á-o*, expansion; *phál-gun*, the spring or opening season; *phun-gí*, a sprout or bud (Lat. *fun-gus*, a sprouting growth); *phal*, a ploughshare (because an expanded blade, or because it breaks open the ground); *phal-í* or *phar-í*, a shield or broad object for defence; and *phar*, a *fr*-uit. The same idea of "expansion" is found in *phá-orá*, a SPADE; *pha-phol-á*, a blister; *phan-í*, a wedge; *phal-áng*, a stride; *phú-há*, a teat or pap; *pháṇṭ-á*, a bough or branch; and *pal-lo*, a sprig or shoot; and the idea of "opening out" is presented in *pháṛ-ná*, to rend; *pháṭ-ná*, to split; *pháṭ-ak*, a gate or opening; *phaṛ-áná*, or *phas-káná*, to split; *phaṭ-á*, a crack; *phaṭ-ná*, to be torn; and even *phuṭ* or *phuṭ-kar*, what is opened out, separated, dispersed, and so an unmatched or "odd" object.

The English equivalent for the Hindî word *pháṭ-ná*, *i.e.* to SPLIT, to SPLINTER, helps us to see that the base *sphaṇḍ* really represents a form *sprit* nasalized, as we

shall show more fully further on. But, in immediate
connection with the present series, we may observe
that the Sanskrit bases *sphuṇḍ, sphaṇṭ, sphuṭ, sphaṭ,*
mean "break," *i.e.* split or spread out, and from
these, by loss of initial and the operation of obvious
phonetic changes, are evolved the bases *bhind*
(s + phund), bhid and *d* becoming *j* (cf. *dyut, jyut,* p.
163) we get *bhāj, bhanj,* to divide, separate, or break.
The last form *bhanj* is the well known analogue of
the Latin *frango,* whence are derived all the words
connected with *frac-ture, frag-ment,* &c., &c., &c. It
is important also to notice that the Latin *frango*
contains the letter *r,* which has been lost in the Sanskrit *bhanj,* thus proving two things, first, that the
Latin is older than the Sanskrit form of this word ;
and, second, that the word *bhanj* is certainly the congener of such words as *bryt*-an, A. S. ; *briot-a,* Icel.;
bris-er, Fr.; *bryte,* Dan.; and the Du. *s·priet,* a *spear,*
bow-*sprit,* a *split* or *splint*-er of wood, the Sans.
sphaṇṭ or *sphaṇḍ.*

In India, a long succession of grammarians preserved from antique times a knowledge of the older
forms of words, and the earnest study of a vast
literature counteracted, to some extent, the ordinary
processes of phonetic corruption ; hence it results
that we have but little difficulty in recognizing our
bases *phal, sphaṇḍ,* &c., in all the foregoing Indian
words. In countries not so favoured, we must not
expect to find this purity ; nevertheless in Persian,
at least, there is sufficient correspondence to enable

us to walk on the solid ground of fact. In Persian, *pál-áyídan* means "to increase;" *pál-údan*, "to be large;" and *pál-ádan*, "to stretch." Here we are clearly dealing with the Sanskrit *phall* or *pul*, "to enlarge." [a] In Persian the letter *p* is never aspirated, on the contrary it is often softened into *b*;[b] hence we meet with *bál-áyánidan*, to extend, enlarge; *bál-án*, increasing; *bál-ish* or *pál-ish*, growth, increase; *pál-ánanda*, augmenting; *bál-ú* or *pál-ú*, a wart or swelling; *bál-úd*, increase; *bál-ín*, a pillow, and *bál-ung*, a cucumber, both being *bul*-ky objects. Other changes are illustrated by *píl*,[c] a swelling; *píl-tan*, bulky; *piyáz*, an onion or *bulb*; *pinda*, a drop, spot (cf. Sans. *piṇḍa*, a ball); and *pind-ish*, a ball of cotton. The leter *l* is, as usual, often replaced by *r*, giving rise to *par-ásh* or *par-wás*, expansion; *bár* or *pár-í*, fruit, flowers; *pár-o*, a shovel, paddle; *par-war*, nourishing; *par-osh* pimples or swellings;— and *pádal*, a flower; *pána*, a wedge; and *páshída*, a pumpkin, also, possibly, take their origin from the base *pul*, " to enlarge."

The bonds of alliance between Aryan and Semitic languages are too slight to allow the scholar to compare such languages with much confidence; still it is worthy of remark that in Arabic also the idea of "expansion" finds expression by a somewhat similar

---

[a] The Sanskrit *pál* will be mentioned anon.

[b] The tenuis becomes, frequently, spiritus asper in Persian; thus the English *grip* (Sans. *grabh*) is, in Persian, *girir-tan*.

[c] Cf. the series of bases containing *pṛi* on p. 178.

sound. Thus, in that language, *bál* means a "spade," and also "affluence;" and *bawl* signifies "bursting out."

When the extension is lateral, the base *pul* (or *pri*, which we shall shortly find is the same thing), is strengthened with a dental, and, in Sanskrit, it becomes *pra-th, pri-th, pa-th*. From these forms arise such words as *pri-thu*, in English *broad* (Germ. *aus-breit-en*); *pri-thwî*, the earth; *pra-thá* or *pra-thiti*, fame, celebrity; *pra-thiman*, greatness; *pra-thima*, chief, excellent; *prithuka*, flattened grain; *pri-thutá*, largeness; *pri-thula*, large; *patra*, a leaf (because *flat*); and *pri-shtha* the back or broad part of the body.[a] In Hindî we meet with *píth*,[b] the back; *pirtam*, the world; *path*, a road or *path*; *pathik*, a traveller; *pát, pattá, pattî*, a leaf; *pátra*, a broad dish; *pát* broad; *prathá*, immemorial custom; *pátan*, a roof. These Hindî words present us with some very corrupt forms; but still further corruption shows itself in the Persian *pahan*, width (*pát*, Hindî, *prithu*, Sans.); *pahná*, broad; and *bádya*, any capacious vessel (*pátra*, Hindî, *prithula*, Sans.). But it is in European languages that the most remarkable changes of this word are to be found; for we recognize the

---

[a] *Prishtha* is the word which explains the use of the dental affix. It is formed of *pri + shthâ* (= *pra + sthâ*), *i.e.* "forth-stand," to be placed, put, or to be forth in all directions, hence *broad*.

[b] This word *píth* is only a phonetic corruption of *prishtha*, the Sanskrit word above given. This affords unanswerable evidence that *pri, pal*, &c., can degenerate into such remnants as *pt* and *pa*.

base *pul+tha* in the word PLATe (*platte*, Fr., *piatto*, Ital., *platt*, Germ.), that is a FLAT or SPREAD out surface;—a BLADe of grass is a BROAD object (A.S. *blad*, Fr. *blé*, Germ. *breit*), as is also a BOARD (Germ. *bret*); a FLOOR is a *flat* (Germ. *platt*) surface, and so are the FLUke of an anchor, a PLAnk of wood (*planke*, Germ., *planche*, Fr.), the PLAn of a country, and PRé, Fr., a meadow.

The SPADe (of which SPOON seems a modification) is another instance of the expression of expanded surface by the base *sphand*, showing a near approach to the form *pal* in the Fr. word *pelle*, a shovel, Ital. *pal-etta*, a small spade; the Fr. *pal-ette*, a painter's *pal-let*, the small tabula on which his pigments are mixed; with a secondary sense in the French word *palette*, "a battledore,"—plainly showing that the sound merely expresses extended surface.

The blade, the flat, or extended vegetable surface is expressed in Latin by *fol-ium*[a] (*tri-folium = trèfLe* Fr.), from which proceed *fol-io*, tin-*foil*, in-*fol-io*, *fol-*ded (*pleat-*ed; *plé*, Fr.); *fol-iol*, *fol-iomor;* hence arise *fol-iage*, *fol-iated*, *fol-iaceous*, *fol-iation*, *fol-iature*, *fol-iér*, Fr. (fluttering pieces of tin). Then we find *fol-leatus*, expanding like a *fol-les; fol-licans*, *fol-liculus* (the envelope of fruit—frumenti vagina, *Cic.*) *fol-ligena*, and *fol-lis*. In French the Lat. *folium* becomes

---

[a] We may notice here the small importance of vowels as a means of discriminating bases. *Fol-* is the same as *pul* and *pal* and *ptl*: the vowel may even be elided altogether, as in *fl-*at and trè-*fl*-e, above given.

N

feuille, feuillage, ef-feuiller, to pick up leaves; and, in the sense of "flower," *fleurette, fleuron* (in printing), *fleuron* (in botany), *fleuraison, fleur-de-liser,* to mark with a hot iron, *fleuriste,* a florist; so also *dé-flor-er,* to take the flowers of virginity; *de-flor-ation,* the act of doing so, to de-*flower.*

Now before we seek to eliminate the onomatop from which the word *flower* derives its sense of expansion, it will be necessary to follow the base *pul* through another channel of derivation. Expansion or enlargement takes place in consequence of distension from *ful*-ness. This word *full,* indeed, presents the base *pul* in one of its earliest meanings; for in this sense it assumes, in Sanskrit, simpler forms, enabling us, by their means, to reach to the ultimate base underlying the whole system. These forms are—*púr, púrv, purv, parv, plu-sh, pru-sh, prá, pṛiṇ, pṛí,* and *pṛi.* All these bases mean *fill;* and the last two are what Professor Max Müller calls "primitive roots." Their claim to that title will be examined in the sequel; but first we must show that in this sense also the base *pul* has been well used. In Sanskrit we get *púr-a,* filling; *púr-ṇatá,* plenty; *pár-aṇa,* fulfilling, and *pár-i,* a cup (both from *pṛi*); the verb *pál,** to nourish; *pál-ana,* cherishing; *pál-a,* a guardian; *púr-*

---

* This base is considered by most Sanskrit scholars to be the causal form of *pá,* to preserve, from *pí,* to drink, to nourish; but the peculiar insertion of *l* in the causal of the verb *pá,* shows that the base arose by the conversion of *pṛi* into *par,* then into *pal* and *pál.*

ta, complete; *púr-ṇa*, able, strong. Hindî gives us *púr-â*, fully; *sam-púrṇ*, full; *púrá-í*, fulness; *púl-â*, *púlí*, and *pol-ak*, bundles of straw; *pál-ná*, to nourish, &c., &c. The prolific vocables *for-ma*, Lat., *for-me*, Fr., *for-mo*, Ital., are also seen in the Hindî *púráí*, fulness; Lat. *am-pul-la*, a stout jar; Fr. *am-poule*, a bubble.

In Persian we find *pur-ídan*, to fill; *pur-â*, fulness; *pur-wár*, fatted, or filled out; *pár*, past, com*pl*eted, &c. In European languages this base frequently recurs in this sense; as, for example, *ple-nus*, *ple-onasm*, *plé-nitude*, *re-ple-nish*, *am-pli-ation*, *am-pli-tude*, *af-flu-ence*, *po-pul-us*, *pl-ebs*, *pl-us*, *plu-rimus*, πίμ-πλη-μι; Lat. *im-ple-re*, Fr. *em-pli-r*, *sup-pli-er*, Eng. *sup-ply*, *re-ple-te*, Fr. *com-plé-ter*, *ple-in*, *accom-pli-r*, to accom-*pli*-sh; Gr. πλέ-ιον, πλοῦ-τος, rich, πλῆ-θος, *ple-thora*, πλε-ος, several, *plu-*rality; Lat. am-*plus*, am-*ple*; A. S. *full*, *fyllan*; Gothic, *fulljan*; Fr. *remplir*, *s'emplir*, *ex-plé-tif*; Ger. *füll-en*, *voll*, *aus-full-end*. The part of the body which is filled and expands is termed the *bel-ly*, clearly a derivative from *fill*; in German *bauch*, and, by metastasis, *leib*; in French *panse* or *ventre*, both of which are obviously allied to the Hindî *peṭ*,[a] *peṭh*, or *peṭú* (*peṭú*, gluttonous); and the Sanskrit *phaṇḍa* or *phâṇḍa*, the belly, in which last we see ex-*pand* almost pure and simple. Addi-

---

[a] By some such changes as the following:—*pri* becoming *par*, then *pal*, and *fal* and *fad* and *fand*, then *vent*(re); the *t* softening to *s*, would make *vens-*, whence *panse*. More probably *panse* came directly from the Sans. *phâṇḍa*, the parent of the Hindî *peṭ*.

tional examples are found in the Greek πλά-τος, dilate, πλά-τυς, Lat. *la*-tus, ample, πλάτιον, Plato, the master of Aristotle, the man with the large chest, πλά-τανος, the *pla*-tanus, the *pla-ne* tree, whose branches spread out, πλά-τεϊα, a large road; also in such words as *pl-ump, bowl, bowel* (*boyau*, Fr., *boel*, Old Fr.), *bulb*, a *ball;* and in *bourse, purse*, a *ba-g.* Again, βύρσα, *bourse*, Ital. *borsa gonfilata*, Fr. *bourse gonflée, enflée, pleine*, &c.; *bour-geons* of flowers, *bu-ds* (akin to *pa-ds, pa-dding*), *bourrée*, a *bun*-dle of small sticks, *bour-reler, bour-let*, a kind of cushion filled with hair, a *pad, bour-relier*, the man who fills horses' collars with flocks. There are also diminutives, as *bour-sicauld*, a small purse and *bour-son*, a small pocket; besides the noun *bour-soufflage*, inflation.

Of this word *bourse* Mr. Wedgwood gives the following congeners:— "It. *bolgia, bolza*, Gris[ons], *bulscha, buscha*, a budget or leather wallet; Sp *bolsa*, a bag, purse, exchange. Hence with the common change of an *l* for an *r* (as Sp. *peluca*, Fr. *perruque*), It. *borsa, borsia, borza*, Fr. *bourse.*

"From the It. form *bolza* seems derived *bolzac-chini*, Sp. *bolzequin*, buskins, originally signifying bags of skin into which the feet were thrust, as Sp. *bolsa*, bag lined with furs or skins to keep the feet warm.—Neumann. The same change from *l* to *r*, as in *bolsa, borsa*, gives It. *borzacchini*, Du. *broseken* (Fr. *brodequin*), E *buskin*. In like manner it seems that the original meaning of *boot* was a leathern bag, as in Sp. *bota*, which signifies both a leathern bag to carry wine, and also boot, a leathern covering for the leg and foot. Du. *bote, boten-schoen* pero, calceus rusticus e crudo corio.—Kil." (vol. i. p. 277.)

But the filling up of any object or person *satisfies* the recipient; and the idea of satisfaction is also expressed by the base we are examining. It meets us in the words *play, ple-ase, ple-asure, pla-cere,* Lat.; *plaire,* Fr.; *be-frie-digen, freund,* Ger.; *fri-end,* Eng.; and in the Sanskrit bases *priṇ, priḍ, spri, pri, piy, pri, pri,* also in the developed bases *sphaṇt, sphaṇḍ, sphuṭ,* and *sphuṇḍ,* the last four meaning *play,* and the rest *please.* It is needless to cite many examples of this most prolific form of the base; they come ready to hand in the Sanskrit *pri-ya,* beloved (Persian *yár,* a friend, *pyár,* affection); *pri-yaka,* a bee; *pri-ti,* gratification; *pre-man,* kindness; *paur-ta,* a pleasing work, &c.; also in the Hindî *pre-m* or *pem,* love; and *pemî,* a lover, &c.

The foregoing has shown us that the verb *pri,*—the past participle of which is *púrṇa,* giving rise to the secondary base *púr* or *pul,* and the tertiary bases *sphuṭ, sphaṇḍ,*[a] &c.,—originates a vast assemblage of words with *pleasure* at one end, and the *span* of an arch at the other, all which words meet at a point in the word *bel-ly,* in which both the ideas of "expansion" and of "satisfaction" find expression. The extreme plasticity of primitive bases having thus been

---

[a] A probable series of phonetic changes being—*pri, pir* or *púr, pul, phûl* or *pál, phall, phad, phand, sphand.* See p. 106 for change of *l* to *d.*

somewhat lengthily demonstrated, we are in a position to carry the inquiry still further, and to endeavour to reach the cause of all, that is, to endeavour to ascertain how it is that the sound *pri* (which is the most primitive of all the forms the base assumed) in the first instance acquired its sense of "extension." To effect this we resolve it into two parts *pr + i*. The *pr*, or rather the *p* only,[a] is the original onomatop from which the prepositions *pra, per, pro, πρὸ, fi* Arabic, *for, forth, forward,* &c. &c. *ad infinitum,* received their birth: it is the very natural expression of out-going—the forward *puff* of ʙreath. That the sound *puff* enters into articulate speech we have distinct evidence in the Persian verb *puf-idan,* to blow, also in the Sanskrit *phût,* an imitative sound occurring frequently in the lighter works;[b] and in the word *phût-kára,* hissing, crying aloud, beside the common English phrase "to be *puffed* up" (Galla *afufa,* Hungarian *fuv-ni,* Scotch *fuff,*—Wedgwood). The letter *p* as the exponent of *ex-p-ulsion* (*expulsum, pulso,* Lat., *pousser,* Fr., *push,* Eng.) is also the ultimate onomatop from which springs the Sanskrit *vij* and *vá,* to ʙlow, *vá-yus,* ᴡind, &c.

The *p* being thus accounted for, there remains but *i,* a simple onomatop expressive of motion, existing quite pure in the Sanskrit *i,* to go, in the Egyptian

[a] The letter *r,* as is well known, imparts a sense of quickness to Aɪyan words, without otherwise altering their sense: cf. **run, rush, rabid, rapid,** &c. &c., and the Sans. *i,* to go, and *ri,* to go, &c.

[b] The *Panchatantram,* for instance.

Hieroglyph *eï*=go; and in the Latin *eo*, &c. This base might be more correctly defined as "the proximate definite,"[a] and may be illustrated by the word *he-re*[b] (*here*, A. S.; *her*, Du.; *hier*, Germ.; *i-dhar*, Hindî; *iha*, Sans.), implying *motion towards the speaker*, and when intensified it takes what, in Sanskrit grammar, is called the *vṛiddhi* substitute, and becomes *ai* (pronounced like the word *eye*), and when strongly aspirated becomes *hi! hi!* (Sans. *hay*, to make a noise) so constantly used when inciting to motion. As a definer of that which is proximate this base gives life to many vocables; as, for example, the Sanskrit *i-ha*, here; *i-hatya*, of this place; *i-tas*, hence; *i-tara*, other (beyond this); *i-dam*, this; *i-dá-nîm*, the present time; *i-va*, like, in this form; *i-ti*, thus, in this way; *i-ttham,* or *i-tthâ*, thus; *i-driś*, this-like; *e-tad*, this-here; and, by phonetic corruption, *a-dya*, to-day (for *i-dyu*=this light, *see* p. 164; in Hindî this word becomes, by still further corruption, *a-b*); *a-tas*, hence (cf. *i-tas*, above); *a-tha*, now; *a-tra*, here. In the modern Hindî we find *i-t*, here; *i-dhar*, hither; *i-ttâ* or *e-tâ*, this much; *i-tnâ* or *e-tnâ*, this many; *ya-hán*, here; *y-ún*, thus (*y* = *i*); *i-tek*, this

[a] The argument that follows shows that the distinction between demonstrative and predicative bases, contended for by Prof. Max Muller, has no existence in fact.

[b] The *h* in these words stands for an ancient sibilant, found in the Sans. *sa*, Lat. *sibi*, still surviving in the English *she*, though lost in *he*, and dentalized in *the* (Sans. *tad*). The sibilant is a definer of the proximate, "the *this*;" the dental defines that which is more remote, "the *that*."

much; *ai-sá* this-like; and, in the Braj dialect, *i-tau*, here. In Bengalí also: *i-ni*, this person; *i-háte*, hereby; *e* or *ei*, this; *e-mot*, thus; *e-kháne*, here; *ei-hetuk*, hence; *ei-sthane*, hither; *ei-ovodhi*, hitherto, &c. These vocables find their equivalents in Europe in such words as *he-re*, *hi-ther*, *he-nce*; *i-ci*, Fr.; *i-d*, *i-dem*, *ea-dem*, *i-bi*, *i-bidem*, Lat., &c., &c., &c.

But there is yet another idea arising out of this proximate definite, for the very acmè of approximation is Self, and subjectively this idea assumes the double form of Personality and Unity. I is the natural exponent of personality, and shows itself on the surface of widely scattered languages *a-ní*, Hebrew (as a suffix *-í*); *a-na'*, Arabic; *a-nak*,[a] in the Egyptian Hieroglyphs; ·*nek*, or ·*nekki*, in the Berber dialect; ·*ñoca*, in the Quichua language; ·*nga*, Burmese; ·*go*, in the Canton dialect; *y-u* in Chinese; *I*, English; *i-k*, Dutch; *a-ku*, Malayan; *i-ch*, German; *j-e*, French; *i-o*, Italian; *s-ɪ-hrih* or *s-ᴇʏ-ree*, Georgian; *e-go*, Latin; ε-γω, Greek; *a-ham*, Sans.; *m-ai-ṇ*,[b] Hindî; *man*, Persian—the last coming round almost to the Semitic *ani*. In its sense of unity—the I—the one—it is of universal recurrence. It is the *e-ka* of Sanskrit, the Hebrew *e-khad*, the *a-ce* of cards, the Pehleví *a-chad*,

---

ᶠ   [a] The base of this word, and, therefore, of the other Semitic forms *aní, ana', nek,* &c., is proved to be a vowel both by the Hebrew suffix -*í*, and also by the personal termination of verbs in the Hieroglyphs. In the latter case it is articulated as *a*, thus ᴹᵉʀ, to love, ᴹᵉʀ-*a*, *I* love; so ᴀᵀᵉᵂ-*a*, *my* father.

   [b] Sounded like the English (m)eye.

the Persian *y-ak* or *e-k*, and the nominal affix -*i* (as *mard-i*, one man), the Japanese *i-ts'*, the Georgian *z-ee;* the German *ei-n*, Norse, *ei-tt*, the Dutch *ee-n*, the French *u-n*, the Italian *u-no*, the English *a-n*, *ane*, *one*. So natural is it to man to express unity by this articulation that no process of decay or length of time seems sufficient to destroy its traces. Thus in the Tamulic group of languages *one* is expressed by the Toduva *won*, the Malayâlam *on-na*, the Tuluva *on-ji*, the Gond *un-di*, the Malabar and Canarese *on-du*, the Uraon-Kol *un-ta*, the Tamil *on-ru*, the Telugu *o-ka*, the last anastomosing with the Ugric group of languages, represented by the Tsheremissian *i-k*, the Lappish *a-kt*, the Esthonian *u-ks*, the Finnish *y-ksi*, the Hungarian *e-gy*, the Vogulian *a-kva*, the Mordvinian *vai-ke*, the Syrianian *ó-tik*, and the Ostiakian *it, i, ja*. Around the Caucasus, also, may be met the Abchasian *a-ka*, the Georgian *e-rthi* or *z-ee*, the Mingrelian *a-rti*, the Suanian *e-shchu*: the Mandshu *e-mu* is clearly the same onomatop, and so, among Mongolic people, is the Aimak *n-i-kka*, the Sokpa *n-e-ge*, and the Ölöt *n-i-ke*. Nor have we yet done with it; for the Taic group supplies us with additional examples in the Kassia *w-ei*, the Shan *n-ei-n*, the Khamti, Laos, and Siamese *n-ü-ng*, and the Ahom *l-i-ng;* the Lohitic group presents the Dhimâl *e-long*, and the Mikir *i-chi;* the Gyami gives us *i-ku*, the Kong-Chinese, or spoken dialect, *y-ut*, and finally we obtain it quite pure in the Chinese *'i*, "one.".

In all these numerous examples it is seen that

various modifications of the sound *i* are used to express "unity" all over the world, and that "unity"
—the one—the I—is also the exponent of proximity
—"here,"—and of motion towards the speaker—
"here," "come here," and likewise of motion in
general—*i*, Sans., "to go." In this last form the
sound became a true vocable, all knowledge of its
onomatopic origin being gone; and, as a symbol of an
idea, *i* with its sense of "motion" could, and did,
conjoin itself with other vocables, as, for instance, *r*,
in *ri*, "go quickly"; and finally superadding *p'*,
"forth," became *pri*, "to go forth," the base of all
the words we have been examining.

The word *flower* has thus led us a long way; yet
however strange may appear the ultimate origin of so
highly organized a word, we have seen that the path
we have trod, though long and devious, has always
been one of solid fact. In no part of this disquisition
has the imaginative faculty had any play; we move
from fact to fact in a tedious but certain and scientific manner; and the rational result at which we
finally arrive is at once the keystone, crown, and test
of the entire argument, by which its truth can be
instantly established. We see that the words *flower*,
expand, fill, &c., spring out of *pri*, which itself means
go-forth, and all its manifold derivatives open their
meanings at once to this master key, by which the
going forth, opening out, filling, satisfying, pleasing,
are seen to be but various forms of the one idea, which
underlies and gives vitality to the whole.

" Bee."

An onomatop is a natural euphony itself, the *suprema lex* of language—it is cause and effect—something like the primitive instinct of animals, it is a music that offers an unlimited diversity of harmonies.

Having expatiated on the remarkable onomatops of Cicero, we bring our reader to the humble *bee* of our gardens and proceed to discuss its onomatop.

Everyone knows what a bee is, but few know why it has been called by that name. The Sanskrit base on which it was built is *pí*, which means *p-ump*, suck, drink, the Chinese *f-ung*, Fr. *b-oire, pi-per*. The Greeks made the vocable πί-ω, πί-νω, the Latins *pi-no, pro-pi-no*, to drink the health, and *bi-bo, poto*, in the Quichua language *u-pi-ani*. The insect is called in Italian *ape, pe-cchia;* in Spanish it is *a-be-ja;* in Burmese *py-ah;* in Japanese *ba-tsi;* in Georgian *b-shey;* and in English *bee;* A. S. *beo;* Icel. *by-fluga* (the sucking-fly); Ger. *bie-ne;* Gael. *be-ach.*

The Latins made many vocables from it, such as *a-pi-s, a-pe-s, a-pi-anus, a-pi-arium, a-pi-arius, a-pi-ostra, a-pi-ostrum, a-pi-cula, po-trix, po-tor, po-tus;* whence the English *po-tion, po-tage, po-table, po-t* or *bu-tt, be-verage,* and *bee-r.* In the interesting letter written by Dr. Livingstone to Mr. Bennett, Insama, a chief of south-eastern Africa, is spoken of as calling his cup and beer, *po-mbo!*

The fertile germ whence the word *bee* had birth is

likewise progenitor of nature's chief, the Sanskrit *pi-tri*, Eng. *fa-ther*, πατήρ, *pa-ter*, *pè-re*, who causes everything to grow for the *pa-bulum vitæ*, the nourishment of man, the head of the family, its protector and defender, and who has been called by the same onomatop all over the globe.

The Sanskrit *pá*, which is only a developed form of *pí*, makes *pi-vámi* in the present tense, and passes to the Greek as πί-ω, πί-νω, reduplicate πε-πο-κα, to drink; the Latin *po-tus*, *po-culum*, changing to the English *be-verage*, in French *boi-sson;* and a poor *boisson* is called *pi-quette*, because of its acidity. The Italians made of it *be-veraggio*, *be-vanda*, *po-zione*, and *vi-nello* (of small strength), French *petit vi-n* (little *wi*-ne) or *pi-quette*, *vin*, *vin-aigre*, and *wine*, being only phonetic corruptions of *pí*, *bí*, or *ví*. In this sense this onomatop gives vitality to such words as the Sanskrit *pí-ti* or *pi-tu*, drink; *pí-tha*, or *pá-thas*, water; *pay-as*, milk; *pá-naka*, beverage; and *pi-yúsha*, the nectar of the gods: *push*-PA (Urdu *pahu*-P), a flower, is formed of *push*, to increase, + *pá*, by drinking; and a tree is called *páda*-PA, or foot-drinker, because deriving its nourishment from the root. In Hindî we meet with *pey*, *pay*, milk; *pain*, a reservoir of water; *pau-h*, a stand where water is kept; *po-khar*, a lake or pond; *py-áná* or *py-áwná*, to make to drink; and *py-ás*, thirst. In the last word the letter *s* is the remains of the word *ish*, to *wish;* so that *pyás* (*pipásá*, *pipásu*, Sans.) is really *pí + ish*, to wish to drink, hence thirst. In Hindî we have also the interesting word *pí-ná*, to drink, to suck, also applied to the smoking or rather sucking of a pipe. From *pínd* come both *pí-pá*, a *ba*-rrel, and *pí-pí*, a *pipe* or *s-pou-t*. In Persian we find the vocables *pi-yála*, a drinking cup; *pá-h* and *pá-zûm*, food, pabulum; and the word *púd*, almost identical with the English *food* (*pud*-ding), Ger. *fud-der*, Eng. *fod-der*. That beautifully articulated and wonderfully constructed language, the Sanskrit, lays bare many of the processes by which onomatops change both form and meaning. Thus there are derivatives or secondary bases springing from *pí* in the sense of "swelling," "increasing." These bases are *pyai*, *pyáy*, *sphây*, and they originate such words as *spháti* and *sphíti*, swelling, increase; *pí-vana* and *pí-vara*, large, fat; *pí-ntá*, fatness;—and, according to Professor Th. Benfey, probably *phe-na*, froth, and *phe-nala*, foamy.

This *pá* of Sanskrit indicates nourishment πα-ειν, *po*-wer, and lives in *pa-ste*, *pa-stry*, *pa-sture*, *pa-rentage*, making in Greek πεί-θομαι, subdue to obedience. In this sense we get the Sanskrit nouns *pi-tri*, the nourisher, the father (Japanese, *fi-to* a man), *pa-ti*, a lord or master,—Zend *pai-tis*, Gr. πό-σις, *po-oir*, possess, *po-u-oir*, and finally *po-wer*,—a master, husband; as well as *po-tatio*, *po-tation*, πο-λλὴ, φιλό-πο-της = *potator*, *po-tion*, *poi-son*, *pui-ssant*, *po-ssible*, Lat. *hos-pes*, *hos-pi-tium*, Fr. *hos·te hô·te*, *ho·telerie*, *ho·tellier*, Eng. *hos·t*, *hos·try* (in the last six the elision of *pi* is marked by a dot).

In Persian *pati*, a master, a husband, becomes *pad*

and *bud*, a master, and *páb*, *púb*, *báb*, *bábá*, are used for "father," while *bá-n* represents a "prince," and *pa-nah*, a protector ; the Arabic *bá*, nobility, and the Turkish *báshá*, a lord or master, may have a similar origin. The Sanskrit *pitri*, father, becomes *padar* or *pidar* in Persian, which by phonetic corruption, changes to *piyar*, whence comes *pír*, an old man, a reverend senior, and *pírana*, "elderly."

The base *pí*, besides its subjective sense of " nourish," was also applied to the object,—the one nourished, and so assumed in Sanskrit the form *pu-tra* a nursling, a child, *pu-er*, a b-oy, derivatives of which are found in the Latin *pu-ella*, *pu-ellaris*, *pu-ellariter*, *pu-ellarius*, *pu-ellascere*, *pu-ellatorius*, *pu-elliter*, *pu-ellula*, *pu-erascere*, *pu-eraster*, *pu-erculor*, *pu-erigenus*, *pu-erilis*, *pu-erilitas*, *pu-eritia*, *pu-ernius*, *pu-erperus*, *pu-eriliter*, *pu-erulur ;* and the Spartan ποῖρ for παῖς = πυερα, a girl.

The following Table exhibits the possible phonetic corruptions of the word *father* in 200 languages. It it designed to show the gradual series of modifications by which words, apparently quite different, may have been evolved from each other. It will be seen that Turanian and Semitic words find their natural places among undoubted derivatives of the Aryan *father.* The *outx* of the Canadian Indians is quite as much like *father* as the Bulgarian *otskve*, and the only

* M. Pictet, in "Les Aryas Primitifs," says (p. 348) that the bases *pa* and *ma* are " répandus au loin dans le monde entier."

reason for considering it to have had an independent origin, is that, from want of a literature, we are unable to trace its history, but in the case of the Bulgarian word we can do so. It will be thought that we are mixing two distinct bases together by including the forms of *táta* under those of *pitri*, and this may, in fact, be the case. We have included them because it is possible to suppose them parts of one series in a way indicated by their arrangement in the Table; and we must leave this arrangement to gain what weight it can. - Enough has been said in different parts of this book to show that words undergo strange transformations by mere phonetic corruption. It is worthy of remark, also, that the Greek language possesses all three forms of our arrangement πατήρ, τέττα, and ἄττα. The obscure Turanian languages, furthermore, still await the investigation of scholars like the brothers Grimm, to point out the laws of permutation at work in their midst. We all know the great results which followed when Humboldt shed the light of his genius on the Kawi language.

PI-TRI = " the nourisher."

N.B.—The letter P, at times, becomes *flatus-asper*,
then *asper*, and finally disappears.

1. *Sanskrit*   -   - pi-tri.
2. *Zend*   -   - - pai-tar.
3. *Persian*   -   - pa-dar.
4. *Algerian* -   - - pé-dér.
5. *Hindi* -   -   - pi-tâ, bâp.
6. *Bengali* -   - . - pi-tâ.
7. *Singhalese*   - pi-ta.
8. *Tamil*   -   - - bi-ta, appa.
9. *Greek* -   -   - πα-τὴρ.
10. *Latin*   -   - - pa-ter.
11. *Italian*   -   - pa-dre, pa-pa.
12. *Spanish* -   -   - pa-dre.
13. *Catalan*   - ·   - pâ-re.
14. *Portuguese*   - - pâ-y, pâ-e.
15. *Sardinian*   -   -· pâ-re.
16. *Gascony* -   -   - pâi-re.
17. *French*   -   - pè-re, pa-pa.
18. *Flemish* -   -   - pe-ar.
19. *Old Rhetian* -   - pā-pa.
20. *Kyriaks (Syria)*   - pé-pé.
21. *Turkish*   -   - pé-pé, bâ-shâ, bâ-bâ.
22. *Tatar*   -   - - ba-ba.
23. *Shilah (Africa)*   - bā-ba.
24. *Leodic (Styria)*   - pe-er.
25. *Lithuanian*   -   - pâ-ts.

26. *Slavonic (Hellenic)* bâ-t.
27. *Gujarâti* - - bâ-p.
28. *Grisons* - - - bâ-b.
29. *Frioul* - - pâ-ri.
30. *Frisian* - - - pâ-p, heine.
31. *Gaelic* - - pa-erinthele.
32. *Wallachian* - - pa-renthie, tatul.
33. *Javanese* - - - pâ-man, tama.
34. *Tranquebar* - - pi-tave.
35. *Malabar* - - - pi-tawe.
36. *Thibetan* - - - pâ, jha-phu.
37. *Tonquin* - - - phu.
38. *Siamese* - - - poo.
39. *Japanese* - - - fi-to [a man].
40. *Chinese* - - - fu.
41. *Frisian d'Hin.* - - fe-er.
42. *Gothic* - - - fa-dar, â-tta.
43. *Anglo-Saxon* - -fa-ðer, vâ-tter.
44. *English* - - - fa-ther.
45. *French Theod.* - fa-der.
46. *Runic* - - - fa-dder.
47. *Swedish* - - fa-der.
48. *Danish* - - - fa-der.
49. *Icelandic* - - fa-der.
50. *Orkney Islands* - fa-vor.
51. *Scotch* - - fa-der, na-thairn.
52. *German* - - - va-ter, vâder.
53. *Dutch* - - va-der, va-yer.
54. *Norwegian* - - va-der.
55. *Walcheren* - - vâ-yer.

o

56. *Swiss* - - - vee-r.
57. *Manx* - - â-yr.
58. *Armenian* - - ha-yr.
59. *Polish* - - o-yere, o-cziecz.
60. *Lusatian (Saxony)* vee-r, vo-shi.
61. *Vandals* - - vo-shc, wo-tz, wo-schzi.
62. *Slavonic (Bohem.)* o-tsche.
63. *Muscovian* - - o-tsche.
64. *Krim Tatary* - - a-tscha.
65. *Bohemian* - - e-ttse, o-tez.
66. *Russian* - - - o-tetsu, pa-pa.
67. *Anc. Slave* - - o-tĭtsĭ.
68. *Servian* - - - o-tse.
69. *Dalmatian* - - o-tse.
70. *Croatian* - - o-tse.
71. *Illyrian* - - o-taz.
72. *Bulgarian* - - o-tskve.
73. *Carniola* - - o-tze.
74. *Coptic (modern)* - jô-t.
75. *Esthonian* - - i-ssa (cf. Bohem. *ettse*.)
76 *Finnish* - - - i-sa.
77. *Lappish* - - i-sa.
78. *Canada (Indians)* ou-tx, ai-stan.
79. *Algonkin (New Eng.)* o-shé, nou-scé (comp. Vandal *voshe*).
80. *Virginia (Indians)* â-oosh.
81. *Chippeway* - - o-sah.
82. *Potewotami* - - o-sah.
83. *Shawnee* - - och-sa.
84. *Miami* - - - ox-sahé, okhsakh.

85. *Pian (Illinois)* - os-sah.
86. *Manticoké* - - os-sac, oschsch.
87. *Massachusetts* - osh.
88. *Ottawa* - - oss.
89. *Micmacs* - - ouch.
90. *Lennap* - - och.
91. *Delaware* - - ook.

From the Chinese *fu*, Tonquin *phu*, and Siamese *poo*, we are led to the following series :—

92. *Ahom* - - - po.
93. *Khamti* - - po.
94. *Laos* - - - po.
95. *Mikir (Bengal)* - po.
96. *White Kharen* - pa.
97. *Kuki (Bengal)* - pa.
98. *Miû (Bengal)* - pâ.
99. *Kami* - - pâ-ei.
100. *Khyeng* or *Shou* pau.
101. *Red Kharen* - phay.
102. *Manipuri* - - ipâ.
103. *Ho (Bengal Pres.)* âpu.
104. *Korwa* - - âpu.
105. *Angami Nága* - apû.
106. *Arung Nága* - apco.
107. *Mithan Nága* - apâ.
108. *Tablung Nága* - opàh.
109. *Murmi (Bengal)* âpâ.
110. *Bodo* or *Kachari* aphâ.
111. *Burmese* - - â-pa, phâ-e.
112. *Madagascar* - - amp-roy.

113. *Kumi (Bengal)* - amp-o.
114. *Hottentot* - - amb-up, ho.
115. *Limbu (Bengal)* amba.
116. *Tungusic* - - am-inmoen.
117. *Tulu* - - - am-me.
118. *Tatar* - - âm-a, a-tcha.
119. *Talain (Bengal)* - mâ.
120. *Rabbinical Heb.* - an.
121. *Samaritan* - ab.
122. *Hebrew* - - ab.
123. *Pehlevi* - - ab, âb-ida.
124. *Syriac* - - - ab-oh.
125. *Moresque* - - âb-bo.
126. *Arabic* - - - ab-a, ab-u.
127. *Samoyed* - - âb-am.
128. *Chaldæan* - - âb-ba.
129. *Amharic* - . â-ba.
130. *Barbary* - - â-ba.
131. *Abyssinian* - ab-ba.
132. *Melindan (Zanz.)* ab-a.
133. *Ethiopic* - - ab-i.
134. *Mech (Bengal)* - appa.
135. *Tamil* - - appa.
136. *Butia* - - - appâ.
137. *Kharria (Bengal)* appâ.
138. *Mundari* - - appu.
139. *Telugu* - - abba.
140. *Kuri* or *Muasi* - abba, bâ.
141. *Anka* or *Hrusso* abba, âu.
142. *Dophla (Bengal)* âbo.

143. *Dhimal (Bengal)* âbâ.
144. *Garo* - - âjâ.
145. *Lepcha* - - abô.
146. *Rajmahali Pahari* abu.
147. *Kandh(Beng.Pres.)* abu, âbâ.
148. *Pani-Kocch* - - awa.
149. *Kiranti* - - bâ.
150. *Santâl* - - bâbâ, âpu.
151. *Juanga* - - bâbâ.
152. *Abor (Bengal)* - bâbâ.
153. *Miri (Bengal)* - bâbâ.
154. *Oraon* - - - baba.
155. *Gond* - - baba.
156. *Ramgarh* - - bûba.

Looking at such words as the Gothic *fadar* (No. 42.), which, by loss of the spiritus asper, becomes *átta*, we may understand how such forms as the following are possible varieties of the same word:

157. *Gothic* - - â-tta.
158. *Germ. Swiss* - ae-tti.
159. *Huron (Canada)* aih-taba.
160. *Biscayan* - - â-ta.
161. *Persian* - - a-tâ, i-tâ.
162. *Cantabrian* - a-tta.
163. *Greek* - - - ă-ττα.
164. *Epirote (Albany)* a-tti.
165. *Latin* - - - a-tta.
166. *Welsh* - - - a-thair, tad.
167. *Irish* - - na-thair, ai-te, oi-de.
168. *Hungarian* - - a-tyank.

169. *Kalmuck* - - à-tey.
170. *Ossetian* - - a-dà.
171. *Siberian* - ᴗ a-tai.
172. *Egyptian Hierog.* a-t°w.
173. *Frisian (Germ.)* - hei-ta.
174.   *Do. (Holland)* - hei-tā.
175.   *Do. (common)* - hei-te.
176. *Vaudois* - - ha-rme.
177. *Carib* - - - ha-ba.
178. *Tangut (Thibet)* hā-pa.
179. *Khasi (Bengal)* - ky-pa.
180. *Chutia* - - tsi-pa.
181.. *Greenland (North)* u-bia, uttata.

The Turanian forms *appa* and *abba*, which are
clearly the representatives of *pa, pu, fu,* readily suggest
how, through some such change as produced the Gond
baba, might have arisen the Khari Nâga *tabâ;* the
analogue of the Livonian *tabes,* the Cornish *taz,*
Breton *tad,* Esthonian *taat,* and the whole of the series
given below :—

182. *Khari Naga* - ta-bâ.
183. *Livonian* - - ta-bes.
184. *Werulic (Germ.)* ta-bes.
185. *Prussian* - - the-wes.
186. *Courlandish* - te-we, te-ws.
187. *Breton* - - taa-d, ta-d.
188. *German Jews'* - thâ-daer.
189. *Cambro-Breton* - ta-d.

190. *Canarese* - - tan-dé.
191. *Breton (Armoric)* ta-d.
192. *Cornish* - - ta-z.
193. *Angolan (Africa)* to-t.
194. *Guaranees (Brazil)* tu-ba, ru-ba.
195. *Mexican* - - ta-tli.
196. *Vilela* - - - ta-te.
197. *Moxa* - - ta-ta.
198. *Sapibocona* - - ta-ta.
199. *Nose-pierced tribe* to-ta.
200. *Anc. German* - to-to.
201. *Frisian* - - to-te.
202. *Lithuanian* - - tē-tis.
203. *Albanian* - - tá-tē.
204. *Karelian* - - ta-to.
205. *Mordvinian* - ta-tai.
206. *Esthonian* - - taa-t.
207. *Polish* - - ta-tus'.
208. *Russian* - - tia-tia.
209. *Erse* - - tai-didh.
210. *Irish* - - - dai-d.
211. *Ossetian* - - da-da.
212. *Laghmani (Afgh.)* tâ-tiyâ.
213. *Greek* - - τέ-ττα.
214. *Latin* - - - ta-ta.
215. *Bohemian* - - ta-ta.
216. *Servian* - - ta-ta.
217. *Bengali* - - tâ-t.
218. *Hindi* - - - tâ-t.
219. *Sanskrit* - - tâ-ta.

·The onomatopic base of all the foregoing different forms of *pí*, is to be found in the noise produced by the in-sucking of the lips, naturally accompanied by a sound like that represented by the letter *p*, preceded by a vocalizing element. We, therefore, describe it as ·*p*, placing a dot in front.

CONCLUSION.

ONOMATOPS are the natural and inevitable expression of the conscious Soul, prompted by the secret impulses of life and motion. The onomatop places before the philosophical mind the first springs of human civilization and advancement, the first humanizing influence, —that which first *marked* the divergence of man and brute. " Man speaks, and no other animal has uttered a word."—*Max Müller*. Speech is the surprizing accomplishment that gives to man his pre-eminence, gives him the power to clothe his thoughts in form,— almost in substance,*—it is even more correct to say that it gives to man the very power of thought itself. Philosophers, at times, go widely astray in their deductions by gliding imperceptibly over primary considerations, and by plunging at the very first into the more recondite parts of a subject. This is the case with what is called Mental Philosophy. It has never yet been perceived that the mental phenomena with which we are familiar can have no existence without

* " Words are living powers, are the vesture, yea, even the body, which thoughts weave for themselves."—*Trench, The Study of Words*, 4th ed , p. 2.

Language.[a] Can we even imagine a being thinking out one thought to a conclusion without the use of words, either pictured to the mind or uttered with the voice? This is a matter of experience. Immediately we begin to think a stream of *words* passes through the mind and presents the idea in varying forms, until it assumes the shape we finally approve, and then we give it utterance in audible language. Mental opera-tions, before the formation of articulate speech, must have been confined to mere sensation, such as the lower creation universally manifests. Locke considered man distinguished from the brute by the possession of *general ideas;* and that great thinker did not fail to see that *Language* plays an important part in the build-ing up and development of our ideas ; but the real part that Language plays, and the extent to which it operates in the whole of our conceptions, he could never accurately determine. Horne Tooke was able to see that what Locke called general *ideas* were in reality but general *terms.* This astute writer remarks that it is an easy thing " upon Locke's own principles, and a physical consideration of the senses and mind, to prove the impossibility of the composition of ideas;" [b] that is, that comprehensive ideas could not exist in the mind until a term or vocable existed, enabling the

---

[a] " We cannot reason without words."—*Bunsen, Christianity and Mankind,* vol. iv. p. 127. The same author, very inconsist-ently, in the preceding page speaks of language as " the product of reason."

[b] Diversions of Purley, vol. i. p. 38

mind to project it, so to speak, upon the retina of its
apprehension.   Onomatops are, indeed, the analogues
in speech, of those projections imagined by great archi-
tects in the active moments of their genius.   Our
reasoning, indeed, leads to the conclusion that connected
thought of any kind is impossible without words, with
which alone it can be carried on.   This being so, all
mental philosophy resolves itself into the history of
language,—the first onomatop was parent to the first
thought, and the parent of all that has resulted from
man's mental power.   Horne Tooke thus clearly expresses himself : " The business of the mind, as far as
regards language, appears to me to be very simple.
It extends no further than to receive impressions, that
is, to have sensations or feelings. *What are called its
operations, are really the operations of language.*" [a]
As we have already said, in our opinion, any connected
thought is impossible without language, and therefore
Reason itself is the offspring of the Word.   MAN
SPOKE BEFORE HE REASONED.   Emotional sound was
first stamped with unvarying sense at a time when the
man-animal was instigated by no other sentiments
than those of animal desire and animal aversion.   The
gregarious impulse so conspicuous in man created the
need for this unvarying sense, and the habit of living
and acting in communities increased the number and
definiteness of uttered sounds, as the necessity for
communicating impressions enlarged.   A long period

[a] Diversions of Purley, vol. 1. p. 51.

must have elapsed before sounds settled by usage into fixed signs of ideas, and the merely animal state must have been, during the interim, considerably departed from by the humanizing tendencies of the speaking creature. Nevertheless this rudimentary stage, in which a few sounds possessed the force of true vocables, was far too imperfect to allow of the expression, and therefore of the conception, of anything beyond sensuous impressions. It was phraseological colloca- tion of vocables, first, probably, resulting from a neces- sity for discriminating similar but not identical objects, that gave birth to what is now called the Reasoning faculty. The desire to discriminate would impel the creature to utter two vocables each expressive of some characteristic, the union of which two vocables, pro- ducing a third and compound word (as in the modern *sea-horse, dog-fish*),—would be the germ of the art of Reasoning, that is, the combination of simple proposi- tions. This theory is not inconsistent with itself ; for no higher process than perception is involved in so compounding words. The speaking creature looks at an object in the water,—"it is dog," is the impres- sion; but still looking on it is seen not to walk like the other beings generally so called, but moves like a fish. "It is fish," now the creature perceives ; and to communicate the impression he repeats the names of the two creatures whose ideas have been aroused at sight of the strange object.* The development of this

---

* See the remarks of Dr. Dan. Wilson, quoted p. 46.

process brought about the categorical arrangement of words in a sentence, and with that the power of reasoning, and all the mental operations of which we are now so proud. For further illustrations of this process the reader is referred to the Introduction, under the Laws of Combination, p. 21 *et seq.*

How much, then, of human interest centres in our present inquiry! We seek that which gave to man the power to construct telegraph, railway, and palace, the power to dig the mine, to navigate the deep, to scan the starry heavens, and to meditate on and to subdue the powers of nature to his use. It is the use of articulate sounds that made man master of the tempest and the sea, master of the lightning, and of the magnetic and invisible electric powers, master of the etherial regions, and of all comprised in the material world. All the achievements of man are based upon the communication of ideas, by means of which succeeding generations amplify and perfect the works of their predecessors; and all communication of ideas is impossible without the λόγος, which both Greek and Hindû so justly reverenced.

But as all animate creation emits sound, how shall we discriminate the human sounds so pregnant with germinative power, from the sounds of the horse, the dog, the elephant, &c.? This presents at once the highest problem in linguistic science, and in a few words we boldly state that· *there is no natural and intrinsic difference between the sounds of the brute and the words of the man,*—the difference is one merely of application. The human mind is what botanists would call a "sport" in animal creation, bringing with it the sense of dissatisfaction or discontent. The lower creation are content in their operations, and are free from a restless impulse to change; man alone is for ever discontented, and is for ever striving to improve or change his condition. At first a mere mental idiosyncrasy fostered by the material (or physical) advantages it procured, and developed by succeeding courses of descendants, each of which by employment of the faculty would exaggerate it by the common laws of nourishment and growth, — as the blacksmith's arm, the dancer's leg, and the philosopher's brain are exaggerated by the hypertrophy arising from constant use. Man was first differentiated from the brute by a peculiar, and, may be, accidental* modification of cerebral matter, which under favourable circumstances succeeded in establishing itself as a permanent condition of being. It is from this peculiarity, which at first need have been but little above sensation, that man, emerging from his primal animal character, would *feel* the advantage of association, and association would of itself occasion the natural sounds he uttered in common with the brute, to be utilized as a means of arresting the attention, or calling to, or urging on associates, these actions being prompted by the acquired desire for change. It is generally

---

* The word "accidental" is here employed in the sense in which it may be said of an unusual or monstrous vegetable growth.

admitted, that all arts and sciences had their origin in the pressing wants of barbarous society ; and it is easy to see that language also is only an " accomplishment "—(it is never inherited, but always personally acquired)—which was gradually brought to the state in which we find it. It is not peculiar in its liability to change; for the whole realm of nature and of art continually progresses. The animals and plants of to-day are not the same as those of the geological epochs,—the men of to-day are not the men of only 2000 years ago,—not only are they changed in language, but in habits, dress, food, and general appearance. "The analogy," says Bunsen,[a] "of the development which proceeds from inorganic to organic life, and in organic life from unconsciousness to consciousness and individuality, with the development of mind, as demonstrably exhibited in the progress of language, that is to say, in the history of the deposit of mind, is very striking." That great scholar then divides language into a *primitive* and inorganic or crystalline formation, every word having the power of totality in it, being neither noun, verb, nor attribute ; a *secondary* or vegetable formation, in which words exhibit a power of change according to genera and species ; and he shows that "finally, the words of the spirit, denoting the relation of one thought and sentence to another, are developed, and give expression to the agency of the mind upon itself." Professor

[a] "Christianity and Mankind," vol iv. p. 134.

Pott held it to be conceivable that the developed. and artificial languages were preceded by a state of the greatest simplicity and entire absence of inflexions; and Professor Max Muller adds that " it is absolutely impossible that it should have been otherwise." [a] The simple uninflected sounds are the primordial onomatops which man first interchanged with his fellow man, as a means of communicating his sensations. How long such a process was continued before the animal ejaculations were consolidated by habit into conventional vocal telegraphy it is impossible to say ; but thus much is clear that the first sound uttered for the purpose of communicating perception or desire, as differing from mere animal sensation, was the first Word—the basis of man's pre-eminence—the perennial spring of sublime thought—nay, the very life of thought itself—the mighty and soul-giving λόγος !

[a] Science of Language, Part I., p. 260.

APPENDIX.

THE LANGUAGES OF DARDISTAN, AND THEIR BEARING ON THE PRESENT INQUIRY.

No account of language can now pretend to scientific completeness which fails to notice, and neglects to incorporate the results of the discoveries of Dr. Leitner into the dialects of Dardistan, Kashmir, Little Thibet, Ladak, Zanskar, &c. That eminent linguist has laboured earnestly and · enthusiastically, — enduring privations, undergoing fatigue, hunger, exposure, — and has risked life itself by wandering among hordes of semi-savages in order that he might contribute sound and perfectly reliable material to philological science.

The scene of Dr. Leitner's labours is one of the greatest interest, for all history and tradition point consentiently to that district as the original home of the Aryan race, if not the very birth-place of the human kind. The result of Dr. Leitner's researches strikingly confirms the traditions of antiquity in this

P

respect;—it is scarcely too much to say that the facts which that excellent scholar has brought to light are of themselves sufficient to establish the Central Asian origin of the Sanskritic family of languages even had not a single tradition of the circumstance lived to our days. Dr. Leitner says, and he has excellent grounds for so saying, "it is my impression from an inquiry into Dardu verbal and other forms that these languages are the dialects from which the Sanskrit was perfected." The extreme importance and engrossing interest of Dr. Leitner's discoveries will be readily admitted if there be only *primá facie* grounds for such a conclusion ; but, as will be seen further on, the Dardu dialects possess an inherent interest apart from this consideration.

We have reserved what we have to say on this matter for a separate heading, because the discovery of the languages of Dardistan is altogether too recent an event to lead us to expect that incidental references to the dialects of that district would be readily apprehended by our readers. We take it that words cited from the Shinâ, Arnyiâ, Khajunâ, Kalâsha-Mânder, &c., without further explanation, would convey but little meaning to the minds of even well-informed philologists. We therefore propose to say a few words here that will tend to show how admirably the languages Dr. Leitner has brought to light support and illustrate the conclusions to which we have already arrived.

But first let us fix these languages in space. The district occupied by the Dardu races is close to the.

spot to which legend and history alike point as the
very cradle of the human race,—a phrase which
means, if we may venture to translate the language
of mythology into the language of philosophy, that
the spirit of enterprize and of unsatisfied desire which
has spread civilization over so large a portion of the
earth, had its rise among the people who, in extremely
antique times, occupied the spot which is now known
as Dardistan. This small triangle of land at the
extreme north of Affghanistan, with Badakshan on
the one side and Kashmîr on the other, from its
inaccessible and remote position, was far out of reach
of the general current of history, and its inhabitants
may fairly be supposed to have there lived on unaffected by the progress of their congeners, and even
unknown to all but the wild tribes of Tatary and
Turkistan.

Having thus indicated the position of these Dards
upon the map, we will now, before proceeding to
fortify our former statements with the help of their
languages, bring forward a few facts calculated to
establish the true position of these dialects in the
complex of human speech. There can be no doubt
that the Dardu races are members of the Aryan
family,—the vocabulary and grammar both proclaim
it; and when we reflect on the isolated position of the
Dardu tribes and their unsophisticated manner of
living, which there is every reason to believe has
been unaffected by the whirlwind of changes that has
again and again swept over more accessible portions

of the earth, we shall then see that the languages
of these primitive tribes furnish material of the first
importance as regards the inquiry upon which we are
now engaged. In support of these assertions we will·
compare some Dardu words with their equivalents
in Sanskrit, Hindî, &c., which will, we think, make
manifest the interesting nature of Dr. Leitner's
labours. We shall first give the ordinary numerals.

	One.	Two.	Three.	Four.	Five.	Six.	Seven.	Eight.	Nine.	Ten.
Indic:—										
Hindí.	ek	do	tin	chár	pánch	chhah	sát	áth	nau	das
Bengali.	eko	du-i	tin	chári	pánch	chhay	sát	át	nay	daś
Gujaruti.	ek	be	taraṇ	cheár	pánch	chha	sát	áth	nau	das
Persian.	yak	dú	sih	chahár	panj	shash	haft	hasht	nuh	dah
Sanskrit.	eka	dwi	tri	chatur	panchan	shash	saptan	ashṭan	navan	daśan
Dardu:—										
Ghilghiti.	eyk	do	tré	tshar	poñ	shá	sath	átsh	nau	dáy
Astori.	eyk	du	tshé	tshar	pòsh	shá	sath	asht	nau	dáy
Kalásha.	ék	dú	tré	tcháu	pondj	shó	sátt	asht	nò	dash
Arnyiá.	í	djú	tróy	tshōr	pōntsh	tshoi	sòt	osht	ñò	djosh

It is clear from an examination of this list that the
Dardu languages can in no respect be considered as
derived from the spoken languages. of the north of
India, as many of the forms are obviously more primitive than those now current in Hindustan. By the
word " primitive" we do not mean simply more like
the Sanskrit prototype, because we are fully persuaded
that the Sanskrit itself is a derivative, or, more properly,
a scholarly elaboration of some barbarous tongue, the ·
living form of which may yet be discovered, if, indeed,
the languages we are now treating of be not the very
same.   Our use of the word "primitive" implies that
the Indian forms of words are phonetic corruptions of
more complex forms which are found in Sanskrit and
also in Dardu ; and therefore the latter could not be
derived from the. Hindî, &c., on the common sense
principle that a word having become corrupt, cannot,
by further corruption, approach nearer to the form
whence it started.   Hence it follows that the Ghilghiti *átsh*, the Astori *asht*, the Kalásha *asht*, and the
Arnyiá *osht*, approaching closely to the Sanskrit *ashṭan*,
represent a phase of language decidedly more antique
than the Hindî and Gujaratî *áṭh*, &c.   Similar reasoning applies to the Ghilghiti *tré*, the Kalásha *trè*,
and the Arnyiá *tróy*, which, by retaining the letter
r found in the Sanskrit *tri*, prove incontestably that
they could not have been derived from the Hindî
and Urdû *tín*, or the Bengalî *tin*, or from any other
dialect in which that letter had once been elided.
Even the Gujaratî *taraṇ*, although retaining the *r*,

is obviously no channel by which *tri* could become *trè*. In Arnyiá, as a remarkable fact, we meet with the letter *i* only as the exponent of unity, which our previous inquiry (p. 184) led us to announce as the ultimate base of all the many diverse words found upon the earth with that meaning. We have now a distinctly Aryan language preserving, or presenting, a form the onomatopic simplicity of which rivals the Chinese.

But it may not unfairly be said that the digits form but a slender foundation on which to establish the independent character of a whole cluster of languages. To show that all parts of the Dardu languages present features of a more primitive nature than do the vernaculars of Hindustan, we will cite other examples of nouns, adjectives, and verbs. And, first, we will compare the substantive verb as follows :—

As = " to exist."

	Arnyiá.	Sanskrit.	Persian.	Pálí.	Prákrit.	Bengálí.	Hindí.
am	asùm	asmi	hastam	asmi, amhi	. . .	âchchhi	
Thou art.	asùs	asi	hastî	asi	. . .	âchchhis	
He is	asùr	asti	hast	atthi	atti, achchhi	âchchhe	Quite lost.
We are	asúsi	'smas	hastîm	asma, amha	. . .	âchchhi	
You are	asúmi	'stha	hastîd	attha	achchhadho	âchchho	
They are	asuni	'santi	hastand	santi	achchhanti	âchchhen	

Here it will be seen that the Arnyiá form preserves the base as in every person, although the vowel of that base has been elided even in Sanskrit. As it is unreasonable to suppose that the English is, or Latin est, could ever have been derived from such forms as the Italian è, so would it be equally unreasonable to hold that the Arnyiá as-, or the Persian has-, could have been derived from the Indian equivalent, which in even the early Prákrits had been corrupted to *atti* or *achchhi*, and now throughout a large part of Hindustan has ceased to be employed at all.

The verb "to be," "exist," tells a very similar tale. In Sanskrit the base is *bhú*, A. S. *beon*, Gaelic *beo*, "alive," Irish *bioth*, "life," Gr. βιος, "life," closely akin to the French *vie*, the Latin *vita*; *v* and *b* being frequently interchangeable. The present tense of this base *bhú* is thus conjugated in the Khajuná language:—

Bhu = "to be,"

	Khajuná.	Sanskrit.	Prákrit.	Hindí.
I am	já bá	bhavâmi	homi	hún
Thou art	um bá	bhavasi	hosi	hai
He is	ai bá	bhavati	hodi	hai
We are	hurtu (?) báu	bhavâmas	...	hain
You are	má báu	bhavatha	...	hain
They are	menig (?) báu	bhavanti	honti	hain

Here again we find the full consonant remaining in a Dardu language when it has been softened to the letter *h* in Prâkrit and the modern languages of India (cf. Mahrattî *honen*, " to be ").

We will now give two tenses from two verbs in the Kalásha dialect which will satisfactorily establish the close accordance of the conjugational system of the Dardu languages with that of the Sanskrit. The verbs we select are *tshishtik*, " to stand," and *juk*, " to eat." The *ik* or *uk* in these words is the sign of the infinitive, leaving *tshisht* and *j* as the respective bases : of these *tshisht* is clearly the same as the Sanskrit *tishth*, the base of what are called the " conjugational" tenses of the verb *sthá*, " to stand"; and the *j* is the Sanskrit *ad*, English *eat*, the *d* passing into *dj*, and then into *j*, as *Deva* becomes *Jovis* (p. 163).

	Kalásha.	*Sanskrit.*
I stand	a tshishtim	tishthâmi
Thou standest	tu tshishti	tishthasi
He stands	se tshishteu	tishthati
We stand	abi tshishtik	tishthâmas
You stand	tuaste tshishta	tishthatha
They stand	eledrús[a] tshishten	tishthanti

[a] This word brings to mind the Turkish *anlar*, " they." If it be the same word it offers a notable instance of mixed Grammar.

	Kalásha.	*Sanskrit.*
I eat	a jum	admi
Thou eatest	tu jus	atsi [ad + si]
He eats	se jui.	atti [ad + ti]
We eat	abi juk	admas
You eat	tuaste júa	attha [ad + tha]
They eat	eledrús jún	adanti

There is much phonetic corruption apparent in the above tenses, still the similarity of principle in the two languages is apparent. The past tenses are even more remarkable, because they preserve the initial augment of Sanskrit, which has completely passed away from modern India. The base *j* now becomes *sh* by a phonetic change, such as *ja* = *cha* = *sha*.

	Kalásha.	*Sanskrit.*
I stood	a a-tshishtis	a-tishtham
Thou stood'st.	tu a-tshishti	a-tishthas
He stood	se a-tshishteu	a-tishthat
We stood	abi a-tshishtimi	a-tishthâma
You stood	tuaste a-tshishtili	a-tishthata
They stood.	eledrús a-tshishtani	a-tishthan
I ate	a-shis [? a + ashis]	âdam [a + adam]
Thou atest	tu a-shi	âdas [a + adas]
He ate	so a-shu	âdat [a + adat]

	Kalásha.	*Sanskrit.*
We ate	abi a-shimi	âdam [a + adam]
You ate	tuaste a-shili	âtta [a + ad + ta]
They ate	eledrus a-shin	âdan [a + adan]

It is most interesting to find this antique method of forming a past tense still surviving among an Aryan people of Central Asia.

Among nouns, &c., presenting forms decidedly more antique than those now current in Hindustan we select the following examples. The Sanskrit is placed first, next the Dardu forms, and finally the Pâlî, Hindî, and other Indian forms.

A "fish," is called in Sanskrit *matsya*, in Arnyiá and Kalásha *matzi*,—in Pâlî *machchho*, in Hindî, *machhlî, máhí, mín*.

A "hand," is in Sanskrit *hasta*, in Arnyiá *hòst*,—in Pâlî *hattho*, in Hindî *háth*, in Mahrattî *hát*.

The "head" is in Sanskrit *śiras*, in Zend *śírsha*,—in Ghilghiti *shìsh*, Astori and Kalásha *shish*,—Hindî *sir*, Persian *sar*.

"Lightning," Sans. *vidyut*, Ghilghiti *bitshus*,—Pâlî *vijjumá*, Prâkrit *vijjú, vijjulí*, Hindî *bijlí*, Mahr. *bíj*.

A "fly," Sans. *makshiká*, Ghilghiti *matshì*, Kalásha *mangajík*,—Pâlî *makkhiká*, Prâkrit *machchhiá*, Hindî *makkhí*.

A "bone," Sans. *asthi*, Ghilghiti *āti*, Kalásha *atì*,—Pâlî and Prâkrit *aṭṭhi*, Hindî *haḍḍí*.

The "eye," Sans. *akshi,* Ghilghiti *atchi,* Kalásha *atch,*—Pâlî *achchhi* or *akkhi,* Hindî *ánkh.*

The "sun," Sans. *surya,* Ghilghiti *súri,* Kalásha *suri,*—Prâkrit *sujjo* or *súro,* Hindî *súraj.*

The "lip," Sans. *oshṭra,* Kalásha *úsht,* Ghilghiti *onti,*—Bengalî *oshṭh,* Hindî *onṭh.*

A "crow," Sans. *káka,* Khajuná *káko,*—Pâlî *káko,* Hindî *kág.*

A "brother," Sans. *bhrátṛi,* Arnyiá *birār,*—Pâlî *bhátiko,* Hindî, *bhá-i.*

A "daughter," Sans. *duhitṛi,* Arnyiá *djùṛr,* Ghilghiti *dihh,*—Persian *dukhtar,* Pâlî *dhíṭá,* Prâkrit *dhí-á,* Hindî *dhiyá, dhí, dhíriyá.*

A "bear," Sans. *ṛiksha,* Ghilghiti *ìtch,* Kalásha *ìtz,*—Prâkrit *richchho,* Hindî *ríchh.*

"To-day," Sans. *adya,* Ghilghiti *átshu,* Astori *ash,* Kalásha *óndja,*—Pâlî *ajja,* Hindî *ánd* Mahrattî *áj.*

"Large," Sans. *vriddha,* Astori *baddo,*—Prâkrit *vaḍḍhako,* Hindî *baṛá, baṛhá.*

"Small," Sans. *kshudra,* Khajuná *djött,*—Pâlî *chuddho,* Hindî *chhoṭá.*

"Middle," Sans. *madhya,* Ghilghiti *majja,* Arnyiá *mújja,* Kalásha *mósthe* (? Sans. *madhya + stha,* mid-sta-tioned),—Pâlî and Prâkrit *majjho,* Hindî *manjhlá* or *manjholá,* Mahrattî *máj.*

"Behind," Sans. *paśchát,* Kalásha *pishto,* Ghilghiti *pittu,* Astori *pato,*—Persian *pasín,* Hindî *píchhá.*

A careful examination of the above words (which could easily be multiplied) will show that in every case the Dardu words are more primitive and complex in their character than are the representatives of the Indian vernaculars with which they are contrasted. The Pâlî and Prâkrit forms have hitherto been deemed the oldest forms derived from Sanskrit which we possess supplying a link between the language of the Vedas and the vernaculars now current in. India. The labours of Dr. Leitner have now brought to our notice a whole family of spoken languages which approach much nearer to the Sanskrit than anything to be found in the Pâlî or the Prâkrits. It is transparently clear that, if the Dardu languages be not themselves the ancient language from whence the Sanskrit, in common with the north Indian languages, were elaborated, they at least constitute phonetically an intermediate link between the Sanskrit on the one hand and the Pâlî on the other. Upon the latter ground only these Dardu languages are of .the greatest interest both to philologists and ethnologists.

A few words will now be given which possess, if possible, still greater interest than those already cited, because the Dardu words preserve forms closely akin to the old Sanskrit, which seem to be *entirely lost* to modern India. A few of such are the following :—

"Dog," Sans. *śwan*, Kalásha *sheon*, Ghilghiti *shú*. The Bengalî equivalent of this is *kukkur*, Hindî *kúkar* or *kuttá*, from a corrupt Sanskrit word *kukkura* of *kurkura*. When the word *śwan* is now used in India it is simply the old Sanskrit word artificially revived.

"Earth," Sans. *kshiti*, Arnyiá *tshuti*.

" Milk," Sans. *kshíra*, Arnyiá *tshìrr*, Kalásha *tshìrr*, Persian *shír*.

" Small," Sans. *súkshma*, Ghilghiti *tshùno*, Astori *tshuno*.

" Above," Sans. *adhi*, Ghilghiti *adje*. *Adhi* is still used as a preposition in India, but cannot be employed as a separate word. The Pâlí form, as a preposition, is *ajjh-*.

There is one word in the Dardu languages that suggests a whole history in itself. The word used to express the *right* hand side is, in the Ghilghiti language, *dachíni*. This word is the same as the Sanskrit *dakshiṇa*, the Pâlí and Prâkrit *dakkhiṇo*, the Hindí *dakhin* or *dáhiná*. The remarkable fact is that in all the languages of India, the equivalents of *dakshiṇa* mean not only the right hand side, but also the *south;* whereas, in the Ghilghiti language, this same word, while still expressing the right hand side, is used to distinguish the *north*. As we know that the *right* hand and *south* were considered identical, because the progenitors of the Hindû people entered India from the west, and advancing westward with the rising sun to the front, they had necessarily the southern country on the right hand side ; so we might infer that the Dards entered the land they now occupy from the *east*, having the *north* on the right hand side, the tradition of which still lives among them in this remarkable vocable. If further evidence should strengthen this assumption, it is not unreasonable to conjecture that the Dards in reality are the representatives of the primitive people from whom those we now call the Sanskrit-speaking races originally separated before penetrating the Hindukush, and before the Vedas were composed, or civilization itself had dawned. It is, furthermore, marvellous that one of these Dardu tribes still calls itself by the name "Arnyiá," which differs only in its nasal twang from "Aryiá" or "Ârya," the well-known name by which the Indo-Germanic peoples anciently distinguished themselves. If this ethnographical speculation prove correct, the Dardu languages would present us with a form of Aryan speech closely akin to, and possibly anterior in linguistic stratum than, the Sanskrit language itself; and which assumed its present shape unaffected by anything that took place in India. Whether there be any real ground for these speculations or not, we have undoubtedly made it evident that these interesting dialects are purely Aryan in character, and present forms more antique than those of the vernaculars of Hindustan, and therefore could not have been derived from the latter, but must have had an independent history.

Having thus established the relationship and primitive character of the Dardu languages, it will be evident that the circumstance that the Arnyiá *i* is the equivalent of the Chinese *'i*, and the Sanskrit *eka*, acquires a special significance. It tells us that these rude people who have, as we have seen, conserved many forms of an older stratum of language, have also in daily use as the exponent of unity the very simple articulation which our previous examination of modern dialects had led us to pronounce as the natural onomatop to express it. It is no less remarkable that the same sound *i* is also used among Dardu people to express "motion to a place";—thus the Kalásha people say *aya i* for "come, mother" (*aya* = mother). This is precisely what we concluded would be the case among a primitive people; and upon that onomatopic sound has been based the more developed form *é*, "come," in the Astori and Ghilghiti dialects, identical with the Latin *e-o*, and forming part of the series we have already given on p. 183, &c. We may thus claim to have tracked to its source the onomatop expressive of *motion*. The Dardu languages help us, also, to the onomatop upon which the ideas *forth, forward*, &c., were erected. This we have suggested (p. 182) is the mere puffing forward of the lips by the expulsion of air; but we adduced in evidence only such derivative forms as the Persian *pufídan*, "to blow," and the Sanskrit *phút*, an imitative noise. The Dardu languages, however, present us with the ono- matop we are seeking in its simple purity; thus, "to blow" or "puff" is, in Ghilghiti *phu tóki*, in Astori *phu teono*, in Arnyiá *phu-istai* (?), in Khajuná *phu- eti*, and in Kalásha *phu-she*. The syllables *tóki*, &c., are the Dardu words for the word "do" or "make;" so that the literal meaning is "make a *phu*," precisely in accordance with our previous statements. In the

Q

Astori and Khajuná dialects the word "fire" is also expressed by the same sound, no doubt from the puffing, noisy sounds emitted from burning timber.

The same sound *phu* or *pu* is found in words expressive of "expansion" in the languages of Dardistan, just as is the case in India; so that the Hindî *phúl*, "a flower," is matched by the Ghilghiti *phunérr*, "a flower," and the Astori *púsho*, "a flower." As in Sanskrit we find that a *fruit*, or that which *expands* out of the flower, represented by the sound *phala*, so do we find in Ghilghiti the same idea expressed by *phamúl*, in Astori by *phalamúl*, and in Khajuná by *phamùl*. A particular kind of fruit, "an apple," is called in Ghilghiti *phalá*, and in Astori *phaló*. All these words are obviously connected with the Sanskrit *phala* and *phalya*, and to the other words previously given under the word "Flower," that have a general sense of swelling, extension, or spreading out. The Dardu words for a "leaf," a spread out surface, as shown in the Ghilghiti *patu*, the Astori *pàttu*, and the Kalásha *prón*, help us to further examples to add to those given on p. 176. To the Hindî forms there given we may add the words *páti, pallá, parṇ, panná, pán,* all of which mean "leaf," and show how constantly a *fl*-at or in-*fla*-ted thing was expressed by some equivalent of *f·l* or *p·l*.

Turning to another onomatop, the history of which we have sketched at p. 26 *et seq.*, we find the Dardu languages express the throat and its operations by a guttural noise, which we represent by "*g*" as an ultimate base. The verb "eat" is in Ghilghiti *khà*, and in Astori *kha*, closely allied to the Hindî *khà-nà* and the Sanskrit base *khâd.* In the Introduction our object was merely to sketch the process of word-formation as revealed by our method of investigation. We made no attempt to trace the words there adduced through other than obvious channels ; so that it may be as well here to mention that our view of the guttural origin of words meaning "throat," &c., is not deduced solely from the few examples there adduced. The following Sanskrit bases, all of which mean "eat," "bite," are sufficient to show that we could say a great deal more on this subject :—With the *g* initial, *grî, gûr, gal, gras, glas, ghas;* with the *g* hardened to *k,* and the final sibilant changed to a cerebral, *krid, kud, kad, khed, khet;* the cerebral changing to a dental, *khâd khad;* and softening the initial, *kshad;* the initial still further softened to a palatal (as in the Eng. *chew,* Germ. *käuen*) gives us *char, charv, chash,* and the series *cham, chham, jam, jim, jham,* which are, obviously, only different intonations of one word. All these guttural exponents of the act of eating and swallowing suggest themselves as congeners of the Dardu form *kha,* and give rise to tribes of derivatives such as the Sanskrit *khâdana,* "food," *khâdin,* "biting," &c., &c., and also the base *khand,* "to bite," "to chew up," and afterwards, metaphorically, "to break," which then gave birth to the vocables *khanda,* "a piece," "portion" (literally

Q 2

"a bite"), and *khaṇḍana*, "destroying," "breaking into bits." Possibly, also, the base *khan*, "to dig," or "incise," with its derivatives *khani*, "a mine," Hindî *khá-i*, "a ditch," &c., arises from the same guttural base, as the *gnaw*-ing of food would not be inaptly represented by the gnawing or scratching into the ground in the very early days of engineering operations. Thus we here, by quite an independent process, arrive at the same conclusion as that given on p. 48, where we show that γράφω, "to draw" or "scratch," is a derivative of *gṛí*, "to eat;" and the change of meaning is not so great as that which turns the French *goût*, Italian *gusto*, Latin *gustus*, into the English dis-*gust*.   )

In support of our analysis of the word "Law," the Dardu languages offer us several words of much interest. The Arnyiá, for instance, offers Liyínni for "the tongue," like the Latin *lingua* (p. 143); and that which is smooth or po-*lish*-ed is called, in Kalásha, Lansht (Gr. λεία, p. 144). The "morning," when everything brightens and shines, is called, in Ghilghiti, Loshtáki, and in Astori Lóshte; and the *light* of a candle is called in Kalásha Lutsh (see p. 152). The same transference of the qualities of the object to the subject, which we remarked upon at p. 146, seems to underlie the Arnyiá Lole, "see, look," and the Ghilghiti Lishí, "spy." In the same way the alliance between that which is *light* or brilliant and that which is *light* or *slight* (see p. 136), is shown by

the Ghilghiti Lôko and Arnyiá Lótz, both meaning
"light," "not heavy;" while the *lax* character of the
base ·*l*· (p. 132) is exemplified by the Ghilghiti word
Láto, "low."

· The licking and smearing action of the tongue,
giving expression to the ideas of "painting," &c.
(see p. 144) is found in the Ghilghiti Likyár and
Astori Likhé, "to write" (Sans. *likh*); and *l* becoming
r, as we have so frequently seen, accounts for the
Ghilghiti *ranyito* and Astori *ranyíto*, "colour,"
"paint?" (Sans. *ranj, langh*).

: A long chapter might be written upon this form
of the base ·*l*·, as the Dardu forms for a particular
kind of colour, "red," are eminently suggestive.
The name of this bright, light, and vivid colour
is, in Ghilghiti *lòîlu*, in Astori *lolo*, and in Kalásha
latshéa,—suggesting at once the Persian *lál*, and the
Sanskrit *lohita* or *rohita*, the last word having also
the meanings "bLood," "*light*-ning," and "in-*flam*-
mation." This word Rohita is of itself sufficient to
show how words acquire new meanings with the
growing necessities of mankind; and it, furthermore,
enables us to see the bond of union between itself
and such other Sanskrit words as Rajas, "the bright
sky," Rajat, "white," Rajaka, "a washerman," one
who brightens soiled garments; Ranja, "a colour;"
Ranj, "to be attached," "de-*light*-ed," or "brightened"
(p. 147); Ranjana, "delighting," "colouring;" Ran-
jaka, "what stimulates pleasure;" Rati, "passion;"
Rama, "a lover;" Ramana, "delighting;" Rasa,

"taste," "*love*," "*lust*," what is *lus*-cious or *lus*-
trous ; R*aśmi*, "a *ray* of light" (Lat. L*aqueus*);
R*ukma*, "clear," "bright," "gold;" R*oka*, "light."
Closely akin to these ideas, all of which are connected
with that which is light, bright, vivid, and pleasing,
are other words also arising from the idea of brightening or the making bright, lustrous, or glowing ; such
as the Sanskrit R*osha*, "anger," from *rush*, "to be
angry" (cf. *rûsh*, "to decorate," "paint"); R*oshaṇa*,
"quicksilver"; R*u* or R*ud*, "to be angry"; R*uj*,
"to burn," "glow," "be in pain ;" and R*oga*,
"disease." All these ideas are fairly deducible from
the *ruddy* glow of anger, passion, or mental burning,
and of that which is light or bright. If further
evidence were needed it is supplied by the Sanskrit
word *lajjâ*, "shame," "bashfulness," from the base
laj, "to be ashamed," deduced from an older form *laj*,
"to shine," or "fry," "stew," "burn." We need
not pursue this matter any further. Any oriental
scholar will perceive the whole vocabulary of derivatives that flow from these suggestive bases ; and that
the argument we have sketched affords excellent
evidence of the primal unity of *raksh*, "to rule," and
laksh, "to shine" (p. 154).

We will add a few more words from the interesting
languages of Dardistan in illustration of other statements made in the text. The Ghilghiti *má*, Astori
mú, Arnyiá *ma*, Kalásha *mái*, and Khajuná *mi*, show
that these languages recognize ·*m*· as a fitting

exponent of personality, "me, my" (p. 35); and the Ghilghiti *tú*, *tùs*, the Astori *tù*, the Arnyiá *tú*, and the Kalásha *tái*, express that which is more remote from self by the consonant ·*t*·, "thee, thou, that one" (see pp. 36, 165). Another letter may here be mentioned as suggesting a history of its own, although not treated in the text. In Ghilghiti *anú* means "this," *áni* means "here," and *anú* means "he (if near)." We find the letter ·*n*· with similar meanings in Astori and Khajuná ; and throughout the inflexion of Ghilghiti pronouns this letter· *n* imparts a sense of nearness to every form of the base, which strongly reminds the inquirer of the Sanskrit *nah*, "to bind," the Latin *ne-xus*, and all that is *near, nigh*, and *next* in our own language.

In support of our etymology of *Jovem* (p. 163), we find in Ghilghiti *des*, and Astori *diès* for "day," forms which more closely approach the Sanskrit *divas* than does the Hindî *din*. "Heaven" is, also, in Kalásha *dí*, like the Sanskrit *div, dyu*, and *dyut*. Finally the word *ga*, meaning "also," "beside," in Ghilghiti, is also added to words as the equivalent of the English "and," showing that such ideas as "beside," "beyond," underlie the copula "and" (see p. 39), and not the notion of "equality," "evenness," as suggested by Mr. Wedgwood.

Another feature of much interest, to which we can here only allude, is the presence of pure onomatops in the languages of Dardistan, such as the verb *phu-tóki*, "to make a *phu*," "to blow," and *ho-tóki*, "to make

a *ho*," " to call " (cf. the Sans. *hwe*, " to call ").
These are really the kind of sounds from which first
language, and then languages, have been developed.
The sound *ho* as the exponent of " noise " naturally
came to be the name of particular. noise, so . that, in
Ghilghiti, this same sound *ho* is used for the noun
" voice " as well as for the verb " call." Possibly
tshukk tóki, " to make *tshukk*," " to be silent," " hush,".
is of similar character. These pertinent facts are more
conclusive as to the natural onomatopic origin of
language, than any amount of abstract reasoning;
and make the process by which words were formed
patent to the sense.

In conclusion we sincerely hope that Dr. Leitner
will continue his researches into the unknown districts
of Central Asia. He has already placed within the
reach of scholars eleven languages which were, before
his recent publications, either entirely unknown, or
known only by name. The material which Dr. Leitner
has already collected from the district of Dardistan,
and which will ever reflect honour on his name, is, as
we trust we have shown, of the greatest interest and
value to Comparative Philology, and to the history
of the human race.

INDEX TO ONOMATOPS.

[For references to the text in explanation of the examples here cited, see the Index Verborum.]

G="throat."

G onomatop of throat, swallow, eat, bite, incise, seize, grasp, drag, draw, engrave:—*gal*, "eat," Sans.; *gula, gustus*, Lat.; *gueule*, Fr.; *greedy, gorge, gnawing, disgust*, Eng.

G is aspirated :—*ghas*, "eat," Sans.

G becomes K :—*hrid, kad*, "eat," Sans.

G becomes K aspirated :—*hha*, "eat," Astori; *hhâ*, "eat," Ghilghiti; *khad*, "eat," *khand*, "bite," Sans.

G becomes CH :—*chew*, Eng.; *char, chash, cham*, "eat," Sans.

G becomes J :—*jam, jim, jham*, "eat," Sans.

G in other senses :—*grip, give*, Eng.; *grah*, "take," Sans.; γραφω, Gr.; *scribere*, Lat.; *écrire*, Fr.; *scribble, describe*, Eng.

G ultimately lost :—*write*, Eng.; *hri*, "take," Sans.

I="here."

I a definer of that which is proximate—self—unity—motion towards the speaker—motion in general :—*i*, "one," Arnyiá; *'i*, "one," Chin.; *I*, Eng.; *i*, "go," Sans.; *iha*, "here," Sans.; *ibi*, *idem*, Lat.; *ici*, Fr. When aspirated, *hi! hi!* Eng.; *hay*, "noise," Sans.

I becomes E:—*e*, "this," Beng.; *ë*, "go," Eg. Hier.; *eka*, "one," Sans.; *eo*, Lat.

I becomes Y:—*yu*, "I," Chinese; *yak*, "one," Pers.; *yûn* "thus," *yahán*, "here," Hindî.

I changes to other vowels:—*an, ace*, Eng.; *un*, Fr.; *wei*, "one," Kassia.

R+I:—*ri*, "go," Sans.; *river*, Eng.

V+R+I:—*vri*, "surround, choose," Sans. (*vi*, prep. "about," Sans.); *vridh*, "increase," Sans.; *vrish*, "rain," Sans.

VRI becomes VAR:—*varsha*, "cloud," Sans.

VRI becomes OR:—*orbs, orbit, optare, ordia*, Lat.

L="lick."

L onomatop of tongue, and the tongue's operations, licking, smearing, shining, brightening, liking, attaching, binding:—*lai*, "tongue," Cochin-Chinese; *lih*, "lick," Sans.; *lap*, "speak," Sans.; *lu'âb*, "viscosity," Arab.; *likh*, "write," Sans.; *lip*, Eng.; *light*, Eng.; *relish*, Eng.; *leash*, Eng.; *link*, Eng.; *la*, "law," Cochin-Chinese; *lex*, Lat.; *loi*, Fr., &c.

L becomes R:—*ruch*, "shine," Sans.; *ranj*, "attach," Sans.; *rub*, Eng. (p. 147).

S+L:—*slime*, Eng.; *sling*, Eng.; *slesha*, "union," Sans.; *salive*, Fr.; *saliva*, Eng.

S+P+L:—*splice*, Eng.; *splayed*, Eng.

G+L.—γλοσσα, Gr.; *gloss, glide, glue, grip*, Eng.; *argilla, gelidus*, Lat.; *glisser, gelé*, Fr.

K+L:—*kil*, "attach," Sans.; *cling, clew, clay, clamp, cramp*, Eng.; *coller*, Lat.

P+L:—*plain, prain*, "embrace," Sans.; *plaister, pleat, plug, plot*, Eng.; *plecta*, Lat.

B+L:—*bloc*, Fr.; *block, blot, braid, brace*, Eng.

F+L:—*flag, fleece, flossy, fold, fail, fool, foul, false,* Eng.

V+L:—*vale, vile, wool,* Eng.; *vallée,* Fr.

M+L:—*mlaid, mraid,* " foolish," Sans.

H+L:—*hlot,* Anglo-Saxon.

Z+L:—*galq,* " tongue," Arabic.

Vowels preceding L:—*il,* " lie," Sans.; *el,* " place," Sans.; *'als,* " sticking," Arab.; *oleum,* Lat.

P=" puff."

Ponomatop of puffing, blowing—a forward puff of breath, motion forward, extending, filling, broadening:—*phu,* " blow," Dardu; *puff,* Eng.; *phût,* " puff," Sans.; *pufidan,* " blow," Pers.; *pulsum,* Lat.; *push,* Eng.; [*foux,* O. Fr.; *pouls,* Fr.]

P becomes B:—*blow, breath,* Eng.

P becomes F:—*fore, forth,* Eng.; *fi,* " for," Arab.; *fuff,* " puff," Scotch.

P becomes V:—*vâ, vij,* " blow," Sans.; *vâyu,* " air," Sans.; *vent,* Fr.; *wind,* Eng.

P+R+I:—*pri,* " fill out" (*lit.* " go forth"), Sans.; *pra,* " forward," Sans.; *per, pro,* Lat.; *prâ,* " fill," Sans.; *pâr,* " completed," Pers.; *pûr,* " fill," Sans.; *pâl,* " nourish," Sans.

PRI becomes PL:—*plus,* Lat.; *plump,* Eng.; *emplir,* Fr.; *pleasure,* Eng.; *platt,* Germ.; *plank, pallet,* Eng.

PRI loses its liquid:—*pûsh,* " enlarge," Sans.; *pûsho,* "flower," Astori; *pahnâ,* " broad," Pers.; *pokhnâ,* " nourish," *pemî,* " lover," *pet,* " belly," *pân,* " leaf," Hindi; *pyâr,* " affection," *yâr,* " friend," Pers.

S+PRI:—*spri,* " please," Sans.; *spread, spade, span, expand,* Eng.

PRI is aspirated:—*phalya,* " flower," Sans.; *phâl,* " flower,"

Hindî; *phalâ,* "apple," Ghilghiti; *phár,* "fruit," Hindî; *pha-mul,* "fruit," Khajuná; *phánda,* "belly," Sans.

S+PRI aspirated :—*sphal, sphar,* "increase," *sphand,* "expand," *spund,* "play," Sans.

PRI becomes BL:—*bloom, blossom, bulb, blade, boil, ball, belly,* Eng. Also BR:—*broad, board,* Eng.; and loses its liquid :—*bauch,* Germ.

PRI becomes FL:—*fill, flower, floor, tin-foil, friend,* Eng.; *ansfullend,* Germ.; *folium, forma,* Lat.

P="suck."

P onomatop of in-sucking, drinking, nourishment, strengthening, power, lordship :—*pî, pá,* "suck," *payas,* "milk," Sans.; πιω, Gr.; *pino,* Lat.; *pînâ,* "drink," *pyás,* "thirst," Hindî. *Pabulum,* Lat.; *púd,* "food," Pers.; *pasture, pastry,* Eng. *Power,* Eng.; *puissant,* Fr.; *poti,* "lord," *pitri,* "father, the nourisher," *putra,* "son, the nourished," Sans.; *panah,* "protector," *pîr,* "old man," Pers.

S+P ;—*spout,* Eng.

S+P aspirated :—*sphíti, spháti,* "increase," *spháy,* "swelling," Sans.

P becomes B:—*bibo,* Lat.; *boire,* Fr.; *bee,* "the sucking creature," Eng.; *ba-tsi,* "bee," Japan.; *bshey,* "bee," Georg.; *beer,* Eng.

P becomes F :—*fung,* "drink," Chinese; *food, fodder, father,* Eng.

P becomes V, &c. :—*vin,* Fr.; *wine, water,* Eng.

T="that."

T onomatop of definition, that which is exterior to self, the second person, the other, there, beyond; as an intensifier, "down":—*the, he, thee, thou, that, there, two, twice, twisting, twinkling,* Eng.

T becomes D :—*dwi,* " two," Sans.; *duo,* Lat.; *duality, dupli-cation, duplicity, diverse,* Eng.; *div,* " twinkle," Sans.; *di,* " heaven," Kalásha; *day,* Eng.; *dyo, dyota,* " lustre," Sans.; *deity,* Eng.

T becomes J :—*jut, jyut,* "shine," *jíva,* " life," *jyotish,* " light," Sans.; *joy, jubility,* Eng.; *jour,* Fr.; *jocus, Jovem,* Lat.

T becomes Z :—*zístan,* " live," Pers.

INDEX VERBORUM.

[The language is added in each case, because the same combination of letters has frequently different significations in different languages.

Translations are given of all words of Oriental, and of a few other little known languages.

For 219 equivalents of the word "Father," see pp. 192-199.]

A.

A, a base in Eg. Hier., 32.
Ab, "now," *Hindi*, 183.
Abeja, *Span.*, 187.
Abhi, "over," *Sans.*, 148.
Above, over, up, *Eng.*, 38.
Accomplir, *Fr.*, 179.
Accomplish, *Eng.*, 179.
Ace, *Eng.*, 184.
Achad, "one," *Pehlevî*, 184.
Achchhâ-achchhâ, *Hindi*, 25.
Âchchhi, &c., *Beng.*, 216.
Achchhi, "eye," *Pâli*, 221.
Αχλυς, *Gr.*, 124.
Ad, "eat," *Sans.*, 218.
Adhas, "down," *Sans.*, 96.
Adhi, "above," *Sans.*, 96, 223.
Adje, "above," *Ghilghiti*, 223.
Adya, "to-day," *Sans.*, 163, 183, 221.
Ægidius, *Lat.*, 107 *note*.

Affluence, *Eng*, 179.
Aflifnan, *Goth.*, 129.
Afufa, "puff," *Galla*, 182.
αγε, *Gr.*, 79.
Agedum, *Lat.*, 79.
Agesis, *Lat.*, 79.
Agglutinate, *Eng.*, 120.
Αγιος, *Gr.*, 104.
Agir, *Fr.*, 79.
Agitate, *Eng.*, 79.
Αγνοια, *Gr.*, 167.
Ago, *Lat.*, 79.
Agraffe, *Fr.*, 123.
Aham, "I," *Sans.*, 184.
Ailment, *Eng.*, 134.
Aisâ, "this-like," *Hindi*, 97, 184.
Âj, "to-day," *Hindi* and *Mahr.*, 221.
Ajja, "to-day," *Pâli*, 221.
Aka, "one," *Abchasian*, 185.
Akkhi, "eye," *Pâli*, 221.
Ακμων, *Gr.*, 109.

Akshi, "eye," *Sans.*, 221.

Akt, "one," *Lappish*, 185.

Aku, "I," *Malay.*, 184.

Äkvä, "one," *Vogulian*, 185.

Alaier, *N. Fr.*, 131.

Alampados, *Port.*, 152.

Âlâpana, "complain," *Sans.*, 79 *note.*

Alas, *Eng.*, 79.

Alegance, *N. Fr.*, 118.

'Alfatat, "mixing," *Arab.*, 138.

Aliaunce, *N. Fr.*, 131.

Alience, *N. Fr.*, 131.

Allegation, *Eng.*, 131.

Alliance, *Eng.*, 119.

Allocare, *Lat.*, 119.

Allogare, *Ital.*, 119.

Allouer, *Fr.*, 118.

Allow, *Eng.*, 135.

Allowance, *Eng.*, 118.

Ally, *Eng.*, 119.

Aloft, *Eng.*, 136 *note.*

Alogar, *Prov.*, 119.

Along, *Eng.*, 130.

'Als, "sticking," *Arab.*, 137.

Alter, *Lat.*, 41.

Am, *Eng.*, 104.

Amhi, &c., *Pâli*, 216.

Αμφιλυκη, *Gr.*, 152.

Ample, *Eng.*, 179.

Ampliation, *Eng.*, 179.

Amplitude, *Eng.*, 179.

Amplus, *Lat.*, 179.

Ampoule, *Fr.*, 179.

Ampulla, *Lat.*, 179.

An, ane, *Eng.*, 185.

An, "breathe," *Sans.*, 32.

Ana', "I," *Arab.*, 184.

Anak, "I," *Eg. Hier.*, 184.

And, *Eng.*, 39, 40.

Anî, "I," *Heb.*, 184.

Âni, "here," *Ghilghiti*, 231.

Ânkh, "eye," *Hindî*, 221.

Anta, "end," *Sans.*, 41.

Antar, "within," *Sans.*, 41.

Antara, "different," *Sans.*, 40.

Antarâla, "interval," *Sans.*, 41.

Anthar, *Goth.*, 40.

Antima, "last," *Sans.*, 41.

Antra, "intestine," *Sans.*, 41.

Anu, "this," *Ghilghiti*, 231.

Anú, "he," *Ghilghiti*, 231.

Anwasancharat, "he traversed," *Sans.*, 97.

Anya, "other," *Sans.*, 41.

Ape, *Ital.*, 187.

Apes, *Lat.*, 187.

Apianus, *Lat.*, 187.

Apiarium, *Lat.*, 187.

Apiarius, *Lat.*, 187.

Apicula, *Lat.*, 187.

Apiostra, *Lat.*, 187.

Apiostrum, *Lat.*, 187.

Apis, *Lat.*, 187.

Arch, "honour," *Sans.*, 165.

Arcilla, *Span.*, 123.

Argentum, *Lat.*, 165.

Argile, *Fr.*, 123.

Argillà, *Ital.*, 123.

Argilla, *Lat.*, 123.

Αργιλλος, *Gr.*, 123.

Arï, "do," *Eg. Hier.*, 24.

Arj, "acquire," *Sans.*, 98.

Arj, "honour," *Sans.*, 165.

Arti, "one," *Mingrelian*, 185.

As, *Eng.*, 97.

As, "exist," *Sans.*, 96, 104.

Ash, "to-day," *Astori*, 221.

Asht, "eight," *Astori*, 213.

Asht, "eight," *Kalásha*, 213.

Ashṭan, "eight," *Sans.*, 213.

Aśman, "stone," *Sans.*, 109.

Asmi, "I am," *Sans.*, 104, 216

Asthi, "bone," *Sans.*, 220.

Âśu, "swift," *Sans.*, 109.

Asùm, &c., "I am," &c., *Arnyiá* (=*Sans.* asmi, &c.), 216.

Âṭ, "eight," *Beng.*, 213.

At, "bind up," *Sans.*, 96.

Atas, "hence," *Sans.*, 183.

Atchi, "eye," *Ghilghiti*, 221.

Âṭh, "eight," *Guj.*, 213.

Âṭh, "eight," *Hindi*, 213.

Atha, "now," *Sans.*, 183.

Āti, "bone," *Ghilghiti*, 220.

Atì, "bone," *Kalásha*, 220.

Atra, "here," *Sans.*, 183.

Âtsh, "eight," *Ghilghiti*, 213.

Âtshu, "to-day," *Ghilghiti*, 221.

Aṭṭhi, "bone," *Páli* and *Prákrit*, 220.

Attonitus, *Lat*, 161.

Au, "and," *Hindi*, 30.

Aujourd'hui, *Fr*, 164.

Aur, "and," *Hindi*, 39.

Ausbreiten, *Germ.*, 176.

Ausfullend, *Germ.*, 179.

Ausspannen, *Germ.*, 170.

Awry, *Eng.*, 113.

B.

Bá, "be," *Khajuná*, 217.

Bâ', "nobility," *Arab.*, 190.

Bâb, "father," *Pers.*, 190.

Bâbâ, "father," *Pers.*, 190.

Babbler, *Eng.*, 45.

Baddo, "large," *Astori*, 221.

Bâdya, "tub," *Pers.*, 176.

Bag, *Eng.*, 180.

Bâl, "spade," *Arab.*, 176

Bâlân, "increasing," *Pers*, 175.

Bâlâyânîdan, "extend," *Pers.*, 175.

Bâlin, "pillow," *Pers.*, 175.

Bâlish, "growth," *Pers.*, 175.

Ball, *Eng*, 180.

Bâlû, "swelling," *Pers*, 175.

Bâlûd, "increase," *Pers.*, 175.

Bâlung, "cucumber," *Pers.*, 175.

Bân, "prince," *Pers.*, 190.

Bâr, "fruit," *Pers*, 175.

Baṛâ, "large," *Hindi*, 221.

Baṛhâ, "large," *Hindi*, 221.

Barrel, *Eng.*, 189.

Bash, "injure," *Sans*, 95.

Bâshâ, "lord," *Turk.*, 190.

Ba-tsi, 'bee," *Japan.*, 187.

Bauch, *Germ.*, 179.

Bausch, *Germ.*, 171.

Bawl, "bursting out," *Arab.*, 176.

Be, "two," *Guj.*, 213.

Beach, *Gael.*, 187.

Bécos, *Phrygian*, 13 *note.*

Bee, *Eng.*, 187.

Beer, *Eng.*, 187.

Befriedigen, *Germ.*, 181.

Bek, *Gr.*, 13 *note.*

Beliman, *A. S.*, 120.

Belly, *Eng.*, 45, 179, 181.

Belong, *Eng.*, 136.

Beluccan, *A. S.*, 120.

Bᵉn, "spring," *Eg. Hier.*, 28.

Bᵉnbᵉn, "spring," *Eg. Hier.*, 28.

R

Beo, *A. S.*, 187.
Beo, *Gael.*, 217.
Beon, *A. S.*, 217.
Beorht, *A. S.*, 153.
Better, *Eng.*, 41.
Bevanda, *Ital.*, 188.
Beverage, *Eng.*, 187, 188.
Beveraggio, *Ital.*, 188.
Bhâ, "shine," *Sans.*, 147.
Bhâ-î, "brother," *Hindi*, 221.
Bhâj, "serve," *Sans.*, 98.
Bhâj, "break," *Sans.*, 174.
Bhâkhâ, "language," *Hindi*, 108.
Bhanj, "break," *Sans*, 174.
Bhas, "shine," *Sans.*, 147.
Bhâs, "shine," *Sans.*, 147.
Bhâshâ, "language," *Hindi*, 108.
Bhâtiko, "brother," *Pâli*, 221.
Bhavâmi, &c., "I am," *Sans.*, 217
Bhid, "break," *Sans.*, 174.
Bhind, "break," *Sans.*, 174.
Bhlâs, "shine," *Sans.*, 147.
Bhlâś, "shine," *Sans.*, 147.
Bhran, "noise," *Sans.*, 162.
Bhrâj, "shine," *Sans.*, 147.
Bhrâś, "shine," *Sans.*, 147.
Bhrâs, "shine," *Sans.*, 147.
Bhrâtṛi, "brother," *Sans.*, 221.
Bhrej, "shine," *Sans.*, 147.
Bhriñś, "shine," *Sans.*, 147.
Bhû, "be," *Sans.*, 217.
Bibo, *Lat.*, 187.
Biene, *Germ.*, 187.
Bihtar, "better," *Pers*, 41.
Bij, "lightning," *Mahr.*, 220.
Bijlî, "lightning," *Hindi*, 220.

Bilaigôn, *Goth.*, 142.
Biography, *Eng.*, 48.
Βιος, *Gr.*, 217.
Bioth, *Irish*, 217.
Birâr, "brother," *Arnyiá*, 221.
Bird, *Eng.*, 45.
Bitshus, "lightning," *Ghilghiti*, 220.
Blabber, *Eng.*, 45.
Black, *Swed.*, 126.
Blad, *A. S.*, 177.
Blade, *Eng.*, 177.
Blæse, *A. S.*, 153.
Blare, *O. Eng.*, 153.
Blaren, *Du.*, 153.
Blaze, *Eng.*, 153.
Blé, *Fr.*, 177.
Bleiben, *Germ.*, 129.
Blend, *Eng.*, 132.
Blifwa, *Swed.*, 129.
Bloc, *Fr.*, 126.
Bloca, *Prov.*, 45, 126
Block, *Eng*, 119, 123, 124, 126, 127, 128.
Block, *Germ.*, 126.
Bloem, *Du.*, 169.
Bloma, *A. S.*, 169.
Bloma, *Goth.*, 169.
Blomme, *Swed.*, 169.
Blood, *Eng.*, 229.
Bloom, *Eng.*, 169.
Blosse, *Germ.*, 126.
Blossom, *Eng.*, 169.
Blostma, *Goth.*, 169.
Blot, *Eng.*, 126.
Blot, *Fr.*, 126.
Blow, *Eng.*, 182.
Blucken, *Du.*, 126.
Blume, *Germ.*, 169.

C.

Caielle, *Picard*, 2.
Calange, *Span.*, 109.
Caligo, *Lat.*, 124.
Cane, *Ital.*, 108.
Cancer, *Lat.*, 122.
Cancro, *Ital.*, 122.
Canis, *Lat.*, 108.
Canonicus, *Lat.*, 109.
Car, *Eng.*, 159.
Carabus, *Lat.*, 122.
Carbo, *Lat.*, 168.
Care, *Eng.*, 79 *note*.
Caru, *A. S.*, 79 *note*.
Catulus, *Lat.*, 108.
Cavus, *Lat.*, 157.
Ceald, *A. S.*, 126.
Ceil, *Eng.*, 157.
Ceinture, *Fr.*, 157.
Cele, *A. S.*, 126.
Celebro, *Lat.*, 168.
Cercle, *Fr.*, 157.
Ceres, *Lat.*, 168.
Chahâr, "four," *Pers.*, 213.
Chaîne, *Fr.*, 157.
Chaise, *Fr.*, 2.
Chakra, "wheel," *Sans.*, 157.
Cham, "eat," *Sans.*, 227.
Char, "eat," *Sans.*, 227.
Châr, "four," *Hindi*, 213.
Chariot, *Eng.*, 159.
Châri, "four," *Beng.*, 213.
Charkh, "wheel," *Pers.*, 157.
Charv, "eat," *Sans.*, 227.
Chash, "injure," *Sans.*, 95.
Chash, "eat," *Sans.*, 227.
Chatt, "cut," *Sans.*, 92.
Chatur, "four," *Sans.*, 213.
Cheâr, "four," *Guj.*, 213.

Chervy, *Russ.*, 158.
Chew, *Eng.*, 227.
Chha, "six," *Guj.*, 213.
Chhah, "six," *Hindi*, 213.
Chham, "eat," *Sans.*, 227.
Chhay, "six," *Beng.*, 213.
Chhed, "cut," *Sans.*, 92.
Chhid, "cut," *Sans.*, 92.
Chhidr, "cut," *Sans.*, 92.
Chill, *Eng.*, 126.
Chho, "cut," *Sans.*, 92.
Chhut, "cut," *Sans.*, 92.
Chhur, "cut," *Sans.*, 92.
Chien, *Fr.*, 108.
Chit, "wake up," *Sans.*, 96.
Chrit, "blaze up," *Sans.*, 96.
Chitter-chatter, *Eng.*, 25.
Chorda, *Lat.*, 159.
Χορδη, *Gr.*, 158.
Chun, "cut," *Sans.*, 92.
Chund, "cut," *Sans.*, 92.
Chunt, "cut," *Sans.*, 92.
Chut, "cut," *Sans.*, 92.
Cicada, *Lat.*, 107 *note*.
Cicala, *Ital.*, 107 *note*.
Ciel, *Fr.*, 157.
Cielo, *Ital.*, 157.
Cigale, *Fr.*, 107 *note*.
Cingolo, *Ital.*, 157.
Cingula, *Lat.*, 157.
Cincta, *Lat.*, 157.
Circem, *Lat.*, 158.
Circhio, *Ital.*, 158.
Circolo, *Ital.*, 157.
Circonférence, *Fr.*, 158.
Circuit, *Eng.*, 158.
Circuitus, *Lat.*, 158.
Circulator, *Lat.*, 158.
Circum, *Lat.*, 158.

Dhwani, "noise," *Sans*, 162.
Di, "heaven," *Kalásha*, 231.
Dia, *Celtic*, 163.
Diable, *Fr.*, 163.
Διασια, *Gr.*, 168.
Did, *Eng.*, 25.
Diès, "day," *Astori*, 231.
Dieu, *Fr.*, 163.
Diewas, *Lettonian*, 163.
Dihh, "daughter," *Ghilghiti*, 221.
Dilatory, *Eng.*, 133.
Din, "day," *Hindi*, 231.
Din, *Eng.*, 162.
Διο, *Gr.*, 163.
Dio, *Ital.*, 163.
Dios, *Span*, 163.
Disgust, *Eng.*, 228.
Dispergere, *Lat.*, 170.
Displayed, *Eng.*, 130.
Div, "shine," *Sans.*, 163,164,231.
Divas, "day," *Sans.*, 231.
Diverse, *Eng.*, 164.
Divinus, *Lat.*, 163.
Divus, *Lat.*, 163.
Divya, "divine," *Sans.*, 163.
Diw, "sound," *Sans.*, 160.
Djósh, "ten," *Arnyiá*, 213.
Djott, "small," *Khajuná*, 221.
Djú, "two," *Arnyiá*, 213.
Djùrr, "daughter," *Arnyiá*, 221.
Do, "two," *Hindi*, 213.
Do, "two," *Ghilghiti*, 213.
Do-do, *Fr.*, 25.
Donar, *O. H. G*, 162.
Donner, *N. H. G.*, 162.
Doubling, *Eng.*, 164, 165.
Dú, "two," *Kalásha*, 213.
Du, "two," *Astori*, 213.
Dú, "two," *Pers.*, 213.

Dū, "give," *Eg. Hier.*, 24.
Duality, *Eng.*, 165.
Dugdugânâ, "make a noise," *Hindi*, 27.
Dūhān, "stand," *Eg. Hier.*, 24.
Duhitri, "daughter," *Sans.*, 221.
Dui, "two," *Beng.*, 213.
Dukhtar, "daughter," *Pers.*, 221.
Duo, *Lat.*, 164.
Duplication, *Eng.*, 164.
Duplicity, *Eng.*, 164.
Dûr-dûr, *Hindi*, 25.
Dūt, "the hand," *Eg. Hier.*, 24.
Duw, *Gael*, 163.
Dwi, "two," *Sans.*, 164, 213.
Dynan, *A. S.*, 162.
Dyne, *A. S.*, 162.
Dyo, "lustre," *Sans.*, 163.
Dyota, "lustre," *Sans.*, 163.
Dyu, "shine," *Sans.*, 163, 231.
Dyut, "shine," *Sans.*, 96, 163, 213.

E.

E, "this," *Beng*, 184.
E, *Ital.*, 39.
È, *Ital.*, 216.
Eadem, *Lat.*, 184.
Eat, *Eng.*, 218.
Ébranler, *Fr.*, 162.
Écrevisse, *Fr.*, 122.
Een, *Du.*, 185.
Effeuiller, *Fr.*, 178.
Εγω, *Gr.*, 184
Ego, *Lat.*, 184.
Egy, "one," *Hung.*, 185.
Ei, "go," *Eg. Hier.*, 183.
Ei, "this," *Beng.*, 184.

Feuillage, *Fr.*, 178.
Feuille, *Fr.*, 178.
Fi, "for," *Arab.*, 148, 182.
Fidem, *Lat.*, 163.
Fil, *Fr.*, 172.
Filament, *Eng.*, 172.
Filature, *Eng.*, 172.
Filth, *Eng.*, 134.
Fi-to, "man," *Japan.*, 189.
Flag, *Eng.*, 133.
Flake, *Eng.*, 126.
Flambeau, *Fr.*, 153.
Flame, *Eng.*, 153.
Flamma, *Lat.*, 153.
Flamme, *Fr.*, 153.
Flare, *Eng.*, 153.
Flash, *Eng.*, 153.
Flat, *Eng.*, 177, 226.
Flax, *Eng.*, 127.
Fleax, *A. S.*, 127.
Fleck, *Germ.*, 126.
Fleece, *Eng*, 127.
Fleur, *Fr.*, 169.
Fleuraison, *Fr.*, 178.
Fleur-de-liser, *Fr*, 178.
Fleurette, *Fr.*, 178.
Fleuriste, *Fr.*, 178.
Fleuron, *Fr.*, 178.
Fleuve, *Fr.*, 131.
Floc, *Fr.*, 127.
Flocc, *A. S.*, 127.
Flock, *Eng.*, 126, 127.
Flocke, *Germ.*, 127, 128.
Flocon, *Fr.*, 127.
Floor, *Eng.*, 177.
Flora, *Lat.*, 169.
Floraison, *Fr.*, 169.
Flos, *Lat.*, 169.
Floss, *Eng.*, 172.

Flossy, *Eng.*, 127.
Flow, *Eng.*, 131.
Fluke, subs., *Eng.*, 177.
Flyse, *A. S.*, 127.
Fodder, *Eng.*, 189.
Foil, *Eng.*, 172.
Fold, *Eng.*, 132.
Folded, *Eng.*, 177.
Foliaceous, *Eng.*, 177.
Foliage, *Eng.*, 177.
Foliated, *Eng.*, 177.
Foliation, *Eng.*, 177.
Foliature, *Eng.*, 177.
Folier, *Fr.*, 177.
Folio, *Eng.*, 177.
Foliol, *Lat.*, 177.
Foliomor, *Lat.*, 177.
Folium, *Lat.*, 38, 45, 169, 177.
Folleatus, *Lat.*, 177.
Folles, *Lat.*, 177.
Follicans, *Lat.*, 177.
Folliculus, *Lat.*, 177.
Folligena, *Lat.*, 177.
Follis, *Lat.*, 177.
Food, *Eng.*, 189.
Fool, *Eng.*, 133, 139.
For, *Eng.*, 24, 182.
Fore, *Eng.*, 24.
Forma, *Lat.*, 179.
Forme, *Fr.*, 179.
Formo, *Ital.*, 179.
Forth, *Eng.*, 24, 182.
Forth, *Eng.*, 225.
Forward, *Eng.*, 24, 182, 225.
Foul, *Eng.*, 134.
Fox, *Eng.*, 161.
Fracture, *Eng.*, 174.
Fragment, *Eng.*, 174.
Frango, *Lat.*, 174.

Freund, *Germ.*, 181.
Friend, *Eng*, 181.
Frondeo, *Lat.*, 171.
Frondescere, *Lat.*, 171.
Frondicamus, *Lat.*, 171.
Frondifer, *Lat.*, 171.
Frondosus, *Lat.*, 171.
Frons, *Lat.*, 171.
Fructeta, *Lat.*, 171.
Fructicare, *Lat.*, 171.
Fructifer, *Lat.*, 171.
Fructuosus, *Lat.*, 171.
Fructus, *Lat.*, 171.
Fruit, *Eng.*, 170, 226.
Frux, *Lat.*, 171.
Fudder, *Germ.*, 189.
Fuff, *Scotch*, 182.
Full, *A. S.*, 179.
Full, *Eng.*, 178.
Füllen, *Germ.*, 179.
Fulljan, *Goth.*, 179.
Fulmen, *Lat.*, 162.
Fulness, *Eng.*, 178.
Fung, " drink," *Chin.*, 187.
Fungus, *Lat*, 173.
Fuvni, *Hung.*, 182.
Fyllan, *A. S.*, 179.

G.

G, a base, 27, 51, 94.
Ga, " and," *Ghilghiti*, 231.
Ga, " also," *Ghilghiti*, 231.
Gabh, " take," *Gael.*, 47.
Gal, " eat," *Sans.*, 27, 227.
Gala, " throat," *Sans.*, 27.
Gam, " go," *Sans.*, 29.
Γαον, *Gr.*, 161.
Γαργαφια, *Gr.*, 27 *note.*
Γαργαρεων, *Gr.*, 27 *note.*
Γαργαρισμος, *Gr.*, 27 *note.*

Γαργαριζω, *Gr.*, 27 *note.*
Gargle, *Eng.*, 27 *note.*
Gargote, *Fr.*, 27 *note*
Gargotier, *Fr.*, 27 *note.*
Gargouille, *Fr.*, 27 *note.*
Gargousse, *Fr.*, 27 *note.*
Gauja, *Goth.*, 161.
Gaunôn, *Goth.*, 161.
Gavi, *Goth.*, 161.
Γη, *Gr.*, 167.
Gelæccan, *A. S*, 120.
Geláss, *Bohem.*, 120.
Gelassen, *Bav.*, 120.
Gelatinate, *Eng.*, 126.
Gelidus, *Lat.*, 126.
Gelihtan, *A. S.*, 152.
Gemius, *Lat.*, 167.
Geno, *Lat.*, 167.
Gerato, *Lat.*, 167.
Germius, *Lat.*, 167.
Gero, *Lat.*, 167.
Gesco, *Lat.*, 167.
Gestio, *Lat.*, 167.
Gestun, *A. S.*, 161.
Giban, *Goth.*, 47, 130.
Gigno, *Lat*, 167.
Gilles, *Fr.*, 107 *note.*
Γινωριξει, *Gr.*, 167.
Γινωσκω, *Gr.*, 167.
Girdle, *Eng.*, 157.
Giriftan, " seize," *Pers.*, 175 *note.*
Girth, *Eng.*, 157.
Give, *Eng.*, 47, 130.
Ghas, " eat," *Sans.*, 26, 227.
Ghu, " sound," *Sans.*, 160.
Ghush, " injure," *Sans.*, 95.
Glacies, *Lat.*, 144.
Glœs, *A. S.*, 153.
Glai, " fade," *Sans.*, 140.

Glaimous, *O. Eng.*, 121.
Glair, *Scotch*, 121.
Glaire, *Fr.*, 121.
Glance, *Eng.*, 153, 168.
Glanz, *Germ.*, 168.
Γλαφυρος, *Gr* , 168.
Glar, *Scotch*, 121.
Glare, *Eng.*, 153, 168.
Glas, "eat," *Sans* , 227.
Glass, *Eng.*, 153, 168.
Glaur, *Scotch*, 121.
Glaze, *Eng.*, 146, 153, 168.
Gleam, *Eng.*, 153, 168.
Glean, *Eng.*, 136.
Gleba, *Lat.*, 125.
Gleissen, *Germ.*, 168.
Glen, *Eng.*, 130.
Glent, *Eng* , 168.
Glesan, *A. S.*, 168.
Glide, *Eng.*, 144.
Glim, *Eng.*, 168.
Glima, *Norse*, 153.
Glimma, *Swed.*, 153.
Glimmen, *Pl. Du.*, 153.
Glimmer, *Eng.*, 153, 168.
Glimmern, *Pl. Du* , 153.
Glimpse, *Eng.*, 153, 168.
Γλισχος, *Gr.*, 144.
Glisser, *Fr.*, 144.
Glisten, *Eng.*, 153, 168.
Glisteren, *Du.*, 153.
Glitenan, *A. S.*, 153.
Glitter, *Eng.*, 153, 168.
Gliua, *Pol.*, 123.
Gliua, *Russ.*, 123
Glóa, *Norse*, 168.
Gloeren, *Du.*, 126.
Γλοιος, *Gr.*, 120.
Glombe, *O. Eng.*, 126.

Glomme, *Dan.*, 126.
Glomung, *A. S.*, 126.
Gloomy, *Eng.*, 126.
Glora, *Norse*, 168.
Gloriam, *Lat.*, 168.
Gloriola, *Lat.*, 168.
Glory, *Eng.*, 168.
Glose, *Eng.*, 168.
Gloser, *Fr.*, 168.
Gloss, *Eng.*, 146, 153, 168.
Γλοσσα, *Gr.*, 141, 146.
Glossare, *Lat.*, 168.
Glouglou, *Fr.*, 27.
Glout, *Eng.*, 126.
Glow, *Eng.*, 168.
Glowan, *A. S.*, 168.
Glowt, *Eng.*, 126.
Glu, *Fr.*, 120.
Glud, *Welsh*, 120.
Glue, *Fr.*, 120.
Gluhen, *Germ.*, 168.
Glum, *Eng.*, 126.
Glupna, *Norse*, 126.
Glus, *Lat.*, 120.
Glutinum, *Lat.*, 120.
Gluyeren, *Du.*, 126.
Glyn, *N. Fr.*, 130.
Gnarigare, *Lat.*, 167.
Gnaritas, *Lat.*, 167.
Gnarus, *Lat.*, 167.
Gnawing, *Eng.*, 228.
Γνωσις, *Gr.*, 167.
Γνωσομαι, *Gr.*, 167.
Go, "cow," *Sans.*, 161.
Go, "I," *Canton*, 184.
Γω, *Gr.*, 167.
Γονη, *Gr.*, 167.
Gorge, *Eng.*, 27.
Gorge, *Fr.*, 27.

Kauritha, *Goth* , 79 *note.*

Kaurs, *Goth.*, 79 *note.*

Keel, *Eng.*, 159.

Κεραννυμι, *Gr.*, 168.

Κεραω, *Gr.*, 168.

Κερας, *Gr.*, 109.

Kha, " eat," *Astori*, 227.

Khà, "eat," *Ghilghiti*, 227.

Khad, "be firm," *Sans.*, 99.

Khaḍ, " cut," *Sans.*, 92

Khad, '' eat," *Sans.*, 227.

Khâd, '' eat," *Sans.*, 227.

Khâdana, "food," *Sans.*, 227.

Khâdin, "biting," *Sans.*, 227.

Khâ-î, " ditch," *Hindî*, 228.

Khal, "aggregate," *Sans.*, 140.

Khan, "cut," *Sans.*, 92, 228.

Khânâ, " eat," *Hindî*, 227.

Khaṇḍ, " bite," *Sans.*, 227.

Khaṇḍ, " cut," *Sans.*, 92.

Khanda, "piece," *Sans.*, 227.

Khanḍana, " destroying," *Sans.*, 228.

Khani, " mine," *Sans* , 228.

Khash, " injure," *Sans.*, 95.

Kheḍ, " eat," *Sans.*, 227.

Kheṭ, "eat," *Sans.*, 227.

Khid, " distressed," *Sans.*, 92.

Khilkhilânâ, '' burst out laughing," *Hindî*, 28.

Khu, "sound," *Sans.*, 160.

Khuḍ, "cut," *Sans.*, 92.

Khuṇḍ, " cut," *Sans.*, 92.

Khur, "cut," *Sans.*, 92.

Ki, " know," *Sans.*, 96.

Kîl, " attach," *Sans.*, 140.

Κιρκος, *Gr.*, 158.

Kirm, "worm," *Hindî*, 48.

Kirminis, *Lith.*, 158.

Κιρνημι, *Gr.*, 168.

Kishk, " injure," *Sans.*, 95.

Kit, " know," *Sans* , 96.

Klạb, *Pol.*, 125

Klabb, *Swed.*, 125.

Klæbe, *Dan.*, 122.

Klæg, *Dan* , 123.

Klænga, *Swed* , 123.

Klag, *Dan.*, 123.

Klam, *Du* , 121.

Klam, "fade," *Sans.*, 140.

Klamm, *Germ.*, 121.

Klamme, *Du.*, 121.

Klamme, *Germ.*, 121.

Klamp, *Du* , 121.

Klampe, *Du.*, 121.

Klanken, *Bav.*, 123.

Klave, *Germ.*, 122.

Kleben, *Germ* , 122.

Kleck, *Germ.*, 126.

Kleeven, *Du.*, 122.

Kleg, *Dan.*, 123.

Κλειω, *Gr.*, 124, 168.

Κλεομαι, *Gr.*, 168.

Κλεος, *Gr.*, 168.

Kley, *Du.*, 123.

Klib, " fail," *Sans.*, 140.

Klijven, *Du* , 122.

Klinken, *Du.*, 123.

Κλιος, *Gr.*, 168.

Kliś, " distressed," *Sans.*, 92.

Klissen, *Du.*, 124.

Klister, *Du.*, 124.

Κλιθρον, *Gr.*, 124.

Klîv, "fail," *Sans.*, 140.

Kloben, *Germ.*, 125.

Klods, *Dan.*, 124.

Klompe, *Du.*, 125.

Klonte, *Du.*, 125.

S

Kuṭṭ, "cut," *Sans.*, 92.

Kuṭṭ, "distressed," *Sans.*, 92.

Kuttâ, "dog," *Hindî*, 222.

L.

L, a base, 94.

La, "law," *C. Ch.*, 143.

La, *Span.*, 127.

La, "lassitude," *C. Ch.*, 143.

La, "call," *C. Ch.*, 143.

Làa, *Port.*, 127.

La'ab, "play," *Arab.*, 142.

La'âb, "viscosity," *Arab.*, 138, 142, 149.

Lab, "hang," *Sans.*, 132.

Labedâ, "club," *Hindî*, 124.

Labh, "obtain," *Sans.*, 145.

Labhasa, "a rope," *Sans.*, 119.

Labi, *Lat.*, 132.

Labia, *Lat.*, 144.

Lablabâ, "clammy," *Hindî*, 121.

Lac, *Fr.*, 130.

Lac, *Prov.*, 120.

Laca, *Port.*, 120.

Laca, *Span.*, 120.

Lacca, *Ital.*, 120.

Lacca, *Lat.*, 120.

Lace, vb., *Eng.*, 119.

Laces, *N. Fr.*, 120.

Lacet, *Fr.*, 120.

Lachchhâ, "a bundle," *Hindî*, 121.

Lâche, *Fr.*, 133.

Lachh, "distinguish," *Sans.*, 145.

Lachlachânâ, "be clammy," *Hindî*, 121.

Lack, *Dan.*, 120.

Lack, *Swed.*, 120.

Lacryma, *Lat.*, 107 *note.*

Lacs, *O. Fr.*, 120.

Lacus, *Lat.*, 130.

Lâd, "load," *Hindî*, 131.

Ladânâ, "to load," *Hindî*, 131.

Ladâ-o, "load," *Hindî*, 131.

Laḍḍu, "sweetmeat," *Sans.*, 120.

Lading, *Eng.*, 131.

Lafaf, "stammering," *Arab.*, 149.

Laff, "joining," *Arab.*, 138, 150.

Lafîf, "crowd," *Arab.*, 138.

Laflafat, "eating voraciously," *Arab.*, 149.

Lafm, "binding," *Arab.*, 138, 150.

Lafq, "joining," *Arab.*, 138.

Lafẓ, "word," *Arab.*, 149.

Lag, "attach," *Sans.*, 119, 129, 139, 141.

Lag, "taste," *Sans.*, 142.

Lag, "near," *Hindî*, 123.

Lâg, "attachment," *Hindî*, 141.

Lag, *Norse*, 116.

Lag, *Icel.*, 116.

Lag, vb., *Eng.*, 129.

Laga, *A. S.*, 116.

Lagân, "holding fast," *Hindî*, 121.

Lagânâ, "apply," *Hindî*, 141.

Lagbhag, "near," *Hindî*, 123.

Lage, *Swed.*, 116.

Laggâ, "attachment," *Hindî*, 141.

Laggî, "staff," *Hindî*, 124.

Laggs, *Goth.*, 129.

Laghb, "become weary," *Arab.*, 139.

Laghîs, "mixture," *Arab.*, 138.

Laghu, "light," *Sans*, 136.
Laghûb, "foolish," *Arab.*, 138.
Lagna, "attached," *Sans.*, 129, 135.
Lagnâ, "attach," *Hindi*, 119.
Lagnâ, "like," *Urdû*, 141.
Lagna, *Port.*, 127.
Lagnaka, "surety," *Sans.*, 141.
Lâgû, "attached to," *Hindi*, 121.
Lagû-â, "paramour," *Hindi*, 141.
Laguda, "club," *Sans.*, 120.
Lâgût, "attachment," *Hindi*, 141.
Lah, *A. S.*, 116.
Lâh, "gum-lac," *Hindi*, 121.
Lahja, "tongue," *Arab.*, 142.
Lâhjâ, "viscosity," *Hindi*, 121.
Lahq, "adhering," *Arab.*, 138.
Lai, "tongue," *C. Ch.*, 143.
Lai, *N. Fr.*, 117, 131.
Laid, *Eng*, 130, 131.
Laie, *N. Fr.*, 116, 117, 131.
Laiel, *N. Fr.*, 117.
Laigon, *Goth.*, 142.
Laine, *Fr.*, 127.
Lainers, *O. Eng.*, 119.
Lair, *Eng.*, 131.
Laisnes, *N. Fr.*, 127.
Laissar, *Prov.*, 133, 135.
Laisser, *Fr.*, 133.
Lait, *N. Fr.*, 135.
Laj, "shine," *Sans.*, 147.
Laj, "ashamed," *Sans.*, 230.
Laj, "burn," *Sans.*, 230.
Lajam, "slime," *Pers.*, 150.
Lajjâ, "shame," *Sans.*, 230.
Lak, "taste," *Sans.*, 142.
Lak, *Du.*, 120.
Laka, *Russ.*, 120.

Laka, *Pol.*, 120.
Lak'a, "adhering," *Arab.*, 138.
Lakar, "club," *Hindi*, 124.
Lake, *Eng.*, 130.
Lâkh, "gum-lac," *Hindi*, 121.
Lakhlakhânâ, "gasp," *Hindi*, 28.
Lakîr, "line," *Hindi*, 144.
Lakh, "mixture," *Arab.*, 138.
Lakkia, *Finn.*, 143.
Λακκος, *Gr.*, 130.
Lakra, "lump," *Hindi*, 124.
Laksh, "shine," *Sans.*, 145, 146, 149, 151, 230.
Lâkshâ, "gum-lac," *Sans.*, 120.
Lakti, *Lith.*, 142.
Lakut, "club," *Hindi*, 124.
Lal, "wish," *Sans.*, 145.
Lâl, "red," *Pers*, 229.
Lâlâ, "saliva," *Sans.*, 144.
Lalâma, "tail," *Sans*, 129.
La'm, "saliva," *Arab*, 148.
Lamb, "hang," *Sans.*, 132.
Lamba, "long," *Hindi*, 129.
Lamdor, "leash," *Hind*, 121.
Lamella, *Lat.*, 109.
Lamlûm, "crowd," *Arab.*, 138.
Lamm, "assembling," *Arab.*, 138.
Lamp, *Eng.*, 153.
Lampadii, *Russ.*, 152.
Lamparas, *Span.*, 152.
Lampas, *Lat.*, 153.
Lampata, "covetous," *Sans.*, 145.
Lampe, *Fr.*, 152, 153.
Lampen, *Du.*, 152.
Lamper, *Dan.*, 152.
Λαμπω, *Gr.*, 152.
Lampor, *Swed.*, 152.

Λαμψις, *Gr.*, 152.

Lampy, *Pol.*, 152.

Lamq, " writing," *Arab.*, 149.

Lamz, " licking," *Arab.*, 149.

Lana, *Ital.*, 127.

Lance, *Eng.*, 130.

Lânchh, " distinguish," *Sans.*, 145.

Land, *Eng.*, 130.

Lane, *Eng.*, 130.

Laners, *N. Fr.*, 133.

Lang, *Scotch*, 129.

Langa, " link," *Sans.*, 123, 141.

Lângala, " plough," *Sans.*, 109.

Langaka, " a lover," *Sans.*, 141.

Langar, a rope, *Pers.*, 119.

Langh, " shine," *Sans.*, 147.

Lânghana, " trespass," *Sans.*, 109.

Langiman, " union," *Sans.*, 141.

Langot, *O. Eng.*, 119.

Langour, *Eng.*, 129.

Langr, *O. Norse*, 129.

Languir, *Fr.*, 129.

Languish, *Eng.*, 129.

Languissant, *Fr.*, 133.

Langûla, " tail," *Sans.*, 129.

Lângula, " tail," *Sans.*, 129.

Lanh, " tongue," *C. Ch.*, 143.

Lanj, " shine," *Sans.*, 147.

Lanja, " tail," *Sans.*, 129.

Lank, *Eng.*, 129.

Lânk, " bird-lime," *Hindî*, 121.

Λανω, *Doric*, 127.

Lansht, " smooth," *Kalásha*, 228.

Lantern, *Eng.*, 153.

Lanterna, *Lat.*, 153.

Lanterne, *Fr.*, 153.

Lanuz, *N. Fr.*, 127.

Lanyards, *Eng.*, 119.

Λαω, *Gr.*, 143.

Lao, " loose," *C. Ch.*, 143.

Lap, " speak," *Sans.*, 79 *note*, 145, 149.

Lap, " speak," *C. Ch.*, 143.

Lap, " bind," *C. Ch.*, 143.

Lapana, " mouth," *Sans.*, 145, 149.

Lapita, " voice," *Sans.*, 149.

Lapsî, " gelatin," *Hindî*, 121.

Lapsus, *Lat.*, 133.

Laptî, " gelatin," *Hindî*, 121.

La'q, " licking," *Arab.*, 142.

Laqs, " laying," *Arab.*, 138.

Laqs, " mixing," *Arab.*, 138.

Laqt, " collecting," *Arab.*, 138.

Laqueus, *Lat.*, 120, 230.

Laqy, " meeting," *Arab.*, 138.

Las, *Dan.*, 133.

Las, " embrace," *Sans.*, 139.

Las, " lust," *Sans.*, 144.

Las, " shine," *Sans.*, 147.

Las, " tenacity," *Hindî*, 121.

Lâsâ, " clammy," *Hindî*, 121.

Lasab, " adhering," *Arab.*, 138.

Lasakuâ, " become viscid," *Hindî*, 121.

Lasam, " tasting," *Arab.*, 148.

Lasb, " adhering," *Arab.*, 138.

Lasb, " licking," *Arab.*, 142.

Laschen, *Du.*, 120.

Lasciare, *Ital.*, 133.

Lasd, " licking," *Arab.*, 142, 148.

Lasf, " joining," *Arab.*, 138.

Lash, vb., *Eng.*, 119, 131, 142.

Lash, " wish," *Sans.*, 145.

Lashan, " support," *Pers.*, 166.

Majja, "middle," *Ghilghiti*, 221.
Majjho, "middle," *Páli* and *Prákrit*, 221.
Makkhî, "fly," *Hindî*, 220.
Makkhikâ, "fly," *Páli*, 220.
Makshikâ, "fly," *Sans.*, 220.
Mâm, "me," *Sans.*, 35.
Man, "I," *Pers.*, 35, 184.
Mangajîk, "fly," *Kalásha*, 220.
Manjhlâ, "middle," *Hindî*, 221.
Manjholâ, "middle," *Hindî*, 221.
Mark, *Eng.*, 146.
Math, "grind," *Sans.*, 92.
Matshî, "fly," *Ghilghiti*, 220.
Matsya, "fish," *Sans.*, 220.
Matzî, "fish," *Arnyiá* and *Kalásha*, 220.
Me, my, mine, *Eng.*, 35.
Μεσος, *Gr.*, 38.
Meum, *Lat.*, 35.
Med, "foolish," *Sans.*, 140.
Medium, *Lat.*, 38.
Melior, *Lat.*, 41.
Met, "foolish," *Sans.*, 140.
Mí, "me," *Khajuná*, 230.
Mil, "embrace," *Sans.*, 140.
Mîn, "fish," *Hindî*, 220.
Mio, *Ital.*, 35.
Mio, *Span.*, 35.
Mlai, "fade," *Sans.*, 134, 139, 140.
Mlaid, "foolish," *Sans.*, 140.
Mlait, "foolish," *Sans.*, 140.
Mlechh, "obfuscated," *Sans.* 134.
Moi, *Fr.*, 35.
Μονος-αρχη, *Gr.*, 165.
More, *Eng.*, 41.
Mósthe, "middle," *Kalásha*, 221.
Mrad, "grind," *Sans.*, 92.

Mraid, "foolish," *Sans.*, 140.
Mrait, "foolish," *Sans.*, 140.
Mraksh, "anoint," *Sans.*, 145, 149.
Mri, "die," *Sans.*, 134.
Mrid, "grind," *Sans.*, 92.
Mriksh, "anoint," *Sans.*, 145.
Mú, "me," *Astori*, 230.
Mū, "give," *Eg. Hier.*, 25.
Mud, "grind," *Sans.*, 92.
Muh, "be faint," *Sans.*, 140.
Mújja, "middle," *Arnyiá*, 221.
Mund, "grind," *Sans.*, 92.
Munt, "grind," *Sans.*, 92.
Murchh, "fade," *Sans.*, 140.
Mûrchhâ, "fainting," *Sans.*, 134.
Mûrkha, "a fool," *Sans.*, 134, 139.
Mush, "injure," *Sans.*, 95.
Mut, "grind," *Sans.*, 92.

N.

Nah, "bind," *Sans.*, 231.
Namela, *Prov.*, 109.
Nângar, "plough," *Hindî*, 109.
Nânghnâ, "trespass," *Hindî*, 109.
Narrare, *Lat.*, 167.
Narro, *Lat.*, 167.
Nasco, *Lat.*, 167.
Nascor, *Lat.*, 167.
Natus, *Lat.*, 167.
Nau, "nine," *Astori*, 213.
Nau, "nine," *Ghilghiti*, 213.
Nau, "nine," *Guj.*, 213.
Nau, "nine," *Hindî*, 213.
Navan, "nine," *Sans.*, 213.
Nay, "nine," *Beng.*, 213.
Near, *Eng.*, 231.

Nege, "one," *Sokpa,* 185.
Nein, "one," *Shan,* 185.
Neither, *Eng.,* 40.
Nek, "I," *Berber,* 184.
Nekki, "I," *Berber,* 184.
Next, *Eng.,* 231.
Nexus, *Lat.,* 231.
Nga, "I," *Burm.,* 184
Nigh, *Eng.,* 231.
Nike, "one," *Ölöt,* 185.
Nikka, "one," *Aimak,* 185.
Nil, "be thick," *Sans.,* 140.
Nitrum, *Lat.,* 109.
Niveau, *Fr.,* 109.
Ñò, "nine," *Arnyiá,* 213.
Nò, "nine," *Kalásha,* 213.
Ñoca, "I," *Quichua,* 184.
Νους, *Gr.,* 167.
Nosco, *Lat.,* 167.
Nrî, "lead," *Sans.,* 96.
Nṛit, "lead forth," *Sans.,* 96.
Ṇu, "sound," *Sans.,* 160.
Ñuh, "nine," *Pers.,* 213.
Νυμφη, *Gr.,* 109.
Nùng, "one," *Khamti, Laos,* and *Siamese,* 185.
Nûsh, "injure," *Sans.,* 95.
Nutria, *Span,* 109.

O.

O, "and," *Bengali,* 39.
Obliegen, *Germ.,* 132.
Obtundere, *Lat.,* 161.
Οδυσσευς, *Gr,* 107 *note.*
Odor, *Lat,* 107 *note.*
Oggi, *Ital.,* 164.
Oil, *Eng.,* 144.
Oka, "one," *Telugu,* 185.

Ωκυς, *Gr.,* 109.
Oleo, *Lat.,* 107 *note.*
Oleum, *Lat.,* 144.
Oliva, *Lat,* 144.
Óndja, "to-day," *Kalásha,* 221.
Ondu, "one," *Malabar* and *Canarese,* 185.
One, *Eng.,* 185.
Onji, "one," *Tuluva,* 185.
Onna, "one, *Malayálam,* 185.
Onomatop, the word, 54.
Onru, "one," *Tamil,* 185.
Onṭh, "lip," *Hindi,* 221.
Onti, "lip," *Ghilghiti,* 221.
Opacus, *Lat.,* 49.
Οφελλω, *Gr.,* 170.
Οφελος, *Gr.,* 170.
Operari, *Lat.,* 49.
Operire, *Lat.,* 49.
Opes, *Lat.,* 49.
Opimo, *Lat.,* 49.
Optare, *Lat.,* 49.
Optimus, *Lat.,* 49.
Opulens, *Lat.,* 49.
Or, other, *Eng.,* 40.
Orare, *Lat.,* 50.
Orbs, orbit, *Lat.,* 50, 113.
Orcare, *Lat.,* 50.
Ordia, *Lat.,* 50.
Ορεγνυμι, *Gr.,* 165.
Ορεγω, *Gr.,* 165.
Orphanus, *Lat.,* 109.
Orphelin, *Fr.,* 109.
Osht, "eight," *Arnyiá,* 213.
Oshṭh, "lip," *Beng.,* 221.
Oshṭra, "lip," *Sans.,* 221.
Οθεν, *Gr.,* 104.
O þer, *A. S.,* 40.
Other, or, *Eng.,* 40.

Ötik, "one," *Syrianian*, 185.

Over, above, up, *Eng.*, 38, 136 *note*

Overwhelm, *Eng.*, 114.

Ox, *Eng.*, 161.

Oxa, *A. S.*, 161.

Oxe, *Dan.*, 161.

P.

P, "forth," a base, 23, 94, 182, 186.

P, "suck," a base, 200.

P, a base in *Eg. Hier.*, 32.

P = f, 38.

Pâ, pî, "suck," *Sans*, 45 *note*, 188.

Pâb, "father," *Pers.*, 190.

Pabulum, *Lat.*, 2 *note*, 188, 189.

Pad, "lord," *Pers.*, 189.

Pâdal, "flower," *Pers.*, 175.

Pâda-pa, "tree," *Sans.*, 188

Padar, "father," *Pers.*, 190.

Padding, *Eng*, 180.

Pads, *Eng*, 180.

Παειν, *Gr.*, 189.

Pâh, "food," *Pers.*, 189.

Pahan, "width," *Pers.*, 176.

Pahnâ, "broad," *Pers*, 176.

Pahup, "flower," *Urdû*, 169, 188.

Paielle, *Picard*, 2.

Paitis, "lord," *Zend*, 189.

Paiṇ, "embrace," *Sans*, 139.

Pain, "reservoir," *Hindi*, 188.

Pâl, "nourish," *Sans.*, 178.

Pâla, "guardian," *Sans.*, 178.

Pâlâdan, "stretch," *Pers.*, 175.

Pâlana, "cherishing," *Sans.*, 178.

Pâlânanda, "augmenting," *Pers*, 175.

Palâṇḍu, "onion," *Sans.*, 173.

Palâsa, "foliage," *Sans.*, 173.

Pâlâyîdan, "increase," *Pers.*, 175.

Paletta, *Ital*, 177.

Palette, *Fr.*, 177.

Pâlish, "growth," *Pers.*, 175.

Pallâ, "leaf," *Hindi*, 226.

Pallava, "sprout," *Sans.*, 173.

Pallet, *Eng.*, 177.

Pallo, "sprig," *Hindi*, 173.

Pâlnâ, "nourish," *Hindi*, 179.

Pâlû, "swelling," *Pers*, 175.

Pâlûdan, "be large," *Pers.*, 175.

Pân, "leaf," *Hindi*, 226.

Pâna, "wedge," *Pers*, 175.

Panah, "protector," *Pers.*, 190.

Pânaka, "beverage," *Sans.*, 188.

Pânch, "five," *Beng.*, 213.

Pânch, "five," *Guj.*, 213.

Pânch, "five," *Hindi*, 213.

Panchan, "five," *Sans.*, 213.

Παιδια-δειπολια, *Gr.*, 168.

Panj, "five," *Pers.*, 213.

Pannâ, "leaf," *Hindi*, 226.

Panse, *Fr.*, 179.

Pâr, "completed," *Pers.*, 179.

Pâraṇa, "fulfilling," *Sans.*, 178.

Parâsh, "expansion," *Pers*, 175.

Paraśu, "axe," *Sans.*, 109.

Parentage, *Eng.*, 180.

Pâri, "cup," *Sans.*, 178.

Pûri, "fruit," *Pers.*, 175.

Parṇ, "leaf," *Hindi*, 226.

Pâro, "shovel," *Pers*, 175.

Parosh, "pimples," *Pers.*, 175.

Parv, "fill," *Sans.*, 178.

Parwar, "nourishing," *Pers.,* 175.

Parwâs, "expansion,"*Pers.,* 175.

Paś, "injure," *Sans ,* 99.

Paś, "see," *Sans ,* 10.

Paśchât, "behind," *Sans ,* 221.

Pash, "injure," *Sans.,* 95.

Pâshîda, "pumpkin," *Pers.,* 175

Pasîn, "behind," *Pers.,* 221

Paste, *Eng.,* 189.

Pastry, *Eng.,* 189.

Pasture, *Eng.,* 189.

Pât, "broad," *Hindi,* 176.

Pat, "fall down," *Sans.,* 96.

Pât, "leaf," *Hindi,* 176.

Pâtan, "roof," *Hindi,* 176.

Πατηρ, *Gr.,* 188.

Pater, *Lat.,* 188.

Path, *Eng.,* 176.

Path, "extend," *Sans ,* 176.

Path, "road," *Hindi,* 176.

Pâthas, "water," *Sans ,* 188.

Pathik, "traveller," *Hindi,* 176.

Pâtî, "leaf," *Hindi,* 226.

Pati, "lord," *Sans.,* 189.

Pato, "behind," *Astori,* 221.

Pâtra, "dish," *Hindi,* 176.

Patra, "leaf," *Sans.,* 176.

Pattâ, "leaf," *Hindi,* 176.

Pattî, "leaf," *Hindi,* 176.

Pâttu, "leaf," *Astori,* 226.

Patu, "leaf," *Ghilghiti,* 226.

Pauh, "water-stand," *Hindi,* 188.

Paurta, "pleasing act," *Sans.,* 181.

Pay, "milk," *Hindi,* 188.

Payas, "milk," *Sans.,* 188.

Pâzûm, "food," *Pers.,* 189.

Pecchia, *Ital.,* 187.

Peg, *Eng.,* 128.

Πειθομαι, *Gr.,* 189.

Πελεκυς, *Gr.,* 109.

Pelle, *Fr.,* 177.

Pellis, *Lat.,* 134.

Pem, "love," *Hindi,* 181.

Pemî, "lover," *Hindi,* 181.

Pen, "embrace," *Sans.,* 139.

Pepî, "drink excessively," *Sans.,* 29.

Pépie, *Fr ,* 29 *note.*

Per, *L.,* 24, 182.

Perceive, *Eng.,* 167.

Percerpere, *Lat.,* 168.

Percipio, *Lat.,* 168.

Père, *Fr.,* 188.

Peṛû, "belly," *Hindi,* 179.

Peṭ, "belly," *Hindi,* 179.

Peth, "belly," *Hindi,* 179.

Peṭû, "gluttonous," *Hindi,* 179.

Pey, "milk," *Hindi,* 188.

Pflegen, *Germ.,* 132.

Phailânâ, "spread," *Hindi,* 173.

Phailâo,"expansion,"*Hindi,* 173.

Phal, "expand," *Sans.,* 90.

Phal, "fruit," *Hindi,* 173.

Phal,"ploughshare," *Hindi,*173.

Phalâ, "apple," *Ghilghiti,* 226.

Phala, "fruit," *Sans.,* 170, 226.

Phalamúl, "fruit," *Astori,* 226.

Phalûng, "stride," *Hindi,* 173.

Phalgu, "spring," *Sans.,* 172.

Phâlgun, "spring," *Hindi,* 173.

Phalî, "shield," *Hindi,* 173.

Phaló, "apple," *Astori,* 226.

Phalya, "flower," *Sans.,* 170.

Phamúl, "fruit, *Ghilghiti,* 226.

Phamùl, "fruit," *Khajund,* 226.

Phaṇa, "hood," *Sans.,* 172.

Πινω, *Gr.*, 187, 188.

Pino, *Lat.*, 187.

Pintâ, "fatness," *Sans.*, 189

Πιω, *Gr* , 187, 188.

Pîpâ, " a barrel," *Hindi*, 45 *note*, 189.

Pipâsâ, "thirst," *Sans.*, 188.

Pipâsu, " thirst," *Sans.*, 188.

Pipe, *Eng.*, 189.

" Pipe " of wine, *Eng.*, 45 *note*.

Piper, *Fr.*, 187.

Pîpî, " a pipe," *Hindi*, 45 *note*, 189.

Piplu, " a freckle," *Sans.*, 20.

Piquette, *Fr.*, 188.

Pîr, " old man," *Pers.*, 190.

Pîrana, " elderly," *Pers* , 190.

Pirtam, " world," *Hindi*, 176.

Pish, " injure," *Sans.*, 95

Píshto, " behind," *Kalásha*, 221.

Pîṭh, " back," *Hindi*, 169, 176.

Pîtha, " water," *Sans* , 188.

Pîti, " drink," *Sans.*, 188.

Pitri, " father," *Sans.*, 188, 189.

Pitri, " the nourisher," *Sans.*, and its congeners, pp. 192-198.

Pittu, " behind," *Ghilghiti*, 221.

Pitu, " drink," *Sans.*, 188.

Pîvana, " large," *Sans.*, 189.

Pîvara, " large," *Sans.*, 189.

Piy, " please," *Sans.*, 181.

Piyâla, " cup," *Pers.*, 189

Piyar, " old man," *Pers.*, 190.

Piyâz, " onion," *Pers.*, 175.

Pîyûsha, " nectar," *Sans.*, 188.

Placed, *Eng.*, 131.

Placere, *Lat.*, 181.

Plaga, *Swed* , 132.

Plaid, *N. Fr.*, 131.

Plain, "embrace," *Sans.*, 139.

Plaindre, *Fr.*, 131.

Plaint, *Eng.*, 131.

Plaint, *N. Fr.*, 131.

Plaire, *Fr.*, 181.

Plaister, *Eng.*, 136.

Plait, *Eng.*, 132

Plait, *N. Fr.*, 131.

Plan, *Eng.*, 177.

Planche, *Fr.*, 177.

Plane-tree, *Eng.*, 180.

Plank, *Eng.*, 177.

Planke, *Germ.*, 177.

Πλατανος, *Gr* , 180.

Platanus, *Lat* , 180.

Plate, *Eng.*, 177.

Πλατεια, *Gr.*, 180.

Πλατιον, *Gr.*, 180.

Πλατος, *Gr.*, 180.

Platt, *Germ.*, 177.

Platte, *Fr.*, 177.

Πλατυς, *Gr.*, 180.

Play, *Eng.*, 181.

Plé, *Fr.*, 177.

Plea, *Eng.*, 131.

Please, *Eng* , 181.

Pleasure, *Eng* , 181.

Pleat, *Eng.*, 132.

Pleated, *Eng.*, 177.

Plebs, *Lat.*, 179.

Plecta, *Lat.*, 127.

Pledge, subs., *Eng.*, 131.

Pledge, vb., *Eng* , 131.

Pleger, *Dan.*, 132.

Plegg, *N. Fr.*, 131.

Plein, *Fr.*, 179.

Pleine, *Fr.*, 180.

Pleintie, *N. Fr.*, 131.

Πλειον, *Gr.*, 179.

T

Prı, " fill," *Sans.*, 178.

Prî, " fill," *Sans.*, 178.

Pri, " go forth," *Sans.*, 186.

· Pṛi, " please," *Sans* , 24, 181.

Pṛî, " please," *Sans* , 181.

Prî, " please," *Sans.*, 181.

Pṛid, " please," *Sans.*, 181.

Priṇ, " fill," *Sans.*, 178.

Pṛıṇ, " please," *Sans.*, 181.

Prınceps, *Lat.*, 165.

Prise, *Eng.*, 20.

Pṛish, " injure," *Sans.*, 95.

Prishtha, " back," *Sans.*, 169, 176

Pṛith, " extend," *Sans.*, 176.

Pṛıthu, " broad," *Sans.*, 176.

Prıthula, " large," *Sans.*, 176.

Pṛithuka, "flattened graın,"*Sans.*, 176.

Pṛithutâ, "largeness," *Sans.*, 176.

Pṛıthwî, " earth," *Sans.*, 176.

Prîti, " pleasure," *Sans.*, 181.

Priya, " beloved," *Sans.*, 181.

Priyaka, " bee," *Sans.*, 181.

Προ, *Gr.*, 24, 182.

Pro, *Lat.*, 182.

Prón, " leaf," *Kalásha*, 226.

Propino, *Lat.*, 187.

Prush, "fill," *Sans.*, 178.

Pûb, " father," *Pers.*, 190.

Pûd, " food," *Pers.*, 189

Pudding, *Eng.*, 189.

Puella, *Lat.*, 190.

Puellaris, *Lat.*, 190.

Puellariter, *Lat.*, 190.

Puellarius, *Lat.*, 190.

Puellascere, *Lat.*, 190.

Puellatorius, *Lat.*, 190.

Puelliter, *Lat.*, 190.

Puellula, *Lat.*, 190.

Πυερα, *Gr.*, 190.

Puerascere, *Lat.*, 190.

Pueraster, *Lat.*, 190.

Puerculor, *Lat.*, 190.

Puerigenus, *Lat.*, 190.

Puerilıs, *Lat.*, 190.

Puerilıtas, *Lat.*, 190.

Puerıliter, *Lat* , 190.

Pueritia, *Lat.*, 190.

Puernius, *Lat.*, 190.

Puerperus, *Lat.*, 190.

Puerulur, *Lat.*, 190.

Puff, *Eng.*, 182.

Puffed up, *Eng.*, 182.

Pufîdan, " blow," *Pers.*, 182, 225.

Puissant, *Fr.*, 189.

Pul, " aggregate," *Sans.*, 140, 170.

Pûl, " aggregate," *Sans.*, 140.

Pûlâ, " bunch,". *Hindi*, 179.

Pûlî, " bunch," *Hındi*, 179.

Pull, *Eng.*, 136.

Pulk, *Esthon.*, 127.

Pulkka, *Finn.*, 127.

Pulsum, *Lat.*, 182.

Pump, *Eng.*, 187.

Puṇyatara, " purer," *Sans.*, 41.

Pûr, " fill," *Sans.*, 178.

Pûra, " filling," *Sans.*, 178.

Purâ, " full," *Pers.*, 179.

Pûrâ, " fully," *Hindi*, 179.

Pûrâ-î, " fulness," *Hindi*, 179.

Purer, *Eng.*, 41.

Purîdan, " fill," *Pers.*, 179.

Pûrṇa, " able," *Sans.*, 178.

Pûrṇatâ, " plenty," *Sans.*, 178.

Purse, *Eng.*, 180.

Pûrta, "complete," *Sans.*, 178.
Purv, " fill," *Sans.*, 178.
Pûrv, " fill," *Sans.*, 178.
Purwâr, "filled," *Pers.*, 179.
Push, "enlarge," *Sans.*, 170, 188.
Pûsh, "enlarge," *Sans.*, 170.
Push, *Eng.*, 182.
Pushpa, "flower," *Sans.*, 169, 170, 188.
Púsho, "flower," *Astori*, 226.
Pushta, "heap," *Pers.*, 170.
Pushṭi, "increase," *Sans.*, 170.
Putra, "boy," *Sans.*, 190.
Πυξις, *Gr.*, 171.
Πυξος, *Gr.*, 171.
Pyah, "bee," *Burm.*, 187.
Pyai, "swelling," *Sans.*, 189.
Pyânâ, "drink," *Hindi*, 188.
Pyâr, "affection," *Pers.*, 181.
Pyâs, "thirst," *Hindi*, 188.
Pyâwnâ, "drink," *Hindi*, 188.
Pyây, "swelling," *Sans.*, 189.

Q.

Qalma, "worm," *Chaldean*, 158.
Q'n, "beat," *Eg. Hier.*, 28.
Q'nq'n, "beat soundly," *Eg. Hier.*, 28.

R.

Râ'â, "guarding," *Arab.*, 166 *note.*
Ra'ab, "chieftain," *Arab.*, 166 *note.*

Rabb, "ruling," *Arab.*, 166 *note.*
Rabbud, "chief," *Armen.*, 166 *note.*
Rabe, *Germ.*, 162.
Rabh, "wish," *Sans.*, 145.
Rabid, *Eng*, 182 *note.*
Râchhas, "demon," *Hindi*, 166.
Raff, "sucking," *Arab.*, 150.
Râff, "preserver," *Arab.*, 166 *note.*
Râfi', "who exalts," *Arab.*, 166 *note.*
Rafif, "shining," *Arab.*, 150.
Rafik, "foolish," *Arab.*, 138.
Roga, "disease," *Sans.*, 230.
Raihts, *Goth.*, 165.
Râj, "govern," *Sans.*, 165.
Râj, "shine," *Sans.*, 147, 154.
Râjâ, "king," *Hindi*, 166.
Râjan, "king," *Sans.*, 165.
Râjaka, "splendid," *Sans.*, 154, 165.
Rajaka, "washerman," *Sans.*, 229.
Râjanya, "soldier," *Sans.*, 165.
Rajas, "sky," *Sans.*, 229.
Rajat, "white," *Sans.*, 229.
Râjih, "excelling," *Arab.*, 166 *note.*
Râjpût, "warrior," *Hindi*, 166.
Râjpûtî, "courage," *Hindi*, 166.
Râjya, "government," *Sans.*, 165.
Rakâsî, "devilish," *Hindi*, 166.
Rakjan, *Goth.*, 165.
Rakhaiyâ, "keeper," *Hindi*, 166.
Rakhnâ, "guard," *Hindi*, 166.
Rakhsh, "lightning," *Pers.*, 151.
Rakhshû, "shining," *Pers.*, 151.
Rakhshîdan, "shine," *Pers.*, 151.

T 2

Rochaka, "pleasing," *Sans.*, 151.
Rochana, "splendid," *Sans.*, 151.
Rochis, "flame," *Sans.*, 151.
Rochishnu, "gaily dressed,"*Sans.*, 151.
Rock, *Eng.*, 123 *note*.
Rodana, "grief," *Sans.*, 79 *note*, 162.
Rodas, "heaven," *Sans.*, 162.
Robān, "stand," *Eg. Hier.*, 24.
Rohita, "red," *Sans.*, 229.
Roi, *Fr.*, 165.
Roj, "day," *Pers.*, 151.
Roka, "light," *Sans.*, 230.
Rook, *Eng.*, 162.
Rosh, "light," *Pers.*, 151.
Rosha, "anger," *Sans.*, 230.
Roshana, "quicksilver," *Sans.*, 230.
Rout, *Eng.*, 162.
Row, *Eng.*, 79 *note*.
Row, *Eng.*, 162.
Roz, "day," *Pers.*, 151.
Ru, "be angry," *Sans.*, 230.
Ru, "sound," *Sans.*, 79 *note*, 160, 162.
Rub, *Eng.*, 147.
Rub, *Gael*, 147.
Rubba, *Norse*, 147.
Ruch, "shine," *Sans.*, 147, 151.
Rud, "be angry," *Sans.*, 230.
Rud, "cry," *Sans.*, 79 *note*, 162.
Ruddy, *Eng.*, 230.
Ruefully, *Eng.*, 162.
Rûftan, "rub," *Pers.*, 147.
Ruj, "burn," *Sans.*, 230.
Rule, *Eng.*, 155.
Ruler, *Lat.*, 165.
Rukma, "bright," *Sans.*, 230.

Rumour, *Eng.*, 162.
Run, *Eng.*, 26, 182 *note*.
Runa, *Germ.*, 162.
Rûnên, *Germ.*, 162.
Runś, "shine," *Sans.*, 147.
Ruobbet, *Lappish*, 147.
Rush, *Eng.*, 26, 95, 182 *note*.
Rush, "be angry," *Sans.*, 230.
Rush, "injure," *Sans.*, 95.
Rûsh, "paint," *Sans.*, 230.
Rusht, "bright," *Pers.*, 151.
Rut, "shine," *Sans.*, 147.
Ruzâb, "saliva," *Arab.*, 149.
Ryn, *A. S.*, 162.

S.

S, a base, 96.
Sa, "with," *Sans.*, 96.
Sâ, "like," *Hindi*, 97.
Sabhâj, "serve," *Sans.*, 98.
Sad, "sit," *Sans.*, 96.
Sagh, "strike," *Sans.*, 99.
Sah, "he," *Sans.*, 96, 183 *note*.
Saha, "with," *Sans.*, 96.
Salf, "levelling," *Arab.*, 137.
Saliva, *Eng.*, 144.
Sam, "with," *Sans.*, 96.
Sama, "like," *Sans.*, 97.
Same, *Eng.*, 97.
Samgam, "go with," *Sans.*, 97.
Sampûrn, "full," *Hindi*, 170.
Sangle, *Fr.*, 157.
Sanj, "be attached," *Sans.*, 98.
Sanjnâ, "conversant with," *Sans.*, 97.
Śankha, "shell," *Sans.*, 109.
Saphala, "fruitful," *Sans.*, 98.

Saptan, "seven," *Sans.*, 213.
Sar, "fade," *Sans.*, 140.
Sar, "head," *Pers.*, 220.
Sarj, "acquire," *Sans.*, 98.
Sash, "injure," *Sans.*, 95.
Sât, "seven," *Beng.*, 213.
Sât, "seven," *Guj.*, 213.
Sât, "seven," *Hindi*, 213.
Sath, "seven," *Astori*, 213.
Sath, "seven," *Ghilghiti*, 213.
Sâtt, "seven," *Kalásha*, 213.
Saurgan, *Goth.*, 79 *note*.
Say, "go," *Sans.*, 98.
Scarabæus, *Lat.*, 122.
Schliessen, *Germ.*, 124.
Schlingeln, *Germ.*, 135.
Schlostern, *Germ.*, 133.
Scortum, *Lat.*, 159.
Scorza, *Ital.*, 159.
Scramble, *Eng.*, 123.
Scriba, *Lat.*, 48.
Scribble, *Eng.*, 48.
Scribere, *Lat.*, 48.
Scrinium, *Lat.*, 48.
Se, "with," *Hindi*, 97.
Seek, *Eng.*, 139.
S'emplir, *Fr.*, 179.
Sen, "breathe," *Eg. Hier.*, 28.
Sensen, "breathe," *Eg. Hier.*, 28.
Seyree, "I," *Georg.*, 184.
Shá, "six," *Astori*, 213.
Shá, "six," *Ghilghiti*, 213.
Shash, "six," *Pers.*, 213.
Shash, "six," *Sans.*, 213.
She, *Eng.*, 183 *note*.
She, "tongue," *Chin.*, 143 *note*.
She-cho, "place," *Chin.*, 143 *note*.
Sheon, "dog," *Kalásha*, 222.

Shin, "lip," *Chin.*, 143 *note*.
Shîr, "milk," *Pers.*, 223.
Shish, "head," *Astori* and *Ka-lásha*, 220.
Shish, "head," *Ghilghiti*, 220.
Shó, "six," *Kalásha*, 213.
Shú, "dog," *Ghilghiti*, 222.
Sibi, *Lat.*, 183 *note*.
Sigh, *Eng.*, 79 *note*.
Sih, "three," *Pers.*, 213.
Sihrih, "I," *Georg.*, 184.
Sil, "collect," *Sans.*, 140.
Śil, "collect," *Sans.*, 140.
Śilâ, "rock," *Sans.*, 123.
Śilîndhrî, "clay," *Sans.*, 123.
Śilî-pada, "club-footed," *Sans.*, 123.
Silqâ, "lying flat," *Arab.*, 137.
Similar, *Eng.*, 97.
Sinsin, "thirst," *Arab.*, 28.
Sir, "head," *Hindi*, 220.
Śiras, "head," *Sans.*, 220.
Sîrsha, "head," *Zend*, 220.
Śish, "injure," *Sans.*, 95.
Sit, *Eng.*, 96.
Σκαραβειον, *Gr.*, 122.
Σκαραβος, *Gr.*, 122.
Σκεπτομαι, *Gr.*, 45.
Skhad, "be firm," *Sans.*, 99.
Σκολιος, *Gr.*, 158.
Slack, *Eng.*, 133.
Slag, *Eng.*, 135.
Slaga, *Swed.*, 135.
Slain, *Eng.*, 135.
Ślath, "loose," *Sans.*, 135, 140.
Ślatha, "loose," *Sans.*, 133.
Slattern, *Eng.*, 133.
Slaw, *A. S.*, 129, 133.
Slay, *Eng.*, 135.

Sleep, *Eng.*, 133.
Slender, *Eng.*, 136.
Śleṣha, "union," *Sans.*, 123.
Śleshmaka, "mucus," *Sans.*, 123.
Śleshman, "mucus," *Sans.*, 123.
Slet, *Du.*, 133.
Slide, *Eng.*, 144.
Slight, *Eng.*, 136, 228.
Slime, *Eng.*, 120.
Slimy, *Eng.*, 144.
Sling, *Eng.*, 135.
Slingern, *Du.*, 135.
Śli-pada, "club-footed," *Sans.*, 123.
Śli-padin, "club-footed," *Sans.*, 123.
Ślish, "shine," *Sans.*, 154, 168.
Ślish, "embrace," *Sans.*, 140.
Slobber, *Eng.*, 133.
Slobbern, *Du.*, 133.
Slog, *Saxon*, 133.
Ślok, "aggregate," *Sans.*, 140.
Ślon, "collect," *Sans.*, 140.
Slouchy, *Eng.*, 133.
Slov, *Du.*, 129.
Slove, *Dan.*, 133.
Sloven, *Eng.*, 133.
Slow, *Eng.*, 129.
Sludge, *Eng.*, 133.
Slug, *Eng.*, 120.
Sluggard, *Eng.*, 129.
Slumber, *Eng.*, 133.
Slumerian, *A. S.*, 133.
Slummer, *Du.*, 133.
Slur, *Eng.*, 133.
Slush, *Eng.*, 133.
Slut, *Eng.*, 133.
Slyk, *Du.*, 133.
Smash, *Eng.*, 95.

So, *Eng.*, 97.
Śoka, "grief," *Sans.*, 79 *note*.
Sommeil, *Fr.*, 133.
Son, *Fr.*, 162.
Sonâ, "sleep," *Hindi*, 133.
Sonare, *Lat.*, 162.
Sonitus, *Lat.*, 162.
Sonno, *Ital.*, 133.
Sono, *Ital.*, 104.
Sorg, *Norse*, 79 *note*.
Sough, *Eng.*, 79 *note*.
Sorrow, *Eng.*, 79 *note*.
Sòt, "seven," *Arnyiá*, 213.
Souhaiter, *Fr.*, 139.
Sound, *Eng.*, 162.
Spade, *Eng.*, 173, 177.
Spaltan, *O. H. G.*, 170.
Span, *Eng.*, 170, 181.
Sparcir, *Span.*, 170.
Spargo, *Lat.*, 170.
Sparpagliar, *Ital.*, 170.
Spaś, "injure," *Sans.*, 99.
Spear, *Eng.*, 174.
Specto, *Lat.*, 45.
Spend, *Eng.*, 170.
Sphal, "expand," *Sans.*, 99, 170.
Σφαλλω, *Gr.*, 133.
Σφαλμα, *Gr.*, 133.
Sphand, "expand," *Sans.*, 170, 171, 177.
Sphand, "play," *Sans.*, 181.
Sphaṇṭ, "play," *Sans.*, 181.
Sphar, "increase," *Sans.*, 170.
Sphâra, "large," *Sans.*, 172.
Sphaṭ, "expand," *Sans.*, 170.
Sphaṭa, "hood," *Sans.*, 172.
Sphâti, "increase," *Sans.*, 189.
Sphây, "swelling," *Sans.*, 189.
Sphira, "large," *Sans.*, 172.

W.

London : Printed by Gilbert & Rivington, St. John's Square, and Whitefriars Street.

A SELECTION FROM

MESSRS. ALLEN & CO.'S

Catalogue of Books

IN EASTERN LANGUAGES.

DICTIONARIES.

Forbes's Hindustani-English Dictionary in the Persian Character, with the Hindi words in Nagari also; and an English Hindustani Dictionary in the English Character; both in one volume. By DUNCAN FORBES, LL.D. Royal 8vo. 42s.

Forbes's Hindustani Dictionary, the Two Volumes in One, in the English Character. Royal 8vo. 36s.

Forbes's Smaller Dictionary, Hindustani and English, in the English Character. 12s.

Robertson's Hindustani Vocabulary. 3s. 6d.

Haughton's Sanscrit and Bengali Dictionary, in the Bengali
Character, with Index, serving as a reversed Dictionary.
4to. 30s.

Williams's (Monier) Sanscrit and English Dictionary. 4to. cloth.
4l. 14s. 6d.

Williams's English and Sanscrit Dictionary. 4to, cloth. 3l. 3s.

Richardson's Persian, Arabic, and English Dictionary. Edition
of 1852. By F. Johnson. 4to. 4l.

Brown's Dictionary, English-Teloogoo and Teloogoo-English,
with a Dictionary of the Mixed Dialects used in Teloogoo.
3 vols. in 2, royal 8vo. 5l.

Campbell's Teloogoo Dictionary. Royal 8vo. 30s.

Morris's Teloogoo Dictionary. 4l. 4s.

Percival's English-Teloogoo Dictionary. 10s. 6d.

Rutler's Dictionary, Tamil and English. 4to. 42s.

Percival's Tamil Dictionary. 2 vols. 10s. 6d.

Molesworth's Dictionary, Mahratta and English. 4to. 42s.

Molesworth's Dictionary, English and Mahratta. 4to 42s

Shapurji Edalji's Dictionary, Guzrattee and English. 21s.

Morrison's Chinese Dictionary. 6 vols. 10l.

Reeves's Dictionary, English-Carnatica and Carnatica-English.
2 vols. 8l.

GRAMMARS.

Forbes's Hindustani Grammar, with Specimens of Writing in the Persian and Nagari Characters, Reading Lessons, and Vocabulary. 8vo. 10*s.* 6*d.*

Platt's (John T.) Hindustani or Urdu Grammar. 12*s.*

Williams's (Monier) Sanscrit Grammar. 8vo. 15*s.*

Wilkin's (Sir Charles) Sanscrit Grammar. 4to. 15*s.*

Forbes's Persian Grammar, Reading Lessons, and Vocabulary. Royal 8vo. 12*s.* 6*d.*

Ibraheem's Persian Grammar, Dialogues, &c. Royal 8vo. 12*s.* 6*d.*

Forbes's Bengali Grammar, with Phrases and Dialogues. Royal 8vo. 12*s.* 6*d.*

Forbes's Arabic Grammar, intended more especially for the use of young men preparing for the East India Civil Service, and also for the use of self instructing students in general. Royal 8vo. 18*s.*

Palmer's (E. H.) Arabic Grammar. (Nearly ready.)

Brown's Teloogoo Grammar. 16*s.*

Babington's Grammar (High Dialect). 4to. 12*s.*

Beschi's Grammar (Common Dialect). 8vo. 7*s.*

Rhenius's Grammar. 8vo. 14*s.*

Stevenson's Marathi Grammar. 17*s.* 6*d.*

Marsden's Malay Grammar. 21*s.*

Marshman's Clavis Sinica, or Chinese Grammar. 2*l.* 2*s.*

Summer's Chinese Grammar. 28*s.*

THEORIES OF HISTORY.

AN INQUIRY INTO THE

THEORIES OF HISTORY,—CHANCE,—LAW,—WILL.

WITH SPECIAL REFERENCE TO THE

PRINCIPLE OF POSITIVE PHILOSOPHY.

By WILLIAM ADAM.

Octavo. 15s.

"The whole book bears the evident mark of maturity of thought. The third chapter is full of thoughtful and able argument, in which the positions of Comté, and even of Mill, are powerfully and successfully assailed."— *Spectator.*

"It is well thought and weightily written. We have not come across a book of the present day for a considerable while so far removed from the common run of writing and of thinking as this one is."—*Athenæum.*

𝕷𝖔𝖓𝖉𝖔𝖓:

W. H. ALLEN & CO., 13, WATERLOO PLACE, S.W.

Lightning Source UK Ltd.
Milton Keynes UK
UKHW02f1928130818
327178UK00005B/267/P